BORIS FORD

Benjamin Britten's Poets

edited by BORIS FORD

Benjamin Britten's Poets

The poetry he set to music

CARCANET

Published with the Aldeburgh Bookshop

First published in Great Britain in 1994 by
Carcanet Press Ltd
Alliance House
Cross Street
Manchester M2 7AQ

Revised edition published 1996, reissued 2013

A CIP catalogue record for this book is available from the British Library

ISBN-10 1 85754 240 1
ISBN-13 978 1 85754 240 0

The publisher acknowledges financial assistance from Arts Council England

Set in Monotype Ehrhardt by XL Publishing Services, Exeter
Printed and bound in England by SRP Ltd, Exeter

Contents

ACKNOWLEDGEMENTS   ix
INTRODUCTION by Boris Ford   xi
COMPOSER AND POET by Peter Porter   xviii

O that I had ne'er been married 1922 *Robert Burns*   1
Beware 1923 *Henry Longfellow*   2
The volunteer 1926 *Herbert Asquith*   3
QUATRE CHANSONS FRANÇAISES 1928 *Victor Hugo, Paul Verlaine*   4
TIT FOR TAT 1928–31 *Walter de la Mare*   6
A Wealden trio 1929 *Ford Madox Ford*   9
The birds 1929 *Hilaire Belloc*   10
A hymn to the Virgin 1930 *Anon.*   11
The sycamore tree 1930 *Trad.*   12
THY KING'S BIRTHDAY 1931 *Henry Vaughan, Anon., Robert*   13
     Southwell, C.W.Stubbs
THREE TWO-PART SONGS 1932 *Walter de la Mare*   18
A BOY WAS BORN 1932–3 *Anon., Thomas Tusser, Christina*   20
     Rossetti, Francis Quarles
TWO PART-SONGS 1933 *George Wither, Robert Graves*   28
Te Deum in C 1934   32
Festival Te Deum 1944 *The Book of Common Prayer*   32
May 1934 *Anon*   33
FRIDAY AFTERNOONS 1933–5 *Anon., William Makepeace*   34
     Thackeray, Jane Taylor, Nicholas Udall, Izaak Walton, Eleanor
     Farjeon
When you're feeling like expressing your affection 1935–6   42
     W.H. Auden
OUR HUNTING FATHERS 1936 *W.H. Auden, Thomas Weelkes?*
     Thomas Ravenscroft   43
Pacifist march 1937 *Ronald Duncan*   46
TWO BALLADS 1937 *Montagu Slater, W.H. Auden*   47
ON THIS ISLAND 1937 *W.H. Auden*   49
Fish in the unruffled lakes 1937 *W.H. Auden*   53
To lie flat on the back 1937 *W.H. Auden*   54
The sun shines down 1937 *W.H. Auden*   55
Song 1937 *Peter Burra*   56
The company of heaven 1937 *Emily Brontë*   57
Night covers up the rigid land 1937 *W.H. Auden*   60
Advance democracy 1938 *Randall Swingler*   61
The red cockatoo 1938 *After Po Chü-i*   62
FOUR CABARET SONGS FOR MISS HEDLI ANDERSON   63
     1937–9 *W.H.Auden*

BALLAD OF HEROES 1939 *Randall Swingler, W.H. Auden*   67
A.M.D.G. 1939 *Gerard Manley Hopkins*   71
LES ILLUMINATIONS 1939 *Arthur Rimbaud*   76
SEVEN SONNETS OF MICHELANGELO 1940 *Michelangelo di Ludovico Buonarroti*   81
What's in your mind? 1939/41 *W.H. Auden*   85
TWO SONGS 1942 *Thomas Lovell Beddoes*   86
Hymn to St Cecilia 1942 *W.H. Auden*   88
Cradle song 1942 *Louis MacNeice*   90
A CEREMONY OF CAROLS 1942 *Trad., Anon., James, John & Robert Wedderburn, Robert Southwell, William Cornyshe*   91
FOLK SONG ARRANGEMENTS, VOL.1 BRITISH ISLES 1943 *W.B. Yeats, Trad.*   96
Rejoice in the Lamb 1943 *Christopher Smart*   100
SERENADE 1943 *Charles Cotton, Alfred Lord Tennyson, William Blake, Anon., Ben Jonson, John Keats*   102
The Ballad of Little Musgrave and Lady Barnard 1943 *Anon.*   107
A shepherd's carol 1944 *W.H. Auden*   111
THIS WAY TO THE TOMB 1945 *Ronald Duncan*   112
THE HOLY SONNETS OF JOHN DONNE 1945 *John Donne*   114
Birthday song for Erwin 1945 *Ronald Duncan*   118
FOLK SONG ARRANGEMENTS, VOL.2 FRANCE 1946 *Trad.*   119
Canticle I: My beloved is mine 1947 *Francis Quarles*   124
A CHARM OF LULLABIES 1947 *William Blake, Robert Burns, Robert Greene, Thomas Randolph, John Phillips*   126
FOLK SONG ARRANGEMENTS, VOL.3 BRITISH ISLES 1947 *Trad.*   129
SAINT NICOLAS 1948 *Eric Crozier*   133
SPRING SYMPHONY 1949 *Anon., Edmund Spenser, Thomas Nashe, George Peele & John Clare, John Milton, Robert Herrick, Henry Vaughan, W.H. Auden, Richard Barnfield, William Blake, Francis Beaumont & John Fletcher*   143
A wedding anthem 1949 *Ronald Duncan*   155
FIVE FLOWER SONGS 1950 *Robert Herrick, George Crabbe, John Clare, Anon.*   157
Canticle II: Abraham and Isaac 1952 *Anon*   162
WINTER WORDS 1953 *Thomas Hardy*   171
If it's ever spring again 1953 *Thomas Hardy*   176
Canticle III: Still falls the rain 1954 *Edith Sitwell*   176
Song 1956 *Edith Sitwell*   178
Hymn to St Peter 1955 *from the Gradual for the Feast of St Peter & St Paul*   178
Antiphon 1956 *George Herbert*   179
The holly and the ivy 1957 *Trad.*   180
SONGS FROM THE CHINESE 1957 *The Book of Songs, Po Chü-i, Wu-ti, Lu Yu*   181

NOCTURNE 1958 *Percy Bysshe Shelley, Alfred Lord Tennyson, Samuel Taylor Coleridge, Thomas Middleton, William Wordsworth, Wilfred Owen, John Keats, William Shakespeare*   184
SECHS HÖLDERLIN-FRAGMENTE 1958 *Friedrich Hölderlin*   192
Um Mitternacht 1959/60 *Johann Wolfgang von Goethe*   195
A MIDSUMMER NIGHT'S DREAM 1960 *William Shakespeare*   196
FOLK SONG FRRANGEMENTS, VOL.4 / MOORE'S IRISH MELODIES; 1960 *Thomas Moore*   202
Jubilate Deo 1961 *The Book of Common Prayer*   207
FOLK SONG ARRANGEMENTS, VOL.5 BRITISH ISLES 1961 *Henry Carey, Trad., Robert Burns*   208
Fancie 1961 *William Shakespeare*   212
FOLK SONG ARRANGEMENTS, VOL.6 ENGLAND 1961 *Trad.*   213
WAR REQUIEM 1961 *Trad., Wilfred Owen, English Missal*   216
Psalm 150 1962 *The Book of Common Prayer*   224
The twelve apostles 1962 *Trad.*   225
King Herod and the cock 1966 *Anon.*   226
Hymn to St Columba 1962 *attr. St Columba*   227
Cantata Misericordium 1963 *Patrick Wilkinson*   228
SONGS AND PROVERBS OF WILLIAM BLAKE 1965 *William Blake*   232
VOICES FOR TODAY 1965 *Jesus Christ, Asoka, Sophocles, Lao Tzu, John Bright, William Penn, Herman Melville, Albert Camus, Lec, Yevgeny Yevtushenko, Friedrich Hölderlin, Alfred Lord Tennyson, Percy Bysshe Shelley, Publius Virgil*   239
THE POET'S ECHO 1965 *Alexandr Sergeevich Pushkin*   244
The 'Golden Vanity' 1966 *Colin Graham*   246
The building of the house 1967 *Psalm 127 from Whole Book of Psalms*   248
The oxen 1967 *Thomas Hardy*   249
Children's crusade 1968 *Bertolt Brecht, H. Keller*   250
WHO ARE THESE CHILDREN? 1969 *William Soutar*   254
Canticle IV: Journey of the Magi 1971 *T.S. Eliot*   259
Canticle V: The death of St Narcissus 1974 *T.S. Eliot*   261
Sacred and Profane 1974–5 *St Godric, Anon.*   263
A BIRTHDAY HANSEL 1975 *Robert Burns*   267
Phaedra 1975 *Robert Lowell (after Racine)*   271
WELCOME ODE 1976 *Thomas Dekker & John Ford, Anon., Henry Fielding*   277
EIGHT FOLK SONG ARRANGEMENTS 1976 *Trad., Thomas Oliphant*   280

BRITTEN'S LIBRARY   287
INDEX OF AUTHORS   289
INDEX OF TITLES   291
INDEX OF FIRST LINES   296

Acknowledgements

The editor and publisher wish to thank the following for their most generous grants towards the cost of publishing this volume:
Mrs Valerie Eliot,
HRH The Princess of Hesse and the Rhine,
The Britten Estate Ltd,
The Norman Scarfe Charitable Trust,
Faber and Faber Ltd.

The editor and publisher also wish to thank the following who have kindly given permission for the use of copyright material:

Boosey & Hawkes Music Publishers Ltd: for 'Cantata Misericordium' by Patrick Wilkinson. Copyright © 1963 by Boosey & Hawkes Music Publishers Ltd, London. 'Six Hölderlin Fragments' translated by Peter Pears and Elizabeth Mayer. Copyright © 1963 by Boosey & Hawkes Music Publishers Ltd, London. 'St Nicolas' by Eric Crozier. Copyright © 1948 by Hawkes & Son (London) Ltd. Reproduced by permission of Boosey & Hawkes Music Publishers Ltd.

Milein Cosman: for Bertolt Brecht, 'The Children's Crusade', translated by Hans Keller.

David Higham Associates: for 'Still falls the rain' by Edith Sitwell, from *Collected Poems* published by Macmillan.

Faber & Faber Ltd.: for 'Fish in the unruffled lakes', 'Johnny', 'O tell me the truth about love', 'Funeral blues', 'Let the florid music praise', 'Now the leaves are falling fast', 'Night covers up the rigid land', 'As it is, plenty', 'Our hunting fathers told the story' and Prologue, 'It's farewell to the drawing-room's civilised cry', 'Out on the lawn I lie in bed', 'The sun shines down on the ships at sea', 'To lie flat on the back with the knees flexed', 'Underneath the abject willow', 'What's in your mind, my dove, my coney' from *The English Auden* 1927–1939; ed. Edward Mendelson; 'Anthem for St Cecilia's Day', 'Calypso: Driver, drive faster and make a good run', 'On this Island' from *W.H. Auden: Collected Poems*, ed. Edward Mendelson; 'Shepherd's Carol' from *For the Time Being* by W.H. Auden; 'When you're feeling like expressing your affection' from W.H. Auden & Christopher Isherwood: *Plays 1928–1938;* extract from *Phaedra* by Robert Lowell; 'The death of St Narcissus' from *Poems Written in Early Youth* by T.S. Eliot; 'Journey of the Magi' from *Collected Poems 1909–1962* by T.S. Eliot; 'Cradle Song for Eleanor' from *The Collected Poems of Louis MacNeice;* extract from 'Composer and Poet' by Peter Porter from *The Britten Companion*, ed. Christopher Palmer; 'Fanfare', 'Villes', 'Phrase', 'Antique', 'Royauté', 'Marine', 'Interlude', 'Being Beauteous', 'Parade',

'Départ' from *Prose poems from Les Illuminations of Arthur Rimbaud*, translated by Helen Rootham.

Faber Music Ltd London: for 'The Poet's Echo' by Alexandr Pushkin, translated by Peter Pears. Copyright © 1967 by Faber Music Ltd London.

The Literary Trustees of Walter de la Mare and The Society of Authors as their representative: for 'Song of Enchantment', 'Autumn', 'Silver', 'Vigil', 'Tit for Tat', 'The Ride-by-Nights', 'The Rainbow', 'The Ship of Rio' by Walter de la Mare.

Penguin Books Ltd: for 'Um Mitternacht' from *Selected Verse* by Goethe, translated by David Luke (Penguin Classics 1964), copyright © David Luke 1964.

Peters, Fraser & Dunlop: for 'The Birds' from ;Complete Verse; by Hilaire Belloc, reprinted by permission of Peters, Fraser & Dunlop Ltd.

Sidgwick & Jackson: for 'The Volunteer' by Herbert Asquith.

Unwin Hyman, of Harper Collins Publishers: for 'The big chariot', 'The old lute', 'The autumn wind', 'The herd-boy', 'Poems in depression, at Wei Village', 'Dance Song', 'The red cockatoo', from *Chinese Poems* by Arthur Waley.

A.P. Watt Ltd on behalf of the Robert Graves Copyright Trust: for 'Tail Piece: A Song to Make You and Me Laugh'.

Judith Williams: for 'Across the darkened sky', 'You who stand at the doors', 'Still though the scene of possible summer recedes' by Randall Swingler.

We regret that it has not proved possible to trace the copyright holders of a few poems in the anthology.

Introduction *by* BORIS FORD

'One of my chief aims is to try and restore to the musical setting of the English language a brilliance, freedom and vitality that have been curiously rare since the days of Purcell.'

Benjamin Britten

That Benjamin Britten was a great composer is perhaps open to discussion; but that he was a great composer of vocal music seems to me indisputable. There are the twelve operas and three dramatic church parables; there are the Spring Symphony and the War Requiem; and there is all the vocal music for solo voice and for choirs. It is a massive achievement and this anthology testifies to a major element in that achievement: the words that Britten set to music. (This anthology omits the words of his operas, though it does include the songs from *A Midsummer Night's Dream*. It also omits the words of the Parables.)

An anthology of Britten's texts might sound like a rather formal and dutiful compilation, likely to be of little abiding interest to anyone but his devout admirers. In fact, it is of the first importance musically, for it not only confirms one's general impression that Britten set poetry of an exceptional quality but that, in terms of its quality and range, this poetry cannot, I believe, be matched by any other composer. Monteverdi set fine poetry, amid much that is tediously artificial, but its range is not great. Schubert, Schumann, Brahms and Wolf set a great volume of poetry, some of it moving and heart-felt; but much of it is pretty poor, sentimental, even bathetic stuff. That may have been, in part, because such was the mixed quality of the poetry that was being written at the time they were composing. And anyway, it is true that poetry of an indifferent and even trite calibre has, throughout the ages, been made into great songs. It has even been claimed that great words can prove a hindrance to the composer, because they have too much life of their own and refuse to take a humble second place to the music. What suffices, as far as the composer is concerned, is that the words provide a theme, a drama, a sentiment, which lend themselves to being transformed into the finished song. And certainly a great proportion of religious and amorous music, and probably the bulk of operatic libretti, would seem to confirm this view.

What this anthology enables one to say is that the quality of the poetry mattered greatly to Britten as a composer. Indeed, poetry of quality mattered greatly to him as a person. His library at Aldeburgh is full of poetry (see Appendix); Rosamund Strode has said that he never travelled anywhere without packing an anthology, one of his favourites being Horace Gregory's *The Triumph of Life* (a *multum in parvo*, as she describes it). Not all the poems Britten set are great poetry; a few of them, during his earlier years up to the Second World War, are somewhat crude political poetry that appealed to his anti-fascist and pacific beliefs; some are hectoring poems by Auden, designed to get Britten to face up to his as yet latent homosexuality. And one or two are ceremonial concoctions like the *Cantata Academica*. But the number of indifferent or banal texts, *out of a total of some 315*, is astonishingly small. Listeners who are familiar with Britten's well-known works know that he set poems by Wordsworth, Keats, Tennyson, Donne, Rimbaud, Blake, Eliot and Owen. What they may not realize is that he set poems by as many as *ninety* known poets and by a great number of anonymous medieval poets. It is a remarkable roll-call of well – and lesser-known names; and their poems which Britten chose are of a great range and variety of topic and mood. In this respect his record is, I believe, incomparable.

The kind of evidence adduced above only substantiates the platitude that Britten was a major composer for the human voice. But what seems seldom to have been asked is why he should have written predominantly vocal music, and what this preoccupation might imply. One obvious, if too obvious, answer is that he must have had a predilection for writing music that interprets and treats of a story or theme, which is what a poem provides. Or one might deduce that he loved the human voice above all instruments. But true as these explanations may be, is it not possible that he was impelled, subconsciously, towards vocal music because it is a human utterance and, where the composer is also the accompanist or conductor, it involves a close human relationship? Britten's first compositions, when he was only a few years old, were written for his mother to sing; subsequently the vast majority of his vocal compositions were written ostensibly for high voice but in fact for Peter Pears to sing, either on his own or in concert with other singers who became close associates, at least for a time.

Britten's and Pears's letters make it abundantly clear that their musical and sexual relationships were very closely intertwined; they both affirmed that their major musical achievements had only been made possible by and through each other. I think one can see throughout Britten's life (without any need to engage in psychological speculation) a constant urge not only to compose, but to engage with others in making music. In part he was anxious to be useful, as he put it; but, more profoundly, he had a rare talent, whether working with professionals or amateurs, adults or children, for communicating and recreating with them the very essence of the music. Accompanying Pears in the *Winterreise*, it was as if he were indeed Schubert. When the works were his own, he was surely realizing himself in the fullest degree. It is significant that though Britten was an outstandingly accomplished pianist, he had no inclination to be a soloist. What he sought, and found, was human relationship through the composing and performing of music.

And this relationship was founded on words: on his dependence on poets and on his unerring choice of poems which perhaps led him into emotional realms where he might not have ventured on his own and where, deprived of the supporting words, he might not have prospered musically to the same degree. It appears that he needed, very frequently, this verbal prompting in order to get going. He always seemed to respond creatively, which swiftly meant responding musically, to the poetry he was so often reading. Auden spoke of his 'extraordinary musical sensitivity in relation to the English language'. And not only to English poetry. When he was introduced by Auden to Rimbaud's *Les Illuminations*, he was immediately eager, according to Sophie Wyss, to set this 'most wonderful poetry' to music; in this instance, and it is not an isolated one, it seems to me that he transformed the poems for the better. Peter Porter, himself an accomplished poet, testifies that 'I had responded to [Donne's] baroque exaggeration very imperfectly until I heard Britten's music for nine of the *Holy Sonnets*'. And Graham Johnson, discussing his 'delicate and civilized amalgam of poetry and music', speaks of being 'surprised and enriched by Britten's uncanny ability to find new and appropriate solutions to problems which others found insoluble.'

This anthology includes virtually all the published poems (and extracts from poems) that Britten set to music, including all the folk songs which he arranged. It is interesting to examine the range of this considerable body of poetry. It may surprise some listeners to learn that the two largest categories are the one hundred traditional and anonymous poems and the seventy-two religious poems. There are fifty poems in foreign languages (Latin, French, Italian, German and Russian); and there are twenty-one poems by Auden, all but two of which were composed between 1936 and 1942. Britten, who described himself in a broadcast in 1963 as 'a dedicated Christian... [though] at the moment I do not find myself worshipping as regularly as perhaps I will', always welcomed the opportunity to set religious texts. He also frequently arranged folk songs (thirty-nine of them) from 1943 until he died. I have included these songs because their texts have an appealing freshness and, very often, a profound innocence, even when somewhat bawdy. Britten's sensitive and brilliant piano accompaniments to these traditional tunes which transform them into art songs are understandably not to the taste of folk-song purists, for these wonderful melodies should ideally be sung unaccompanied. But the words remain intact: they are a significant if increasingly forgotten part of our poetic heritage – this account does not apply to the words that Moore had supplied to the Irish folk melodies that Britten arranged.

It used to be said that it was Auden and Pears who supplied Britten with suggestions for most of his texts, if not with the actual texts themselves. Auden certainly supplied the texts for *Our Hunting Fathers* and he also sent Britten a number of his own poems, though Britten did not set all of them to music. Indeed, it says something for Britten's innocence or magnanimity that he set many of them for public performance, since they tended to contain coded injunctions to Britten about his sexual hesitations and what Auden saw as Britten's bourgeois cosiness. Britten said that the person who developed his love for poetry was Auden: he was bowled over by Auden's intellectual brilliance and for a few years, between 1936 and 1942, he was undoubtedly influenced quite strongly, if more and more reluctantly, by him. But it is hard to discover what his influence amounted to, as far as Britten's reading of poetry was concerned, except that Auden introduced him to Rimbaud's and Eliot's poetry – at the very end of his life, when he was desperately weak, Eliot's was the only poetry Britten could read.

Pears's influence, on the other hand, must surely have been continuous, and Myfanwy Piper once said that Pears 'did consider himself to be the literate one'. But according to Rosamund Strode, who worked closely with Britten for many years, the true picture is that there was an ongoing discussion and exchange of ideas between two people who were living together. And of course they had their differences: thus Pears was originally against setting Eliot's *Journey of the Magi* as Canticle IV, whereas Britten was adamant that he wanted to set it and that he would never cut a line of Eliot. It is interesting that Pears is explicitly credited with having selected the texts for only one work, the Blake *Songs and Proverbs*. There was also their major collaboration on the libretto for *A Midsummer Night's Dream*, which was a triumph achieved at top speed. In my view everything points to Britten's being responsible for the great bulk of his texts: pencilled annotations in his own volumes of poetry confirm that it was certainly he who made the selection of lines and verses to be used or, perhaps more significantly, to be omitted.

In this anthology the texts of poems are given complete, where possible. Where Britten took his texts from poems which are too long to reproduce here, I have most often included additional lines or verses so as to provide the poetic context and also a more complete passage of poetry. The verses and lines that Britten omitted are indicated between square brackets. The following are some of the major instances:

a. Britten extracted twenty lines from Wordsworth's *Prelude*, Book X on the French Revolution, and eighteen lines from Keats's *Sleep and Beauty*, for inclusion in his *Nocturne*. I have printed eighty-two and eighty-four lines respectively from these poems.

b. I have included the whole of Blake's *Auguries of Innocence* from which Britten extracted only four lines for his *Songs and Proverbs of William Blake*.

c. In the *Spring Symphony* Britten uses three verses and two lines from Barnfield's 'The teares of an affectionate shepheard'; I print twenty-four of Barnfield's thirty-eight very decorative verses. I have also included all sixteen verses, as against Britten's six, of Auden's 'Out on the lawn I lie in bed'.

d. In his *Five Flower Songs* Britten includes a fourteen-line 'poem' by Crabbe which he entitles 'Marsh flowers'. In fact these lines are extracted and then shuffled up from two separate tales, from which I have included quite long extracts so as to restore something of Crabbe's dramas.

In all of these instances Britten needed a fairly short passage which would fit into a small 'anthology' on a particular theme. In other instances a poem might have seemed too long for the occasion for which the composition was commissioned or designed – many of Britten's compositions were commissioned and, as always, he was meticulous in meeting the needs of the occasion. But in many other cases one finds that he has omitted a line or two, perhaps a verse here or there, for reasons that seem to have nothing to do with timing, for only a singing minute is saved, or with the public occasion. Unfortunately Britten's journals and letters throw very little light on how he set about selecting and editing his texts.

Suffice it to say that he tends to omit lines about violence and cruelty: for instance the description in 'The ballad of Little Musgrave' where Lord Barnard 'cut her paps from off her breasts', or the couplet from Titania's song, 'And pluck the wings from painted butterflies, /

To fan the moonbeams from his sleepy eyes' which Britten no doubt felt to be a wholly frivolous excuse. At a more serious level he omits the lines about Noye's proposal to offer God a sacrifice of beasts and fowls in thanks for his and his family's delivery from the flood. (Alas, we have not space for *Noye's Fludde*.) Britten also tends to omit passages that describe or hint at intimate relations between men, or which describe close encounters between a man and a woman. It is interesting that he virtually never omits any lines from folk songs, which often include barely concealed sexual innuendoes. But apart from the Michelangelo sonnets and a few folk songs and ballads, it is true that his *oeuvre* does not include anything resembling the great love cycles and songs of Schubert, Schumann, Brahms and Wolf, though his library included such poetry.

The poems are arranged not by author but in the sequence in which Britten set them. This enables one to see the way his taste for poetry developed, and also the increasing poetic complexities and subtleties that he was prepared to tackle. Burns, somewhat surprisingly, was almost his first and last poet; de la Mare, as one would expect, was an early favourite. He set four French poems in his teens, the first of fifty poems in foreign languages, up till the group of poems by Pushkin on which he worked, with the guidance of Slava and Galina Rostropovich, in 1965 and for which Peter Pears provided translations; and one finds him setting a number of anonymous and religious poems early on, and then regularly throughout his life. The main Auden years were 1936–7, followed by *Paul Bunyan* in 1941. From quite early, in 1932, and throughout his life Britten gathered together small anthologies, as one might call them, of poems on a common theme: *A Boy was Born* (1932–3), *Friday Afternoons* (1933–5), *A Ceremony of Carols* (1942), *Serenade* (1943), the *Spring Symphony* (1949), *Nocturne* (1958), *Sacred and Profane* (1974–5); as well as numerous anthologies of poems by single authors: de la Mare, Auden, Hopkins, Rimbaud, Michelangelo, Donne, Blake, Hardy, Hölderlin, Owen, Soutar and Burns – these alone would surely place Britten in a 'poetry class' of his own, for many of their poems are of considerable verbal intensity and awkwardness which must have demanded of the composer great musical tact and subtlety. Indeed one might have thought that many of them were all but impossible to set to music until Britten successfully did so. 'I never realised words could be set with such ingenuity and colour', Britten said of Purcell. And so one might justly say of Britten himself.

Towards the end of his life Britten mastered the contrasted problems of setting two great poems by Eliot and, at the opposite end of the spectrum, a group of medieval sacred and profane poems. And in 1960 he took on the 'tremendous challenge' of setting Shakespeare's 'heavenly words' in *A Midsummer Night's Dream*. As his life was ending he managed to arrange yet another group of folk songs.

The texts of the poems are predominantly those that Britten used, and even where recent editions may contain more authentic versions of some poems, I have usually felt it best to use the texts that Britten read and on which he worked so feelingly.

My thanks are due to Philip Reed and his colleagues at the Britten-Pears Library at Aldeburgh for their help in finding and checking the information included in this anthology; and also to colleagues at Carcanet Press.

BORIS FORD
1993/6

Benjamin Britten was born in 1913 and died in 1976.

Titles

All the poems in this anthology are headed by the title Britten gave that work. Where the work consists of a group of poems, the title uses capital initials (Our Hunting Fathers); for a single poem, the title is in lower case, (O that I had ne'er been married).

Each poem is then given its usual title, in italics (*Beware*); followed, where that differs, by the title Britten gave it, in roman between inverted commas ('The three kings').

Composer and Poet *by* PETER PORTER

(This essay is a shortened version of a chapter first published in
The Britten Companion, edited by Christopher Palmer.)

Not since the days when musician and poet were the same person has
there been a great composer whose art is as profoundly bound up with
words as Benjamin Britten's. There are many special clauses which
need to hedge this statement round, but it remains, I believe, true in
essentials. Born into a world of professionalism in art Britten was
faced, in the 1930s, with a profession profoundly wrenched from its
natural alliances, an artistic atmosphere inimical to the recognition of
the common source of poetry and music in the imagination. Britten's
whole instinct was in the other direction: he had an antediluvian sense
of the unity of musical and poetic vision.

The whole corpus of Britten's work is informed by a deeply poeti-
cal feeling. Vocal compositions predominate in his output, but this is
not the whole or even the main part of the case. Instead, it can be said
that what poets have prefigured in words, he has reworked in music.
This recognition of the fact that even a superb piece of poetry leaves
something more to be said is what makes so many of his settings so
masterful. By fertilizing his musical mind in poetry, Britten gets back
to the unfractured sensibility of the pre-classical past (that is, music
before Purcell). There are composers greater than him who wrote a
great deal of vocal music, some of it, such as Mozart's operas and
Bach's cantatas, the most splendid in a long history of word-setting.
But their inspiration is more universal than Britten's, and their mas-
tery of instrumental music shows that the profoundest analogy which
may be developed around their art is with philosophy. Poetry is un-
friendly to philosophy, if not inimical to it, though it may live on equal
terms with theology. The one great predecessor whose creative per-
sonality springs equally from an instinctive poetical nature is
Schubert: for both Schubert and Britten the world in which music
grows is a poetical place – i.e., it is human, speculative, aphoristic and
spontaneous.

For someone not attracted especially to the technique of develop-
ment, the setting of poems to music is an obvious and natural recourse.
Right through his creative life, Britten gave direction to his genius and

staked out claims on the inchoate by identifying himself with poets and poems. His humanism saved him from the turmoil which followed the break-up of the nineteenth-century symphonism with its attendant idealism and demonism. It is not surprising that Britten, like Schubert, is a great melodist: he finds shapes in notes as memorably limned as the shapes in verse he is using. Perhaps other musicians have had equally good taste in poetry, but Britten is most unusual among composers of the highest level of invention in making settings of so much great and near-great verse.

Britten's depth of concern for literature is *sui generis*, something far more profound than his being a composer in a country whose greatest artistic achievements have been in poetry. How far his early friendship with Auden led him towards the more esoteric of the authors whose words he set is not easy to guess, though compositions such as *Friday Afternoons* and *A Boy was Born*, both pre-Auden, show an already highly developed and original taste in English verse. The poems Britten chose from de la Mare's extensive anthology *Come Hither for Friday Afternoons* show him not just seizing on works which will please schoolboy choristers, but selecting poems with a strong individuality, a definite idiosyncrasy, and no touch of the 'poetic' or half-timbered. The most beautiful tune in the set is fitted to the most mysterious poem, 'A New Year Carol'. Early on, Britten revealed that paramount ability which distinguishes him from many accomplished vocal composers – the finer the poem, the greater the composition it gives rise to.

Several of the poets whose works now mean the most to me I first understood only after hearing his settings of their verse. Thus I had read John Donne but had responded to his baroque exaggeration very imperfectly until I heard Britten's music for nine of the *Holy Sonnets*. There, in his equally extravagant declamation, with its quick-changing moods, its matching of imagery with musical virtuosity, and its reliance on a range of vocal devices from bitter parlando to the most saturated melisma, I found a way into Donne's world. Donnes's universe of auto-angst spoke to me for the first time. Britten's settings are not alien to Donne's poetry: on the contrary, they show the listener how poetical Donne is, and they underline that in linking itself to poetry music may be returning to its true home – at least, when the composer has a genius for song. Poetry, by selection, becomes what Wallace Stevens calls 'a supreme fiction'. A musical genius, knowing where this supreme fiction lies, can serve it in terms of his own art. His technical requirements and the poet's are best matched when they achieve the closest approach to the original and imaginative template. All this is perhaps a roundabout way of saying that living poetry produces living music and respect for the original is best shown by richness of invention. Such is certainly what happens in Britten's Donne songs.

Even more eye- (and ear-) opening for me was the discovery of Christopher Smart's Bedlam poem *Jubilate Agno*, which I first met in Britten's festival cantata, *Rejoice in the Lamb*. I now know the whole torso (only about half of this antiphonal poem has survived) almost by heart, and it has become a key work in my own interior map. Britten's selection of passages for setting reveals an innate understanding of what will go well with music and what will not. He chooses verses from the celebrated passage about Jeoffry, Smart's cat, and Jeoffry's antagonist, the mouse, but he also picks lines which are by no means among the best known. 'Hallelujah from the heart of God and from the hand of the artist inimitable' might be said to cry out for music, as also might the whole passage beginning 'For the instruments are by their rhimes'. But it took a more original mind to discern what could be done with 'For I am in twelve hardships, but he that was born of a virgin shall deliver me out of all', and 'For I am under the same accusation with my saviour – for they said, he is beside himself', and the sublime excerpt 'For at that time malignity ceases and the devils themselves are at peace. / For this time is perceptible to man by a remarkable stillness and serenity of soul.' Britten's musical dramatizing of the poem serves Smart so imaginatively that direct antiphonal exchange is not missed. His selection from the poem becomes a microcosm of the whole of Smart's euphoric Pelagian outpouring. Knitted together in music of rhythmic exactness and great melodic simplicity, the text takes on a wholeness which is true to the unique vision Smart was serving. I can think of no other composer who would have perceived the musical potential of the poem, nor of anyone else undaunted by its oddity, its departure from canons of sense and taste.

My point is not to claim *Rejoice in the Lamb* as one of Britten's greatest compositions: it is perhaps too slender a piece for that. But I am convinced that it enshrines some of the purest responses ever made by a musician to the very heart of that mystery which we know as poetry.

Britten had already shown his originality of inspiration in selecting passages from Rimbaud's *Les Illuminations*, but Rimbaud was the centre of a posthumous cult. The passages selected again reveal Britten's excellent judgement in choosing what suits music. They are not necessarily the most striking parts of the collection, if one judges on purely literary grounds, but they are concrete and rhetorical at once, or they are aphoristic and prophetic. The heart of the cycle is 'Being Beauteous', a poem which needs music to make its greatest impact.

Britten turns the strange tribal poetry of *Les Illuminations* into the musical equivalent of Douanier Rousseau paintings, most notably in 'Antique' and 'Marine'. And when the oracle speaks, its utterance is the purest lyricism, a sort of definition by strangeness – as in 'Phrase' and 'Départ'.

Britten's willingness to write music to texts in foreign languages other than latin has often been remarked upon: his works with foreign language texts tend to be regarded as his most mechanical creations, as *exercises de style*. Such is Peter Pears's view of *Les Illuminations* in his article on Britten's songs in the *Britten Symposium* (pp. 65–6). The opposite seems the case to me: exotic texts lead to Britten's most intense visions. The foreign language brings out an answering hermeticism, a command to the oracular. This is nowhere more evident than in the *Sechs Hölderlin-Fragmente* of 1958. Britten recognized instantly what Hölderlin pieces would sit well with music, and without bypassing the poet's pervasive Philhellenism, sought out that same sense of strangeness which inhabits Smart's more circumstantial apocalyptics.

Not all six poems are properly called fragments – certainly 'Sokrates und Alcibiades' and 'Die Heimat' are highly organized works (Britten fragments the latter by setting only some of its stanzas), but 'Hälfte des Lebens' and 'Die Linien des Lebens' stand in German poetry like uncut gems, pieces of dazzling brilliance from a mind driven mad by the unbearable ordinariness of life. There is a temptation to assert that only a foreigner would dare to add music to so perfect a lyric as 'Hälfte des Lebens', but Britten's willingness to set equally famous poems from the inheritance of his own literature (Keats's sonnet 'To Sleep', Shelley's 'On a poet's lips I slept') show that his confidence in his ability to find notes for the most finished structure is undaunted. However, it is to Hölderlin's madness, as to Smart's, that he turns for his deepest insights (and to desolate Hardy, whose poem 'Before Life and After' distils a love for nescience well beyond the ordinary compass of despair). The four-line epigram which the poet wrote on a piece of wood for his protector Zimmer towards the end of his long and gentle insanity, 'Die Linien des Lebens', is matched by Britten with music of the utmost severity and consolation. 'Die Linien des Lebens' is one of those poems which, once encountered, can seem to irradiate the mind like some fissionable pile. Again, writing as a poet who has had his own invention triggered off by certain works, I am grateful to Britten for directing me to the Hölderlin quatrain. His music lit up the poem for me, and now the two conditions of art, Hölderlin's verse and Britten's music, exist together and independently for me.

Two other Britten song collections must be mentioned here. These are *Winter Words* and *Who are these children?* Thomas Hardy's poetry has attracted many English composers, though not as many as the epigrammatic verse of music-hating Housman. Again, though, only Britten has avoided all touch of the dreaded English pastoral, and reproduced Hardy's urban lyricism and particularly his Victorian or Darwinian doubt. Hardy contributed a wry prefatory note to *Winter Words*, remarking that it was unusual for a man of his advanced years to still be coming before the public with new works. Britten has glossed this by stressing the contrast between, but also the sly alliance of, youth and age in his songs. Most of the poems follow Hardy's musings about the transitoriness of existence, from the autumnal vision of 'A day-close in November' to the breathless renewal of 'Proud Songsters'. 'Before Life and After' is a great poem, and an even greater song – the greatest single song that Britten ever wrote, in my view. Only after meeting the inexorable yet cutting lyricism of this song is one's emotional focus directed back to Hardy. It is schoolmasterly dogma that poetry must be concrete, that it should deal with things not ideas. Yet Hardy uses nothing but abstractions, and makes a masterpiece with them. Who but Britten would have seen this masterly poem still needs the bitter-sweet additive of music to make it complete? For too long before Britten the English genius for music was separated from the more consistently developed English genius for poetry. Bringing them back together to inherit the tradition of Dowland and Purcell would be effected only by a composer whose temperament was poetic and whose love of literature was deep.

The last of my choices of Britten's masterpieces which is also an example of his pioneering taste in purely literary terms is *Who are these children?* written late in his career (1969–71). The commission came from Scotland, which may have pointed Britten's researches north of the border, but only his own instinct took him to William Soutar, the strange invalid poet who died in Perth in the early 1940s. Soutar was that rare thing, a caustic original, and one of the finest poets in the long course of Scottish literature. He wrote in both Scots and English, and his vision is toughened and deepened by looking out from the confinement of an upper room (Emily Dickenson's case). He has something in common with William Blake, writing proverbial poems, snatches of childhood rhyme and concealed prophesies, and is equally at home in formal verse and fierce demotic. The shape of Britten's cycle resembles that of his Blake songs, being a mixture of the proverbial and the lyrical, and alternating Scots and English as well. This is for me by far the most successful of Britten's late vocal (non-operatic) works, and I like to think that its quality is reflected from Soutar's special imagination.

It further develops Britten's perennial themes of the clash of innocence and experience, and the malice of war. The last song is an epigram on that symbol of nobility, an oak tree.

> The auld aik's doun:
> The auld aik's doun:
> Twa hunna year it stüde or mair, ...
> We were sae shair it wud aye be there,
> But noo it's doun, doun.

You can fit out your regret in your own terms as you listen to Britten's setting, so original and traditional at once. Is it civilisation, western tonality, British certainty, human steadfastness, or uncompromising truth which is being honoured in its passing? Could it even be the power of poetry itself which has fallen?

I have deliberately left the libretti of Britten's operas out of the main debate, since I think that the requirements of specially produced dramatic texts alter literary expectations entirely. However, two special relationships with librettists must at least be mentioned. They are with Shakespeare and Auden. I think it fair to say that Britten and Peter Pears rewrote Shakespeare brilliantly in their opera, and did so without adding more than one line to his play. *A Midsummer Night's Dream* is a quintessence, with Britten's music replacing the music, of the verse in Shakespeare's full text. By filleting the play into its three levels of operation – the fairies, the lovers and the mechanicals – Britten was able to expand where the dream status demanded it (the scenes of the reconciled lovers' awakening, for instance) and compress elsewhere. In and out of the magic wood pass the denizens of the dream. Shakespeare's spirit is fully honoured, but the lineaments of musical theatre are substituted for the harangues and tableaux of the play. The fairies are the deepest layer, connected via Bottom to the mechanicals; the lovers and the court are the thin soil of the upper world. The fact that I consider this to be Britten's most beautiful opera (not perhaps his most perfect: I would count *The Turn of the Screw* to be that) is a measure of his tact and imagination in his relations with poetry, especially supreme poetry.

The full story of Britten's friendship with Auden may never be told. Much of it anyway is the concern of his biographer. How far Britten's remarkable certainty when choosing poetry for setting was helped by Auden's tutelage is difficult to tell. Certainly, he never showed the slightest influence of Auden's cranky views of how music and poetry work together. Uncle Wizz affected many people as a bully, whether he intended to or not. Yet Auden's powerful personality worked usually in benign ways, and I can see, throughout Britten's career, vestiges of an approach to poetry which is distinctly Audenish. Clarity, unexpectedness, a fondness for litanies, aphoristic brevity, and a predominant enthusiasm for the crisp and real are all qualities in Britten's vocal music, and Auden's poetry and his productions as an anthologist. Britten's song-cycles of mixed origin show a poetic taste which reflects Auden's many popular compilations. The *Nocturne*, for instance, and the *Serenade* are excellent pocket anthologies, much more like Auden's vision of poetry than any other literary person's.

Britten's imagination pivots on nodes of value which if not necessarily verbal are sited in poetical humanism. And he never profanes the spirit of poetry, never uses it merely as a vehicle for more transcendent things. It is significant that, despite his knowledge of literature, he never supplied his own texts for any work. If the total commitment of a composition like *Parsifal* was beyond him, so was the sense of profanation by ego which that work carried with it. His use of words is never over-reaching, which may be why he turns so often to forms such as the sonnet, the epigram, the antiphon, and the sparse lyrico-dramatic exchanges as are to be found in the miracle plays. To recognize that a poem of such ripe perfection as the Keats sonnet in the *Serenade* could still be made to bear the further weight of music was a daring epiphany. He saw that such sweetness had to be made more sweet, and this he did. The result is paradoxically a purification of Keat's mawkishness.

There is so much of the created world in Britten's music. One is always discovering something new in his delineation of character and place. Smart's line 'For nature is more various than observation tho' observers be innumerable' is Britten's slogan as he adds music to his poetically recorded universe. It should also be the watchword of all who listen to Britten's music and claim to comprehend it.

PETER PORTER

1993

The Poetry

O that I had ne'er been married (1922)

This setting was first performed on 20 May 1976 in the Britten-Pears Library by Peter Pears and Roger Vignoles.

ROBERT BURNS *O that I had ne'er been married*

O that I had ne'er been married,
I wad never had nae care,
Now I've gotten wife and bairns,

porridge   An' they cry crowdie ever mair.
Ance crowdie, twice crowdie,
Three times crowdie in a day;
Gin ye crowdie ony mair,
Ye'll crowdie a' my meal away.

woeful, terrify   Waefu' want and hunger fley me,
Glowrin' by the hallen en';
fought   Sair I fecht them at the door,
indoors   But aye I'm eerie they come ben.
Ance crowdie, ...

Beware (1923)

HENRY LONGFELLOW *Beware* (from the German)

I know a maiden fair to see,
    Take care!
She can both false and friendly be,
    Beware! Beware!
    Trust her not,
She is fooling thee!

She has two eyes, so soft and brown,
    Take care!
She gives a side-glance and looks down,
    Beware! Beware!
    Trust her not,
She is fooling thee!

[And she has hair of a golden hue,
    Take care!
And what she says, it is not true,
    Beware! Beware!
    Trust her not,
She is fooling thee!

She has a bosom as white as snow,
    Take care!
She knows how much it is best to show,
    Beware! Beware!
    Trust her not,
She is fooling thee!

She gives thee a garland woven fair,
    Take care!
It is a fool's-cap for thee to wear,
    Beware! Beware!
    Trust her not,
She is fooling thee!]

Epitaph 1926

HERBERT ASQUITH *The volunteer*
'Epitaph'

Here lies the clerk who half his life had spent
Toiling at ledgers in a city grey,
Thinking that so his days would drift away
With no lance broken in life's tournament:
Yet ever 'twixt the books and his bright eyes
The gleaming eagles of legions came,
And horsemen, charging under phantom skies,
Went thundering past beneath the oriflamme.†

[And now those waiting dreams satisfied;
From twilight to the halls of dawn he went;
His lance is broken; but he lies content
With that high hour, in which he lived and died.
And falling thus, he wants no recompense,
Who found his battle in the last resort;
Nor needs he any hearse to bear him hence,
Who goes to join the men of Agincourt.]

†oriflamme: a banderole of two or three points
of red silk attached to a lance.

Quatre Chansons Françaises 'Four French Songs' (1928)

These songs were first performed in a broadcast on 30 March 1980, and at the Aldeburgh Festival on 10 June 1980, by Heather Harper and the English Chamber Orchestra conducted by Steuart Bedford.

VICTOR HUGO   *Nuits de Juin (June Nights)*

L'Été, lorsque le jour a fui, de fleurs couverte
La plaine verse au loin un parfum enivrant;
Les yeux fermés, l'oreille aux rumeurs entr'ouverte,
On ne dort qu'à demi d'un sommeil transparent.

In summertime, at close of day, a heady scent rises from the flower-covered meadows. With eyes closed and ears half-open, only a transparent half-sleep is possible.

Les astres sont plus purs, l'ombre paraît meilleure:
Un vague demi-jour teint le dôme éternel;
Et l'aube douce et pâle, en attendant son heure,
Semble toute la nuit errer au bas du ciel.

The stars seem brighter, the darkness deeper; a faint half-light streaks the eternal dome and the pale, peaceful dawn, awaiting its time, seems to hover at the edge of the sky all the night long.

PAUL VERLAINE   *Sagesse (Wisdom)*

Le ciel est, par-dessus le toit,
     Si bleu, si calme!
Un arbre, par-dessus le toit,
     Berce sa palme.

Above the roof, the sky is so blue, so calm! Above the roof, a tree-branch sways.

La cloche, dans le ciel qu'on voit,
     Doucement tinte.
Un oiseau sur l'arbre qu'on voit
     Chante sa plainte.

The bell in the sky gently tolls. A bird in the tree sings its sad song.

Mon Dieu, mon Dieu, la vie est là,
     Simple et tranquille.
Cette paisible rumeur-là
     Vient de la ville!

Oh God, life is there, simple and tranquil. I can hear the peaceful sounds of the town.

–Qu'as-tu fait, ô toi que voilà
     Pleurant sans cesse,
Dis, qu'as-tu fait, toi que voilà,
     De ta jeunesse?

What have you done, you there, weeping ceaselessly? Tell me, what have you done with your young life?

VICTOR HUGO   *L'Enfance* (*Childhood*)

L'enfant chantait; la mère au lit, exténuée,
Agonisait, beau front dans l'ombre se penchant;
La mort au-dessus d'elle errait dans la nuée;
Et j'écoutais ce râle, et j'entendais ce chant.

The child was singing; the mother, stretched out on the bed, lay dying, her beautiful face turned towards the darkness. Death hovered in the mists above her. I listened to that death-rattle, and I heard that song.

L'enfant avait cinq ans, et près de la fenêtre
Ses rires et ses jeux faisaient un charmant bruit;
Et la mère, à côté de ce pauvre doux être
Qui chantait tout le jour, toussait toute la nuit.

The child was five years old, and outside the window the sound of his games and his laughter were enchanting. The poor sweet creature sang all day, and the mother coughed all night.

La mère alla dormir sous les dalles du cloître
Et le petit enfant se remit à chanter –
La douleur est un fruit; Dieu ne le fait pas croître
Sur la branche trop faible encor pour le porter.

The mother was laid to rest beneath the stones in the cloister, and the little child took up his song again. Sorrow is a fruit: God does not permit it to grow on a branch too weak to bear it.

PAUL VERLAINE   *Chanson d'Automne* (*Autumn Song*)

Les sanglots longs
Des violons
   De l'automne
Blessent mon coeur
D'une langueur
   Monotone.

The slow sobbing of the violins of autumn wounds my heart with monotonous languor.

Tout suffocant
Et blême, quand
   Sonne l'heure,
Je me souviens
Des jours anciens
   Et je pleure;

Breathless and pale, as the hour strikes, I remember former days and weep;

Et je m'en vais
Au vent mauvais
   Qui m'emporte
Deça, delà,
Pareil à la
   Feuille morte.

and I let the rough wind toss me this way and that, like a dead leaf.

Tit for Tat (1928–31, rev. 1968)

These five settings from boyhood of poems by Walter de la Mare, for voice and piano, were first performed in the revised version on 23 June 1969 at the Aldeburgh Festival by John Shirley-Quirk and Britten. They were dedicated 'For Dick de la Mare June 4th 1969'.

WALTER LA MARE

A song of enchantment

A song of enchantment I sang me there,
In a green-green wood, by waters fair,
Just as the words came up to me
I sang it under the wild wood tree.

Widdershins turned I, singing it low,
Watching the wild birds come and go;
No cloud in the deep dark blue to be seen
Under the thick-thatched branches green.

Twilight came; silence came;
The planet of evening's silver flame;
By darkening paths I wandered through
Thickets trembling with drops of dew.

But the music is lost and the words are gone
Of the song I sang as I sat alone,
Ages and ages have fallen on me–
On the wood and the pool and the elder tree.

Autumn

There is a wind where the rose was;
Cold rain where sweet grass was;
   And clouds like sheep
   Stream o'er the steep
Grey skies where the lark was.

Nought gold where your hair was;
Nought warm where your hand was;
   But phantom, forlorn,

Beneath the thorn,
Your ghost where your face was.

Sad winds where your voice was;
Tears, tears where my heart was;
    And ever with me,
    Child, ever with me,
Silence where hope was.

Silver

Slowly, silently, now the moon
Walks the night in her silver shoon;
This way, and that, she peers, and sees
Silver fruit upon silver trees;
One by one the casements catch
Her beams beneath the silvery thatch;
Couched in his kennel, like a log,
With paws of silver sleeps the dog;
[From their shadowy cote the white breasts peep
Of doves in a silver-feathered sleep;]
A harvest mouse goes scampering by,
With silver claws, and silver eye;
And moveless fish in the water gleam,
By silver reeds in a silver stream.

Vigil

Dark is the night,
    The fire burns faint and low,
Hours – days – years
    Into grey ashes go;
I strive to read,
    But sombre is the glow.

Thumbed are the pages,
    And the print is small;
Mocking the winds
    That from the darkness call;
Feeble the fire that lends
    Its light withal.

O ghost, draw nearer;
    Let thy shadowy hair

Blot out the pages
That we cannot share;
Be ours the one last leaf
By Fate left bare!

Let's Finis scrawl,
And then Life's book put by;
Turn each to each
In all simplicity:
Ere the last flame is gone
To warm us by.

Tit for tat

Have you been catching of fish, Tom Noddy?
Have you snared a weeping hare?
Have you whistled, 'No Nunny,' and gunned a poor bunny,
Or a blinded bird of the air?

Have you trod like a murderer through the green woods,
Through the dewy deep dingles and glooms,
While every small creature screamed shrill to Dame Nature,
'He comes – and he comes!'?

Wonder I very much do, Tom Noddy,
If ever, when off you roam,
An Ogre from space will stoop a lean face
And lug you home:

Lug you home over his fence, Tom Noddy,
Of thorn-sticks nine yards high,
With your bent knees strung round his old iron gun
And your head dan-dangling by:

And hang you up stiff on a hook, Tom Noddy,
From a stone-cold pantry shelf,
Whence your eyes will glare in an empty stare,
Till you are cooked yourself!

Tit for Tat (1928–31, rev. 1968)

A Wealden trio: the song of the women (1929, rev. 1967)

This carol for unaccompanied women's voices was first performed on 19 June 1968 at the Aldeburgh Festival by The Ambrosian Singers, conducted by Philip Ledger. It was dedicated 'For Rosamund' [Strode].

FORD MADOX FORD   *The song of the women*

A Wealden trio

1st Voice When ye've got a child 'ats whist for want of food,
　And a grate as grey's y'r 'air for want of wood,
　And y'r man and you ain't nowise not much good;
Together Oh –
　It's hard work a-Christmassing,
　Carolling,
　Singin' songs about 'the Babe what's born'.
2nd Voice When ye've 'eered the bailiff's 'and upon the latch,
　And ye've feeled the rain a-trickling through the thatch,
　An' y'r man can't git no stones to break ner yit no sheep to watch –
Together Oh –
　We've got to come a-Christmassing,
　Carolling,
　Singin' of the 'Shepards on that morn'.
3rd Voice, more cheerfully 'E was a man as poor as us, very near,
　An' 'E 'ad 'is trials and danger,
　An' I think 'E'll think of us when 'E sees us singin' 'ere;
　For 'is mother was poor, like us, poor dear,
　An' she bore Him in a manger.
Together Oh –
　It's warm in the heavens, but it's cold upon the earth,
　And we ain't no food at table nor no fire upon the hearth;
　And it's bitter hard a-Christmassing,
　Carolling,
　Singin' songs about our Saviour's birth;
　Singin' songs about the Babe what's born;
　Singin' of the shepards on that morn.

The birds (1929)

Set for voice and piano, and dedicated 'for my mother'. It was performed at his mother's funeral and his sister's wedding.

HILAIRE BELLOC *The birds*

When Jesus Christ was four years old,
The angels brought Him toys of gold,
Which no man ever bought or sold.
And yet with these He would not play,
He made Him small fowl out of clay,
And blessed them till they flew away;

Thou hast created
them, O Lord
Tu creasti Domine.

Jesus Christ, Thou child so wise,
Bless mine hands and fill mine eyes,
And bring my soul to Paradise.

A hymn to the Virgin (1930)

This anthem, for mixed voices unaccompanied, was first performed on 5 January 1931 at St John's Church, Lowestoft, by the Lowestoft Musical Society.

ANON. (c. 1300) (tr. Ian Hamnett) *A hymn to the Virgin*

one	Of on that is so fayr and bright
like a star of the sea	*Velut maris stella,*
	Brighter than the day is light,
mother and virgin	*Parens et puella:*
	Ic crie to the, thou see to me,
lady	Levedy, preye thi Sone for me,
so good	*Tam pia,*
	That ic mote come to thee
	Maria.
	Al this world was for-lore
by the sinning Eve	*Eva peccatrice,*
	Tyl our Lord was y-bore
of you his mother	*De te genetrice.*
hail	With *ave* it went away
	Thuster nyth and comz the day
of salvation	*Salutis;*
	The welle springeth ut of the,
goodness	*Virtutis;.*
	Levedy, flour of alle thing,
rose without thorn	*Rosa sine spina,*
	Thu bere Jhesu, hevene king,
by divine grace	*Gratia divina:*
	Of alle thu ber'st the pris,
	Levedy, quene of paradys
elected	*Electa:*
	Mayde milde, moder *es*
thou wert made	*Effecta.*

The sycamore tree (1930, rev. 1967)

This carol, for unaccompanied choir, was first performed in its revised version on 19 June 1968 at the Aldeburgh Festival, by The Ambrosian Singers conducted by Philip Ledger. It was dedicated 'For Imo' (Imogen Holst).

TRAD.   *The sycamore tree;* (*'I saw three ships'*)

As I sat under a sycamore tree,
A sycamore tree, a sycamore tree,
I looked me out upon the sea
On Christ's Sunday at morn.

I saw three ships a–sailing there,
A–sailing there, a–sailing there,
Jesu, Mary and Joseph they bare
On Christ's Sunday at morn.

Joseph did whistle and Mary did sing,
Mary did sing, Mary did sing,
And all the bells on earth did ring
For joy our Lord was born.

O they sail'd into Bethlehem!
To Bethlehem, to Bethlehem;
Saint Michael was the steerèsman.
prow   Saint John sat in the horn.

And all the bells on earth did ring
On earth did ring, on earth did ring
'Welcome be thou Heaven's King,
On Christ's Sunday at morn!'

Thy King's Birthday (1931)

This 'Christmas suite' for soprano and alto soloists and mixed chorus might be considered a trial run for the slightly later Christmas anthology, A Boy Was Born;. The first performance of the whole work did not take place until 1991, when it was given by the Britten Singers, directed by Stephen Wilkinson, at the Aldeburgh Festival. But Britten did revise two of the songs, 'New Prince, New Pomp' and 'Sweet was the Song', and these were performed at the 1955 and 1966 Aldeburgh Festivals respectively.

HENRY VAUGHAN *Christ's nativity*

Awake, glad heart! get up and sing!
It is the birthday of thy King.
   Awake! Awake!
   The sun doth shake
Light from his locks, and all the way,
Breathing perfumes, doth spice the day.

Awake! awake! hark how th' wood rings,
Winds whisper, and the busy springs
   A concert make.
   Awake! Awake!
Man is their high priest, and should rise
To offer up the sacrifice.

I would I were some bird, or star,
Fluttering in woods, or lifted far
   Above this inn
   And road of sin;
Then either star or bird should be
Shining or singing still to Thee.

I would I had in my best part
Fit rooms for Thee! or that my heart
   Were so clean as
   Thy manger was!
But I am all filth, and obscene;
Yet, if Thou wilt, Thou canst make me clean.

Sweet Jesu! will then. Let no more
This leper haunt and soil Thy door!
    Cure him, ease him,
     O release him!
And let once more by mystic birth,
The Lord of life be born in earth.

ANON. (early 17th century)   *Sweet was the song*

Sweet was the song the Virgin sung,
When she to Bethlem Juda came,
And was delivered of a Son,
That blessed Jesus hath to name.
Lulla, lulla, lulla, lullaby;
Lulla, lulla, lulla, lullaby, sweet Babe, sang she.
My Son and eke a Saviour born,
Who hast vouchsafed from on high
To visit us that were forlorn;
Lalula, lalula, lalulaby, sweet Babe, sang she,
And rocked Him sweetly on her knee.

ANON. (17th century)   *Preparation*

Yet if His Majesty, our sovran lord,
Should of his own accord
Friendly himself invite,
And say, 'I'll be your guest tomorrow night,'
How should we stir ourselves, call and command
All hands to work. 'Let no man idle stand!

'Set me fine Spanish tables in the hall;
See they be fitted all;
Let there be room to eat
And order taken that there want no meat.
See every sconce and candlestick made bright,
That without tapers they may give a light.

'Look to the presence: are the carpets spread,
dais   The dazie o'er the head,
The cushions in the chairs,
And all the candles lighted on the stairs?
Perfume the chambers, and in any case
Let each man give attendance in his place.'

Thus, if a king were coming, would we do;
And 'twere good reason too;
For 'tis a duteous thing
To show all honour to an earthly king,
And after all our travail and our cost,
So he be pleased, to think no labour lost.

But at the coming of the King of Heaven
All's set at six and seven;
We wallow in our sin,
Christ cannot find a chamber in the inn.
We entertain Him always like a stranger,
And, as at first, still lodge Him in the manger.

ROBERT SOUTHWELL   *New Prince, new pompe*

He... spared not his own son, but delivered him up for us all.
  (Romans 8:32)
The Lord is very pitiful, and of tender mercy. (James 5:11)

Behold a silly tender Babe,
    In freesing Winter night;
In homely manger trembling lies,
    Alas a pitteous sight:

[The Innes are full, no man will yeeld
    This little Pilgrime bed;
But forc'd he is with silly beasts,
    In Crib to shroud his head.]

Despise not him for lying there,
    First what he is enquire:
[An orient pearle is often found
    In depth of dirty mire,

Waigh not his Crib, his wooden dish,
    Nor beasts that by him feede:
Waigh not his Mothers poore attire,
    Nor Josephs simple weede.

This stable is a Princes Court,
    The Crib his chaire of state:
The beasts are parcell of his pompe,
    The wooden dish his plate.

The persons in that poore attire,
    His royall livories weare,]
The Prince himselfe is come from heaven,
    This pomp is prized there.

[With joy approach o Christian wight,
    Doe homage to thy King;
And highly prize this humble pompe, †
    Which he from heaven dooth bring.]

† Britten has 'praise' instead of 'prize'.
Britten made a somewhat different selection of Southwell's verses for inclusion in
A Ceremony of Carols (see p.94).

C.W. STUBBS   *The carol of King Cnut*

O, merry rang the hymn
Across the fenlands dim;
O Joy the day!
When Cnut the king sailed by,
O, row, my men, more might
And hear that holy cry,
Sing Gloria!

It was the Christmas morn
Whereon the Child was born,
O Joy the day!
On lily banks among,
Where fragrant flowers throng
For maiden posies sprung?
Ah nay! ah nay!

It was the winter cold
Whereon the tale was told,
O Joy the day!
What hap did then befall
To men and women all,
From that poor cattle stall,
O Gloria!

The shepherds in a row
Knelt by the cradle low,
O Joy the day!
And told the angel song
They heard their sheep among,
When all the heavenly throng
Sang Gloria!

Sing joy, my masters, sing,
And let the welkin ring,
O Gloria!
And Nowell, Nowell! cry,
The Child is King most High,
O sovran victory!
Sing Joy the day!

Three Two–Part Songs (1932)

These songs, for boys' or women's voices and piano, were first performed on 12 December 1932 at a Macnaghten–Lemare concert at the Ballet Club (Mercury Theatre), London.

WALTER DE LA MARE   *The ride-by-nights*

Up on their brooms the Witches stream,
Crooked and black in the crescent's gleam;
One foot high, and one foot low,
Bearded, cloaked, and cowled, they go.
'Neath Charlie's Wain they twitter and tweet,
And away they swarm 'neath the Dragon's feet,
With a whoop and a flutter they swing and sway,
And surge pell-mell down the Milky Way.
Between the legs of the glittering Chair
They hover and squeak in the empty air.
Then round they swoop past the glimmering Lion
To where Sirius barks behind huge Orion;
Up, then, and over to wheel amain
Under the silver, and home again.

The rainbow

I saw the lovely arch
Of Rainbow span the sky,
The gold sun burning
As the rain swept by.

In bright-ringed solitude
The showery foliage shone
One lovely moment,
And the Bow was gone.

The ship of Rio

There was a ship of Rio
    Sailed out into the blue,
And nine and ninety monkeys
    Were all her jovial crew.
From bo'sun to the cabin boy,
    From quarter to caboose,
There weren't a stitch of calico
    To breech 'em – tight or loose;
From spar to deck, from deck to keel,
    From barnacle to shroud,
There weren't one pair of reach-me-downs
    To all that jabbering crowd.
But wasn't it a gladsome sight,
    When roared the deep-sea gales,
To see them reef her fore and aft,
    A-swinging by their tails!
Oh, wasn't it a gladsome sight,
    When glassy calm did come,
To see them squatting tailor-wise
    Around a keg of rum!
Oh, wasn't it a gladsome sight,
    When in she sailed to land,
To see them all a-scampering skip
    For nuts across the sand!

A Boy Was Born, Op. 3 (1932–3, rev. 1955)

These choral variations for men's, women's and boys' voices were initially broadcast by the BBC; on 23 February 1934, and first performed at a London Macnaghten-Lemare concert on 17 December of the same year. They were dedicated 'To my Father'.

ANON. (16th century)   *A boy was born (Puer natus)*

A boy was born in Bethlehem;
Rejoice for that, Jerusalem.
Alleluya.

[For low he lay within a stall,
Who rules for ever over all:]

He let himself a servant be,
That all mankind he might set free:

Then praise the Word of God who came
To dwell within a human frame:

[And praised be God in threefold might,
    And glory bright,
Eternal good and infinite.]

ANON. (before 1536)   *Lullay, Jesu*

Mine own dear mother, sing lullay.
Lullay, Jesu, lullay, lullay.
Mine own dear mother, sing lullay.
So blessed a sight it was to see,
How Mary rocked her Son so free;
    So fair she rocked and sang 'by-by.'

'Mine own dear Son, why weepest Thou thus?
Is not Thy father King of bliss?
Have I not done that in me is?
    Your grievance, tell me what it is.'

'Therefore, mother, weep I nought,
But for the woe that shall be wrought
To me, ere I mankind have bought.

['Mother, the time ye shall see
Th[at] sorrow shall break your heart in three,
So foul the Jews shall fare with me.

'When I am naked, they will me take,
And fast bind me to a stake,
And beat me sore for man his sake.

'Upon the Cross they shall me cast,
Hand and foot, nail me fast;
Yet gall shall be my drink at last;
    Thus shall my life pass away.]

'Ah, dear mother! yet shall a spear
My heart in sunder all to-tear;
No wonder though I careful were.

'Now, dear mother, sing lullay,
    And put away all heaviness;
Into this world I took the way,
    Again to [heaven] I shall me dress,
Where joy is without end ay
    Mine own dear mother…

ANON. (before 1529)   *Worship we this holy day*   'Herod'

furious   Herod that was both wild and wode,
             Full much he shed of Christian blood,
             To slay that Child so meek of mood,
             That maid Mary bare, that clean may. †

laden   Mary with Jesu forth yfraught,
             As the angel her taught,
             To flee the land till it were sought,
             To Egypt she took her way.

faith   Herod slew with pride and sin
             Thousands of two year and within;
             The body of Christ he thought to win
             And to destroy the Christian fay.

             Now Jesus that didst die for us on the Rood,
             And didst christen innocents in their blood,
             By the prayer of Thy mother good,
             Bring us to bliss that lasteth ay.

             † Britten set the verses in the order 1,3,2,4

A Boy Was Born, Op. 3 (1932–3, rev. 1955)   [21

ANON. (15th century) *Jesu, as Thou art our Saviour*

> *Jesu, Jesu, Jesu, Jesu,*
> *Save us all through Thy virtue.*

Jesu, as Thou art our Saviour
That Thou save us fro dolour.
Jesu is mine paramour.
> *Blessed be Thy name, Jesu.*

Jesu was born of a may,
Upon Christëmas Day,
She was may beforn and ay,
> *Blessed be Thy name, Jesu.*

[Three kingës comen fro Segent,
To Jesu Christ they brought present.
Lord God Omnipotent,
> *Save us all through Thy virtue.*

Jesu died and shed His blood
For all mankind upon the Rood;
He grant us grace of happës good,
> *I beseech Thee, sweet Jesu.*

Jesu, for Thy mother's sake,
Keep us fro the fiendës black;
Against Him that we may wake;
> *And save us all through Thy virtue.*]

ANON. (15th century) *Now is Christmas ycome* 'The three kings'

[Now is Christmas ycome,
Father and Son together in one,
Holy Ghost, as ye be one,
together   in fere-a,
God send us a good New Year-a!

I would you sing for an I might,
Of a Child is fair in sight,
His mother him bare this endernight
                    so still-a
And as it was His will-a.]

There came three kings fro Galilee
Into Bethlehem, that fair city,
To seek Him that ever should be

A Boy Was Born, Op. 3 (1932–3, rev. 1955)

by right-a,
Lord and king and knight-a.

[As they came forth with their offering,
They met with Herod, that moody king,
this tide-a,
And this to them he said-a:

'Of whence be ye, you kingës three?'
'Of the East, as you may see,
To seek Him that ever should be
by right-a,
Lord and king and knight-a.'

When you at this child have be,
Come home again by me,
Tell me the sight that you have see,
I pray you;
Go you no other way-a.']

They took their leave, both old and ying,
Of Herod, that moody king;
They went forth with their offering
by light-a,
By the star that shone so bright-a.

Till they came into the place
Where Jesus and His mother was,
Offered they up with great solace
in fere-a
Gold, incense, and myrrh-a.

[The Father of heaven an angel down sent
these   To thiccy three kings that made present
this tide-a,
And this to them he said-a.

'My Lord hath warned you every one,
By Herod king you go not home;
slay   For an you do, he will you slone
destroy   and strye-a,
And hurt you wonderly-a.']

Forth then went these kingës three,
Till they came home to their country:
Glad and blithe they were all three
together   Of the sight that they had see
bydene-a.†

[† Britten did not set the last line of v.11 and all of v.12.]

A Boy Was Born, Op. 3 (1932–3, rev. 1955)   [23

In the bleak mid-winter
    Frosty wind made moan,
Earth stood hard as iron,
    Water like a stone;
Snow had fallen, snow on snow,
    Snow on snow,
In the bleak mid-winter,
    Long ago.

[Our God, heaven cannot hold him
    Nor earth sustain;
Heaven and earth shall flee away
    When he comes to reign:
In the bleak mid-winter
    A stable-place sufficed
The Lord God Almighty
    Jesus Christ.

Enough for him, whom Cherubim
    Worship night and day,
A breastful of milk,
    And a mangerful of hay;

Enough for him, whom Angels
    Fall down before,
The ox and ass and camel
    Which adore.

Angels and Archangels
    May have gathered there,
Cherubim and Seraphim
    Throngèd the air:
But only his mother
    In her maiden bliss
Worshipped the Belovèd
    With a kiss.

A Boy Was Born, Op. 3 (1932–3, rev. 1955)

What can I give him?
Poor as I am?
If I were a shepherd
I would bring a lamb;
If I were a wise man
I would do my part;
Yet what I can I give him –
Give my heart.]

ANON. (before 1536)   *Lully, lulley, lully, lulley*

Lully, lulley, lully, lulley,
mate   The falcon hath borne my make away.

He bare him up, he bare him down,
He bare him into an orchard brown.

In that orchard there was an hall,
That was hangëd with purple and pall.

And in that hall there was a bed,
It was hangëd with gold so red.

And in that bed there lieth a knight,
His woundës bleeding, day and night.

By that bedside kneeleth a may,
And she weepeth both night and day.

And by that bedside there standeth a stone,
Corpus Christi written thereon.

ANON. (15th century)   *Noel*

Good day, good day,
My Lord Sir Christemas, good day.
Good day, Sir Christemas our King,
For every man, both old and ying,
Is glad of your coming.

Godes Son, so much of might
From heaven to earth down is light
And born is of a maid so bright.

THOMAS TUSSER (1558) *Christmas*

holly   Get ivy and hull, woman, deck up thine house,
And take this same brawn for to seethe and to souse;
Provide us good cheer, for thou knowest the old guise,
Old customs that good be, let no man despise.
At Christmas be merry and thank God of all,
And feast thy poor neighbours, the great and the small.
Yea, all the year long have an eye to the poor,
And God shall send luck to keep open thy door.
Good fruit and good plenty do well in thy loft,
Then lay for an orchard and cherish it oft.
The profit is mickle, the pleasure is much;
At pleasure with profit few wise men will grutch.
For plants and for stocks lay aforehand to cast,

Christmas to   But set or remove them, while Twelve-tide do last.
Twelfth Night

ANON. (15th century) *Welcome Yule*

Noel, noel, noel, noel.
[Welcome Yule, thou merry man,
In worship of this holy day.]
Welcome be thou, heaven-king,
Welcome born in one morning,
Welcome for whom we shall sing
Welcome Yule.

[Welcome be ye, Stephen and John,
Welcome Innocents every one,
Welcome Thomas, Martyr one:

Welcome be ye, good New Year,
together   Welcome Twelfth Day, both in fere,
beloved   Welcome Saintès lief and dear:

Welcome be ye, Candlemas,
Welcome be ye, queen of bliss,
Welcome both to more and less:]

Welcome be ye that are here,
Welcome all, and make good cheer,
Welcome all another year.
Noel, noel, noel, noel.

26]   A Boy Was Born, Op. 3 (1932–3, rev. 1955)

FRANCIS QUARLES *A Christmas carol*

Wassail, wassail.
Lully, lully,
Noel, Noel!
Herod that was so wild and wode.

Glory to God on high, and jolly mirth
'Twixt man and man, and peace on earth!
Mine own dear mother Jesu! Jesu!

This night a Child is born;
This night a Son is given;
This Son, this Child
Hath reconciled
Poor man that was forlorn,
And the angry God of heaven.
Hosanna, sing Hosanna!

Now, now that joyful day,
That blessed hour is come,
That was foretold
In days of old,
Wherein all nations may
Bless, bless the virgin's womb.
Hosanna, sing Hosanna!

Let heaven triumph above,
Let earth rejoice below;
Let heaven and earth
Be filled with mirth,
For peace and lasting love
Atones your God and you.
Hosanna, sing Hosanna!
Sing Noel.

A Boy Was Born, Op. 3 (1932–3, rev. 1955)   [27

Two Part-Songs (1933)

These two songs, for chorus and piano, were first performed on 11 December 1933 at a Macnaghten-Lemare concert at the Ballet Club (Mercury Theatre), London.

GEORGE WITHER *A love sonnet* 'I lov'd a lass'

I loved a lass, a fair one,
    As fair as e'er was seen;
She was indeed a rare one,
    Another Sheba Queen:
But, fool as then I was,
    I thought she loved me too:
But now, alas! sh'as left me,
    Falero, lero, loo!

Her hair like gold did glister,
    Each eye was like a star,
She did surpass her sister,
    Which passed all others far;
She would me honey call,
    She'd – oh, she'd kiss me too!
But now, alas! sh'as left me,
    Falero, lero, loo! &c.

[In summer time to Medley
    My Love and I would go:
The boatman there stood ready
    My Love and I to row;
For cream there would we call,
    For cakes and for prunes too:
But now, alas! sh'as left me,

Many a merry meeting
    My Love and I have had;
She was my only sweeting,
    She made my heart full glad;
The tears stood in her eyes
    Like to the morning dew:
But now, alas! sh'as left me,]

And as abroad we walkëd,
    As lovers' fashion is,
Oft as we sweetly talkëd
    The sun would steal a kiss;
The wind upon her lips
    Likewise most sweetly blew:
But now, alas! sh'as left me,

Her cheeks were like the cherry,
    Her skin as white as snow;
When she was blithe and merry
    She angel-like did show;
Her waist exceeding small,
    The fives did fit her shoe:
But now, alas! sh'as left me,

[In summer time or winter
    She had her heart's desire;
I still did scorn to stint her
    From sugar, sack, or fire:
The world went round about,
    No cares we ever knew:
But now, alas! sh'as left me,

As we walked home together,
    At midnight, through the town,
To keep away the weather
    O'er her I'd cast my gown;
No cold my Love should feel,
    Whate'er the heavens could do:
But now, alas! sh'as left me,

Like doves we would be billing,
    And clip and kiss so fast,
Yet she would be unwilling
    That I should kiss the last:
They're Judas kisses now,
    Since that they proved untrue:
For now, alas! sh'as left me,

To maidens' vows and swearing
    Henceforth no credit give;
You may give them the hearing,
    But never them believe;
They are as false as fair,
    Unconstant, frail, untrue:
For mine, alas! has left me,

'Twas I that paid for all things,
    'Twas others drank the wine;
I cannot now recall things,
    Live but a fool to pine;
'Twas I that beat the bush,
    The bird to others flew:
For she alas! hath left me,

If ever that Dame Nature,
    For this false lover's sake,
Another pleasing creature
    Like unto her would make,
Let her remember this –
    To make the other true:
For this, alas! hath left me,

No riches now can raise me,
    No want make me despair,
No misery amaze me,
    Nor yet for want I care;
I have lost a world itself:
    My earthly heaven, adieu!
Since she, alas! hath left me,
    Falero, lero, loo!]

ROBERT GRAVES *Song: Lift-boy* 'Lift-boy'

Let me tell you the story of how I began:
I began as the boot-boy and ended as the boot-man,
With nothing in my pockets but a jack-knife and a button,
With nothing in my pockets but a jack-knife and a button,
With nothing in my pockets.

Let me tell you the story of how I went on:
I began as the lift-boy and ended as the lift-man,
With nothing in my pockets but a jack-knife and a button,
With nothing in my pockets but a jack-knife and a button,
With nothing in my pockets.

I found it very easy to whistle and play
With nothing in my head or my pockets all day,
With nothing in my pockets.

But along came Old Eagle, like Moses or David;
He stopped at the fourth floor and preached me Damnation:
'Not a soul shall be savèd, not one shall be savèd.
The whole First Creation shall forfeit salvation:
From knife-boy to lift-boy, from ragged to regal,
Not one shall be savèd, not you, not Old Eagle,
No soul on earth escapeth, even if all repent –'
So I cut the cords of the lift and down we went,
With nothing in our pockets.

Can a phonograph lie?

A song very neatly contrived to make you and me
Laugh.

Te Deum in C (1934)

This setting, for solo treble, choir and organ (or strings, and harp or piano) was first performed on 13 November 1935 at St Michael's, Cornhill, London. It was 'Written for Maurice Vinden and the Choir of St Mark's, N. Audley Street, London'.

Festival Te Deum Op. 32 (1944)

This setting, for chorus and organ, was first performed on 24 April 1945 in St Mark's Church, Swindon. It was 'Written for the Centenary Festival of St Mark's, Swindon'.

TE DEUM   *The Book of Common Prayer*

We praise thee, O God: we acknowledge thee to be the Lord.
All the earth doth worship thee, the Father everlasting.
To thee all Angels cry aloud: the Heavens, and all the Powers therein.
To thee Cherubim and Seraphim continually do cry,
Holy, Holy, Holy, Lord God of Sabaoth;
Heaven and earth are full of the Majesty of thy Glory.

The glorious company of the Apostles praise thee.
The goodly fellowship of the Prophets praise thee.
The noble army of Martyrs praise thee.
The holy Church throughout all the world doth acknowledge thee,
The Father of an infinite Majesty;
Thine honourable, true, and only Son;
Also the Holy Ghost, the Comforter.

Thou art the King of Glory, O Christ.
Thou art the everlasting Son of the Father.
When thou tookest upon thee to deliver man,
    thou didst not abhor the Virgin's womb.
When thou hadst overcome the sharpness of death, thou didst
    open the Kingdom of Heaven to all believers.
Thou sittest at the right hand of God, in the glory of the Father.

We believe that thou shalt come to be our Judge.
We therefore pray thee, help thy servants,
   whom thou hast redeemed with thy precious blood.
Make them to be numbered with thy Saints in glory everlasting.
O Lord, save thy people, and bless thine heritage.
Govern them, and lift them up for ever.
Day by day we magnify thee;
And we worship thy Name, ever world without end.
Vouchsafe, O Lord, to keep us this day without sin.

O Lord, have mercy upon us, have mercy upon us.
O Lord, let thy mercy lighten upon us, as our trust is in thee.
O Lord, in thee have I trusted; let me never be confounded.

May (1934)

A unison song with piano accompaniment.

ANON.   *Now is the month of maying*   'May'

> Now is the month of maying,
> When merry lads are playing, fa la,
> Each with his bonny lass
> Upon the greeny grass. Fa la.
>
> The Spring, clad all in gladness,
> Doth laugh at Winter's sadness, fa la.
> And to the bagpipe's sound
> The nymphs tread out their ground. Fa la.
>
> Fie then, why sit we musing,
> Youth's sweet delight refusing, fa la?
> Say, dainty nymphs, and speak,
> Shall we play barley-break? Fa la.

Friday Afternoons Op. 7 (1933–5)

These twelve children's songs with piano accompaniment were dedicated 'To R.H.M.B. and the boys of Clive House, Prestatyn, 1934'. R.H.M.B was Britten's brother and Headmaster of the school.

ANON. (17th century)   *Begone, dull care*

Begone dull care, I prithee begone from me.
Begone, dull care, you and I shall never agree.
Long time has thou been tarrying here and fain thou would'st me kill,
But, i' faith, thou never shalt have thy will.

Too much care will make a young man turn grey,
And too much care will turn an old man to clay.
My wife shall dance and I will sing, and merrily pass the day,
For I hold it one of the wisest things to drive dull care away.

WILLIAM MAKEPEACE THACKERAY   *A tragic story*

There lived a sage in days of yore,
And he a handsome pigtail wore,
But wondered much and sorrowed more,
Because it hung behind him.

He mused upon this curious case,
And swore he'd change his pigtail's place,
And have it hanging at his face,
Not dangling there behind him.

Says he, 'The mystery I've found,
I'll turn me round.' He turned him round,
He turned him round, he turned him round,
But still it hung behind him.

Then round and round, and out and in,
All day the puzzled sage did spin;
In vain it mattered not a pin,
The pigtail hung behind him.

And right and left, and round about,
And up and down, and in and out
He turned, but still the pigtail stout
Hung steadily behind him.

And though his efforts never slack,
And though he twist, and twirl, and tack,
Alas! still faithful to his back
The pigtail hangs behind him.

JANE TAYLOR *Cuck-oo!*

Cuck-òo, Cuck-òo!
What do you do?
    'In April
I open my bill;
    In May
I sing night and day;
    In June
I change my tune;
    In July
Far – far I fly;
    In August
Away I *must.*'

ANON. *Ee-oh!*

The fox and his wife they had a great strife,
They never eat mustard in all their whole life;
They eat their meat without fork or knife,
    And lov'd to be picking a bone, *ee-oh!*

The fox jumped up on a moonlight night;
The stars they were shining, and all things bright;
'Oho!' said the fox, 'it's a very fine night,
    For me to go through the town, *ee-oh!*'

The fox, when he came to yonder stile,
ears   He lifted his lugs and he listened a while.
'Oh, ho!' said the fox, 'it's a very short mile
    From this unto yonder wee town, *ee-oh!*'

The fox when he came to the farmer's gate,
Who should he see but the farmer's drake;
'I love you well for your master's sake,
 And long to be picking your bone, *ee-oh!*'

The grey goose she ran round the farmer's stack,
'Oh, ho!' said the fox, 'you are plump and fat;
You'll grease my beard and ride on my back,
 From this into yonder wee town, *ee-oh!*'

The farmer's wife she jumped out of bed,
And out of the window she popped her head.
'Oh, husband! oh, husband! The geese are all dead,
 For the fox has been through the town, *ee-oh!*'

The farmer he loaded his pistol with lead,
And shot the old rogue of a fox through the head;
'Ah, ha!' said the farmer, 'I think you're quite dead;
 And no more you'll trouble the town, *ee-oh!*'

TRAD. *A New Year carol*

Here we bring new water
 from the well so clear,
For to worship God with,
 this happy New Year.

Sing levy dew, sing levy dew,
 the water and the wine;
The seven bright gold wires
 and the bugles that do shine.

Sing reign of Fair Maid,
 with gold upon her toe, –
Open you the West Door,
 and turn the Old Year go.

Sing reign of Fair Maid
 with gold upon her chin, –
Open you the East Door,
 And let the New Year in.

Sing levy dew...

NICHOLAS UDALL   *I mun be maried a Sunday*

I mun be maried a Sunday;
I mun be maried a Sunday;
Who soever shall come that way,
I mun be maried a Sunday;.

Royster Doyster is my name;
Royster Doyster is my name;
A lustie brute I am the same;
I mun be maried a Sunday.

Christian Custance have I founde;
Christian Custance have I founde;
A Widowe worthe a thousande pounde:
I mun be maried a Sunday.

Custance is as sweete as honey;
Custance is as sweete as honey;
I hir lambe, and she my coney;
I mun be maried a Sunday.

When we shall make our weddyng feast,
When we shall make our weddyng feast,
There shall bee cheere for man and beast;
I mun be maried a Sunday.

I mun be married...

ANON.   *There was a man of Newington*

There was a man of Newington,
And he was wondrous wise.
He jumped into a quick-set hedge,
And scratched out both his eyes.

But when he saw his eyes were out,
With all his might and main
He jumped into another hedge,
And scratched them in again.

IZAAK WALTON *Fishing song*

O the gallant fisher's life,
    It is the best of any!
'Tis full of pleasure, void of strife,
    And 'tis beloved by many:
        Other joys
        Are but toys;
        Only this
        Lawful is;
        For our skill
        Breeds no ill,
But content and pleasure.

In a morning up we rise
    Ere Aurora's peeping;
Drink a cup to wash our eyes;
    Leave the sluggard sleeping.
        Then we go
        To and fro
        With our knacks
        At our backs
        To such streams
        As the Thames,
If we have the leisure.

[When we please to walk abroad
    For our recreation,
In the fields is our abode,
    Full of delectation:
        Where in a brook,
        With a hook,
        Or a lake,
        Fish we take;
        There we sit
        For a bit,
Till we fish entangle.

We have gentles in a horn,
    We have paste and worms too;
We can watch both night and morn,
    Suffer rain and storms too.
        None do here
        Use to swear;

                Friday Afternoons Op. 7 (1933–5)

Oaths do fray
Fish away:
We sit still
And watch our quill;
Fishers must not wrangle.]

If the sun's excessive heat
    Makes our bodies swelter,
To an osier-hedge we get
    For a friendly shelter;
        Where in a dike,
        Perch or pike,
        Roach or dace,
        We do chase;
        Bleak or gudgeon,
        Without grudging:
We are still contented.

[Or we sometimes pass an hour
    Under a green willow,
That defends us from a shower –
    Making earth our pillow:
        Where we may
        Think and pray,
        Before death
        Stops our breath:
        Other joys
        Are but toys,
And to be lamented.]

ANON.   *The useful plough*

A country life is sweet,
In moderate cold and heat,
To walk in the air,
How pleasant and fair,
In every field of wheat.
The fairest of flowers
Adorning the bowers
And every meadow's brow;
So that, I say, no courtier may
Compare with them who clothe in grey,
And follow the useful plough.

They rise with the morning lark,
And labour till almost dark,
Then folding their sheep
They hasten to sleep,
While every pleasant park
Next morning is ringing
With birds that are singing
On each green tender bough.
With what content and merriment
Their days are spent, whose minds are bent
To follow the useful plough.

ELEANOR FARJEON   *Jazz-man*

Crash and Clang! Bash and Bang!
And up in the road the Jazz-man sprang!
The One-Man-Jazz-Band playing in the street,
Drums with his Elbows, Cymbals with his Feet,
Pipes with his Mouth, Accordion with his Hand,
Playing all his Instruments to Beat the Band!

Toot and Tingle! Hoot and Jingle!
Oh, What a Clatter! how the tunes all mingle!
Twenty children couldn't make as much noise *as*
The Howling Pandemonium of the One-Man-Jazz!

ANON.   *There was a monkey*

There was a monkey climbed up a tree,
When he fell down, then down fell he.

There was a crow sat on a stone,
When he was gone, then there was none.

There was an old wife did eat an apple,
When she'd eat two, she'd eat a couple.

There was a horse a-going to the mill,
When he went on, he stood not still.

There was a butcher cut his thumb,
When it did bleed, the blood did come.

There was a lackey ran a race,
When he ran fast, he ran apace.

patching

There was a cobbler clouting shoon,
When they were mended, they were done.

smoothed

There was a chandler making candle,
When he them strip, he did them handle.

There was a navy went into Spain,
When it returned, it came again.

ANON.   *Old Abram Brown*

Old Abram Brown is dead and gone
You'll never see him more;
He used to wear a long brown coat
That buttoned down before.

When you're feeling like expressing your affection (1935–6?)

This song, of uncertain origin, may have been written for a film produced by John Grierson's GPO Film Unit, and its words are probably by Auden. It was first performed in public on 15 June 1992 at the Aldeburgh Festival by Lucy Shelton and Ian Brown.

attributed to W.H. AUDEN   'When you're feeling like expressing your affection'

When you're feeling like expressing your affection
For someone night and day,
Take up the 'phone and ask for your connection,
We'll give it right away.
Eve or Adam, anyone you ask for
We'll find somehow.
Sir or Madam, if you get a taste for
Paris, Berlin, Moscow,
Enter any telephone kiosk O,
Have your say,
Press button A,
Here's your number now.

Our Hunting Fathers Op. 8 (1936)

This symphonic cycle for high voice and orchestra, to a text devised by Auden, was first performed on 25 September 1936 at the Norfolk and Norwich Triennial Music Festival by Sophie Wyss and the London Philharmonic Orchestra conducted by Britten. It was dedicated 'To Ralph Hawkes, Esq.' Britten commented that 'Auden has done me some glorious words. Real stunners.'

W.H. AUDEN 'Prologue'

They are our past and our future; the poles between which our desire unceasingly is discharged.

A desire in which love and hatred so perfectly oppose themselves, that we cannot voluntarily move; but await the extraordinary compulsion of the deluge and the earthquake.

Their finish has inspired the limits of all arts and ascetic movements.

Their affections and indifferences have been a guide to all reformers and tyrants.

Their appearances amid our dreams of machinery have brought a vision of nude and fabulous epochs.

O pride so hostile to our charity.

But what their pride has retained we may by charity more generously recover.

ANON. *Rats away*

I command all the rats that are hereabout
That none dwell in this place, within or without:
Through the virtue of Jesus that Mary bore,
Whom all creatures must ever adore;
And through the virtue of Mark, Matthew, Luke and John,
All four Archangels that are as one;
Through the virtue of Saint Gertrude, that maid clean,
God grant in grace
That no rats dwell in the place
That these names were uttered in;
And through the virtue of Saint Kasi,
That holy man who prayed to God Almighty

Of the scathes they did
His meadows amid
By day and by night.
God bid them flee and go out of every man's sight.
Dominus, Deus, Sabaoth, Emmanuel, great name of God,
Deliver this place from rats and from all other shame.
God save this place from all other wicked wights,
Both by days and by nights,
Et in Nomine Patris et Filii et Sancti Spiriti.

THOMAS WEELKES (?) *Messalina*

Ay me, alas, heigh ho, heigh ho!
Thus doth Messalina go
Up and down the house a-crying,
For her monkey lies a-dying.
Death, thou art too cruel
To bereave her of her jewel;
Or to make a seizure
Of her only treasure.
If her monkey die
She will sit and cry:
Fie, fie, fie, fie, fie!

THOMAS RAVENSCROFT *Hawking for the partridge*   'Dance of Death'

Sith sickles and the shearing scythe,
Hath shorn the fields of late,
Now shall our hawks and we be blithe.
Dame Partridge ware your pate:
Our murdering kites
In all their flights
Will seld or never miss
To truss you ever and make your bale our bliss.

Whurret	Duty	Beauty [Love,] whurret, hey dogs hey:
	[Cater]	[Tray]
	Quando	[Timble]
	Travel	Trover
	Jew	Damsel

Ware haunt, hey	Sempster	Faver	
	Minx	Dido	
	Civil	Leymon,	let fly
	Wanton	Sugar	
	Mistress	Tricker	
	Crafty	Minion	
	Dancer	Jerker	
	Quoy	Stately	
	Ruler	German, whurr, whurr, let fly.	

O well flown, eager kite, mark!
We falconers thus make sullen kites
Yield pleasure fit for kings,
And sport with them in those delights,
And oft in other things.

W.H. AUDEN *'Epilogue'*

Our hunting fathers told the story
    Of the sadness of the creatures,
Pitied the limits and the lack
    Set in their finished features;
Saw in the lion's intolerant look,
    Behind the quarry's dying glare,
Love raging for the personal glory
    That reason's gift would add,
The liberal appetite and power,
    The rightness of a god.

Who nurtured in that fine tradition
    Predicted the result,
Guessed love by nature suited to
    The intricate ways of guilt?
That human ligaments could so †
    His southern gestures modify
And make it his mature ambition
    To think no thought but ours,
To hunger, work illegally,
    And be anonymous?

† Britten has 'company' instead of 'ligaments'.

Pacifist march (1937)

RONALD DUNCAN *Pacifist march*

Blood, mud and bitterness have been used in painting our history
That's been smudg'd with the stain of war.
Empire we've stolen, swollen,
Our imperial greed for more.
May the strength we've misused in violence swing into science
and make more music.

Chorus In our heart we've no hate but complaint against the
chainstore state;
We will build peace for earth's plenty.
March, stride to resist strong with force not with fist.
Against all war we shan't cease to construct force for peace,
Now we're kept poor and merely exist to die, why?
March, stride to resist strong with force not with fist.
March!... march!... march!... march!... march!

Through winters of weariness we have waited in queues
of uneasy length,
For the dole or the cinema.
Though Means Test insults, assaults,
Our culture, native dignity.
Though the generous soil won't understand our Cradle's lack
or our table's want.

Hills old in tenderness have been slaked and torn by high explosives,
Petrol pump and the tin fruit sign.
We've tolerated, painted,
Corrugated iron for our roof.
Patiently we've continued to collect coupons thro' slump
on farms that could feed.

Men born from laziness strive and struggle, muddle and fumble
T'wards peace or forgetfulness.
Centuries of suffering, shuffling
Years of revolving and resolving.
Gradually from our heart's wilderness the will for life thrusts
firm for peace.

Two Ballads (1937)

These ballads for two voices and piano were first performed at the Wigmore Hall, London, on 15 December 1936, by Sophie Wyss and Betty Bannerman and Adolph Hallis, piano. Auden's ballad was addressed directly to Britten.

MONTAGU SLATER *Mother Comfort*

Dear, shall we talk or will that cloud the sky?
Will you be Mother Comfort or shall I?
If I should love him where would our lives be?
And if you turn him out at last, then friendship pity me!
My longing, like my heart, beats to and fro,
Oh that a single life could be both Yes and No.
Will you be Mother Comfort or shall I?
Ashamed to grant and frightened to refuse.
Pity has chosen: Power has still to choose.
But darling, when that stretched out will is tired
Surely your timid prettiness longs to be overpower'd?
Sure gossips have this sweet facility
To tell transparent lies and, without pain, to cry.
Will you be Mother Comfort or shall I be Mother Comfort?
Will you be Mother Comfort or shall I?

W.H. AUDEN *Song* 'Underneath the abject willow'

Underneath an abject willow,
    Lover, sulk no more:
Act from thought should quickly follow.
    What is thinking for?
Your unique and moping station
    Proves you cold;
Stand up and fold
    Your map of desolation.

Bells that toll across the meadows
    From the sombre spire
Toll for these unloving shadows
    Love does not require.
All that lives may love; why longer

Bow to loss
With arms across?
Strike and you shall conquer.

Geese in flocks above you flying,
    Their direction know,
Icy brooks beneath you flowing,
    To their ocean go.
Dark and dull is your distraction:
    Walk then, come,
    No longer numb
Into your satisfaction.

On this Island Op. 11 (1937)

These five songs by Auden, for high voice and piano, were first performed on 19 November 1937 by Sophie Wyss and Britten at Broadcasting House Concert Hall, London. They were dedicated 'To Christopher Isherwood'.

W.H. AUDEN *Song*

Let the florid music praise,
    The flute and the trumpet,
Beauty's conquest of your face:
In that land of flesh and bone,
Where from citadels on high
Her imperial standards fly,
    Let the hot sun
    Shine on, shine on.

O but the unloved have had power,
    The weeping and striking,
Always; time will bring their hour:
Their secretive children walk
Through your vigilance of breath
To unpardonable death,
    And my vows break
    Before his look.

'Now the leaves are falling fast'

Now the leaves are falling fast,
Nurse's flowers will not last;
Nurses to the graves are gone,
And the prams go rolling on.

Whispering neighbours, left and right,
Pluck us from the real delight;
And the active hands must freeze
Lonely on the separate knees.

Dead in hundreds at the back
Follow wooden in our track,
Arms raised stiffly to reprove
In false attitudes of love.

Starving through the leafless wood
Trolls run scolding for their food;
And the nightingale is dumb,
And the angel will not come.

Cold, impossible, ahead
Lifts the mountain's lovely head
Whose white waterfall could bless
Travellers in their last distress.

'Seascape'

Look, stranger, at this island now
The leaping light for your delight discovers,
Stand stable here
And silent be,
That through the channels of the ear
May wander like a river
The swaying sound of the sea.

Here at the small field's ending pause
Where the chalk wall falls to the foam, and its tall ledges
Oppose the pluck
And knock of the tide,
And the shingle scrambles after the suck-
ing surf, and the gull lodges
A moment on its sheer side.

Far off like floating seeds the ships
Diverge on urgent voluntary errands;
And the full view
Indeed may enter
And move in memory as now these clouds do,
That pass the harbour mirror
And all the summer through the water saunter.

'Nocturne' (from *The Dog Beneath the Skin* II)

Now through night's caressing grip
Earth and all her oceans slip,
Capes of China slide away
From her fingers into day
And the Americas incline
Coasts towards her shadow line.
Now the ragged vagrants creep
Into crooked holes to sleep:
Just and unjust, worst and best,
Change their places as they rest:
Awkward lovers lie in fields
Where disdainful beauty yields:
While the splendid and the proud
Naked stand before the crowd
And the losing gambler gains
And the beggar entertains:
May sleep's healing powers extend
Through these hours to our friend.
Unpursued by hostile force,
Traction engine, bull or horse
Or revolting succubus;
Calmly till the morning break
Let him lie, then gently wake.

'As it is, plenty'

As it is, plenty;
As it's admitted
The children happy
And the car, the car
That goes so far
And the wife devoted:
To this as it is,
To the work and the banks
Let his thinning hair
And his hauteur
Give thanks, give thanks.

All that was thought
As like as not, is not;
When nothing was enough
But love, but love
And the rough future
Of an intransigent nature
And the betraying smile,
Betraying, but a smile:
Then that is not, is not;
Forget, Forget.

Let him not cease to praise
Then his spacious days;
Yes, and the success
Let him bless, let him bless:
Let him see in this
The profits larger
And the sins venal,
Lest he see as it is
The loss as major
And final, final.

On this Island Op. 11 (1937)

Fish in the unruffled lakes (1937)

For high voice and piano.

W.H. AUDEN *Fish in the unruffled lakes*

Fish in the unruffled lakes
The swarming colours wear,
Swans in the winter air
A white perfection have,
And the great lion walks
Through his innocent grove;
Lion, fish, and swan
Act, and are gone
Upon Time's toppling wave.

We till shadowed days are done,
We must weep and sing
Duty's conscious wrong,
The Devil in the clock,
The Goodness carefully worn
For atonement or for luck;
We must lose our loves,
On each beast and bird that moves
Turn an envious look.

Sighs for folly said and done
Twist our narrow days;
But I must bless, I must praise
That you, my swan, who have
All gifts that to the swan
Impulsive Nature gave,
The majesty and pride,
Last night should add
Your voluntary love.

To lie flat on the back (1937)

This setting for tenor and piano was first performed by Neil Mackie and John Blakeley in a BBC Radio 3 recital on 23 April 1985.

W.H. AUDEN   'To lie flat on the back'

To lie flat on the back with the knees flexed
And sunshine on the soft receptive belly,
Or face down, the insolent spine relaxed,
No more compelled to cower or to bully,
Is good; and good to see them passing by
Below on the white sidewalk in the heat,
The dog, the lady with parcels, and the boy:
There is the casual life outside the heart.

Yes, we are out of sight and earshot here.
Are you aware what weapon you are loading,
To what that teasing talk is quietly leading?
Our pulses count but do not judge the hour.
Who are you with, from whom you turn away,
At whom you dare not look? Do you know why?

The sun shines down (1937)

W.H. AUDEN 'The sun shines down'

The sun shines down on the ships at sea,
It shines on you and it shines on me
Whatever we are or are going to be.

Tomorrow if everything goes to plan,
Tomorrow morning you'll be a man:
Let wishes be horses as fast as they can.

The dogs are barking, the crops are growing,
But nobody knows how the wind is blowing:
Gosh, to look at we're no great catch;
History seems to have struck a bad patch.

We haven't the time – it's been such a rush –
Except to attend to our own little push:
The teacher setting examinations,
The journalist writing his falsifications,

The poet reciting to Lady Diana
While the footmen whisper 'Have a banana',
The judge enforcing the obsolete law,
The banker making the loan for the war,

The expert determining the long-range gun
To exterminate everyone under the sun,
Would like to get out but can only mutter: –
'What can I do? It's my bread and butter.'

In your house tonight you are flushed and gay;
Twenty-one years have passed away;
Tomorrow morning's another day.

If we can't love, though miles apart,
If we can't trust with all our heart,
If we can't do that, then we're in the cart.

Song (1937)

This setting for tenor and piano was first performed on 22 November 1983 by Neil Mackie and Iain Burnside at a concert celebrating the 70th anniversary of Britten's birth at the Wigmore Hall, London.

PETER BURRA *Not even summer yet* 'Song'

Not even summer yet
Can make me quite forget
That still most blessed thing,
The early spring.

I watched the red–tipped trees
Burst into greeneries;
Saw the swift blossom come
Like sea dissolved in foam.

But in the lover's ways,
The summer of his days
Is come from such a spring
As poets cannot sing.

The company of heaven (1937)

This setting, for soprano, tenor, chorus and orchestra, was originally broadcast by the BBC on 29 September 1937, by Sophie Wyss, Pears and the BBC Chorus and Orchestra, conducted by Trevor Harvey. Its first concert performance was conducted by Philip Brunelle on 10 June 1989 at Snape Maltings Concert Hall.

EMILY BRONTË   *A day dream*   'The company of heaven'

[On a sunny brae alone I lay
One summer afternoon;
It was the marriage-time of May
With her young lover, June.

From her Mother's heart seemed loath to part
That queen of bridal charms,
But her Father smiled on the fairest child
He ever held in his arms.

The trees did wave their plumy crests,
The glad birds carolled clear;
And I, of all the wedding guests,
Was only sullen there.

There was not one but wished to shun
My aspect void of cheer;
The very grey rocks, looking on,
Asked, 'What do you do here?'

And I could utter no reply:
In sooth I did not know
Why I had brought a clouded eye
To greet the general glow.

So, resting on a heathy bank,
I took my heart to me;
And we together sadly sank
Into a reverie.

We thought, 'When winter comes again,
Where will these bright things be?

All vanished, like a vision vain,
An unreal mockery!

'The birds that now so blithely sing,
Through deserts frozen dry,
Poor spectres of the perished Spring
In famished troops will fly.

'And why should we be glad at all?
The leaf is hardly green,
Before a token of the fall
Is on its surface seen.'

Now whether it were really so
I never could be sure;
But as, in a fit of peevish woe,
I stretched me on the moor,]

A thousand thousand gleaming fires
Seemed kindling in the air;
A thousand thousand silvery lyres
Resounded far and near:

Methought the very breath I breathed
Was full of sparks divine,
And all my heather-couch was wreathed
By that celestial shine.

And while the wide Earth echoing rang
To their strange minstrelsy,
The little glittering spirits sang,
Or seemed to sing, to me:

'O mortal, mortal, let them die;
Let Time and Tears destroy,
That we may overflow the sky
With universal joy.

['Let Grief distract the sufferer's breast,
And Night obscure his way;
They hasten him to endless rest,
And everlasting day.]

'To Thee the world is like a tomb,
A desert's naked shore;
To us, in unimagined bloom,
It brightens more and more.

The company of heaven (1937)

'And could we lift the veil and give
One brief glimpse to thine eye
Thou would'st rejoice for those that live,
Because they live to die.'

[The music ceased – the noonday Dream
Like dream of night withdrew
But fancy still will sometimes deem
Her fond creation true.]

Night covers up the rigid land (1937)

This setting for soprano and piano was first performed on 22 November 1985 by Patricia Rozario and Graham Johnson at the Wigmore Hall, London.

W.H.AUDEN   *Song*   Night covers up the rigid land

Night covers up the rigid land
　　And ocean's quaking moor,
And shadows with a tolerant hand
　　The ugly and the poor.

The wounded pride for which I weep
　　You cannot staunch, nor I
Control the moments of your sleep,
　　Nor hear the name you cry,

Whose life is lucky in your eyes,
　　And precious is the bed
As to his utter fancy lies
　　The dark caressive head.

For each love to its aim is true,
　　And all kinds seek their own;
You love your life and I love you,
　　So I must lie alone.

O hurry to the fêted spot
　　Of your deliberate fall;
For now my dream of you cannot
　　Refer to you at all.

Advance democracy (1938)

Set for double chorus, unaccompanied.

RANDALL SWINGLER   *Across the darkened sky*
· 'Advance democracy'

Across the darkened sky
The frosty searchlights creep
Alert for the first marauder
To steal upon our sleep.
We see the sudden headlines
Float on the muttering tide,
We hear them warn and threaten,
We wonder what they hide.

There are whispers across the tables,
Talks in a shutter'd room,
The price of which they bargain
Will be a people's dream.

Ah there's a roar of war in the factories,
And idle hands on the street,
And Europe held in nightmare
By the thud of marching feet.

Now sinks the sun of surety,
The shadows growing tall
Of the big bosses plotting
Their biggest coup of all.

Is there no strength to save us?
No power we can trust,
Before our life and liberties
Are powdered into dust?

Time to arise Democracy
Time to rise up and cry
That what our father fought for
We'll not allow to die.

Time to resolve divisions,
Time to renew our pride.
Time! Time! Time! Time!
Time to decide.

Time to burst our house of glass,
Rise as a single being
In one resolve arrayed:
Life shall be for the people
That's by the people made.

The red cockatoo (1938)

This setting, for voice and piano, was first performed at the Aldeburgh
Festival on 15 June 1991 by Lucy Shelton and Ian Brown.

after PO CHÜ-I (tr. Arthur Waley)   *The red cockatoo*

Sent as a present from Annam –
A red cockatoo.
Coloured like the peach-tree blossom,
Speaking with the speech of men.
And they did to it what is always done
To the learned and eloquent.
They took a cage with stout bars
And shut it up inside.

Four Cabaret Songs for Miss Hedli Anderson (1937–9)

Hedli Anderson, for whom these songs for voice and piano were composed, first performed 'Johnny' in May 1937 and 'Tell me the truth… ' on 19 May 1938. The text of 'Johnny' given here is Auden's 'approved' version, which Britten (or perhaps Auden himself) altered when being set to music.

W.H. AUDEN *Four cabaret songs for Miss Hedli Anderson*

O tell me the truth about love

Some say that Love's a little boy
      And some say he's a bird,
Some say he makes the world go round
      And some say that's absurd:
But when I asked the man next door
      Who looked as if he knew,
His wife was very cross indeed
      And said it wouldn't do.

Does it look like a pair of pyjamas
      Or the ham in a temperance hotel,
Does its odour remind one of llamas
      Or has it a comforting smell?
Is it prickly to touch as a hedge is
      Or soft as eiderdown fluff,
Is it sharp or quite smooth at the edges?
      O tell me the truth about love.

[The history books refer to it
      In cryptic little notes,
And it's a common topic on
      The Trans-Atlantic boats;
I've found the subject mentioned in
      Accounts of suicides,
And even seen it scribbled on
      The backs of railway guides.

Does it howl like a hungry Alsatian
          Or boom like a military band,
Could one give a first-class imitation
          On a saw or a Steinway Grand,
Is its singing at parties a riot,
          Does it only like Classical stuff,
Will it stop when one wants to be quiet?
          O tell me the truth about love.]

I looked inside the summer-house,
          It wasn't ever there,
I've tried the Thames at Maidenhead
          And Brighton's bracing air;
I don't know what the blackbird sang
          Or what the roses said,
But it wasn't in the chicken-run
          Or underneath the bed.

Can it pull extraordinary faces,
          Is it usually sick on a swing,
Does it spend all its time at the races
          Or fiddling with pieces of string,
Has it views of its own about money,
          Does it think Patriotism enough,
Are its stories vulgar but funny?
          O tell me the truth about love.

Your feelings when you meet it, I
          Am told you can't forget.
I've sought it since I was a child
          But haven't found it yet;
I'm getting on for thirty-five,
          And still I do not know
What kind of creature it can be
          That bothers people so.

When it comes, will it come without warning
          Just as I'm picking my nose,
Will it knock on my door in the morning
          Or tread in the bus on my toes,
Will it come like a change in the weather,
          Will its greeting be courteous or bluff,
Will it alter my life altogether?
          O tell me the truth about love.

Four Cabaret Songs for Miss Hedli Anderson (1937–9)

Funeral blues

Stop all the clocks, cut off the telephone,
Prevent the dog from barking with a juicy bone,
Silence the pianos and with muffled drum
Bring out the coffin, let the mourners come.

Let aeroplanes circle moaning overhead
Scribbling on the sky the message He Is Dead,
Put crêpe bows round the white necks of the public doves,
Let the traffic policemen wear black cotton gloves.

He was my North, my South, my East and West,
My working week and my Sunday rest,
My noon, my midnight, my talk, my song;
I thought that love would last for ever: I was wrong.

The stars are not wanted now: put out every one,
Pack up the moon and dismantle the sun,
Pour away the ocean and sweep up the woods;
For nothing now can ever come to any good.

Johnny

O the valley in the summer where I and my John
Beside the deep river would walk on and on
grass   While the flowers at our feet and the birds up above
Argued so sweetly on reciprocal love,
And I leaned on his shoulder; 'O Johnny, let's play':
But he frowned like thunder and he went away.

O that evening   O that Friday near Christmas as I well recall
When we went to the Charity Matinee Ball,
The floor was so smooth and the band was so loud
And Johnny so handsome I felt so proud;
'Squeeze me tighter, dear Johnny, let's dance till it's day':
But he frowned like thunder and he went away.

Shall I ever forget at the Grand Opera
When music poured out of each wonderful star?
hung like ivy   Diamonds and pearls they hung dazzling down
gold and silver   Over each silver or golden silk gown;
'O John I'm in heaven,' I whispered to say:
But he frowned like thunder and he went away.

O but he was as fair as a garden in flower,
As slender and tall as the great Eiffel Tower,
When the waltz throbbed out on the long promenade
O his eyes and his smile they went straight to my heart;
'O marry me, Johnny, I'll love and obey':
But he frowned like thunder and he went away.

O last night I dreamed of you, Johnny, my lover,
You'd the sun on one arm and the moon on the other,
The sea it was blue and the grass it was green,
Every star rattled a round tambourine;
Ten thousand miles deep in a pit there I lay:
But you frowned like thunder and you went away.

Calypso

Driver, drive faster and make a good run
Down the Springfield Line under the shining sun.

Fly like the aeroplane, don't pull up short
Till you brake for Grand Central Station, New York.

For there in the middle of that waiting hall
Should be standing the one that I love best of all.

If he's not there to meet me when I get to town,
I'll stand on the pavement with tears rolling down.

For he is the one that I love to look on,
The acme of kindness and perfection.

He presses my hand and he says he loves me
Which I find an admirable peculiarity.

The woods are bright green on both sides of the line;
The trees have their loves though they're different from mine.

But the poor fat old banker in the sun-parlour car
Has no one to love him except his cigar.

If I were the head of the Church or the State
I'd powder my nose and just tell them to wait.

For love's more important and powerful than
Even a priest or a politician.

Four Cabaret Songs for Miss Hedli Anderson (1937–9)

Ballad of Heroes Op. 14 (1939)

This work, for tenor or soprano solo, chorus and orchestra, was dedicated 'To Montagu and Enid Slater' and first performed, by Walter Widdop and the London Co-operative Chorus and L.S.O, at the Festival of 'Music for the People' (5 April 1939) in the Queen's Hall, London. The conductor was Constant Lambert. The poems were not the result of a collaboration between Auden and Swingler, but were put together by Britten, apparently without consulting Auden.

RANDALL SWINGLER   'You who stand at your doors'

You who stand at your doors, wiping hands on aprons,
You who lean at the corner saying: 'We have done our best,'
You who shrug your shoulders and you who smile
To conceal your life's despair and its evil taste,

To you we speak, you numberless Englishmen,
To remind you of the greatness still among you
Created by these men who go from your towns
To fight for peace, for liberty, and for you.

They were men who hated death and loved life,
Who were afraid, and fought against their fear,
Men who wished to create and not to destroy,
But knew the time must come to destroy the destroyer.

For they have restored your power and pride,
Your life is yours, for which they died.

W.H. AUDEN   *Danse macabre*

It's farewell to the drawing-room's civilized cry,
The professor's sensible whereto and why,
The frock-coated diplomat's social aplomb,
Now matters are settled with gas and with bomb.

The works for two pianos, the brilliant stories
Of reasonable giants and remarkable fairies,
The pictures, the ointments, the frangible wares
And the branches of olive are stored upstairs.

For the Devil has broken parole and arisen,
He has dynamited his way out of prison,
Out of the well where his Papa throws
The rebel angel, the outcast rose.

[Like influenza he walks abroad,
He stands by the bridge, he waits by the ford,
As a goose or a gull he flies overhead,
He hides in the cupboard and under the bed.

O were he to triumph, dear heart, you know
To what depths of shame he would drag you low;
He would steal you away from me, yes, my dear,
He would steal you and cut off your beautiful hair.

Millions already have come to their harm,
Succumbing like doves to his adder's charm;
Hundreds of trees in the wood are unsound:
I'm the axe that must cut them down to the ground.

For I, after all, am the Fortunate One,
The Happy-Go-Lucky, the spoilt Third Son;
For me it is written the Devil to chase
And to rid the earth of the human race.]

The behaving of man is a world of horror,
A sedentary Sodom and slick Gomorrah;
I must take charge of the liquid fire
And storm the cities of human desire.

[The buying and selling, the eating and drinking,
The disloyal machines and irreverent thinking,
The lovely dullards again and again
Inspiring their bitter ambitious men.

I shall come, I shall punish, the Devil be dead,
I shall have caviar thick on my bread,
I shall build myself a cathedral for home
With a vacuum cleaner in every room.

I shall ride the parade in a platinum car,
My features shall shine, my name shall be Star,
Day-long and night-long the bells I shall peal,
And down the long street I shall turn the cartwheel.

So Little John, Long John, Peter and Paul,
And poor little Horace with only one ball,
You shall leave your breakfast, your desk and your play
On a fine summer morning the Devil to slay.]

For it's order and trumpet and anger and drum
And power and glory command you to come;
[The graves shall fly open and let you all in,
And the earth shall be emptied of mortal sin.]

The fishes are silent deep in the sea,
The skies are lit up like a Christmas tree,
The star in the West shoots its warning cry:
'Mankind is alive, but Mankind must die.'

So good-bye to the house with its wallpaper red,
Good-bye to the sheets on the warm double bed,
Good-bye to the beautiful birds on the wall,
It's good-bye, dear heart, good-bye to you all.

SWINGLER   'Still though the scene of possible Summer recedes'

Still though the scene of possible Summer recedes,
And the guns can be heard across the hills
Like waves at night: though crawling suburbs fill
Their valleys with stench of idleness like rotting weeds,
And desire unacted breeds its pestilence
Yet still below the soot the roots are sure
And beyond the guns there is another murmur,
Like pigeons flying unnoticed over continents
With secret messages of peace: and at the centre
Of the wheeling conflict the heart is calmer,
The promise nearer than ever it came before.

Europe lies in the dark.
City and flood and tree;
Thousands have worked and work
To master necessity.
To build a city where
The will of love is done
And brought to its full flower
The dignity of man.

Pardon them their mistakes,
The impatient and wavering will.
They suffer for our sakes,
Honour, honour them all.
Dry their imperfect dust,
The wind blows it back and forth,
They die to make men just
And worthy of the earth.

To you we speak, you numberless Englishmen,
To remind you of the greatness still among you
Created by these men who go from your towns
To fight for peace, for liberty, and for you.

Ballad of Heroes Op. 14 (1939)

A.M.D.G. (1939)

This setting of seven poems by Gerard Manley Hopkins was intended to be performed by Pears and his group of 'Round Table Singers' in November 1939, but owing to the outbreak of the war this plan fell through. The work's opus number 17 was withdrawn and given instead to *Paul Bunyan*. Two of the seven songs, 'The Soldier' and 'Prayer I', were crossed out by Britten on the manuscript. It is not known why the work was abandoned. The first complete performance was given by the London Sinfonietta Voices in the Purcell Room, London, on 21 August 1984. A.M.D.G. (*Ad majorem Dei gloriam*, 'To the greater glory of God') is the motto of the Jesuit order of which Hopkins was a member.

GERARD MANLEY HOPKINS   *Oratio Patris Condren:*
O Jesu vivens in Maria

Jesu that dost in Mary dwell,
Be in thy servants' hearts as well,
In the spirit of thy holiness,
In the fullness of thy force and stress,
In the very ways that thy life goes,
And virtues that thy pattern shows,
In the sharing of thy mysteries;
And every power in us that is
Against thy power put under feet
In the Holy Ghost the Paraclete
　　To the glory of the Father.Amen.

Rosa mystica

'The Rose in a mystery' – where is it found?
Is it anything true? Does it grow upon ground?
It was made of earth's mould, but it went from men's eyes,
And its place is a secret, and shut in the skies,
　　In the Gardens of God, in the daylight divine
　　Find me a place by thee, Mother of mine.

But where was it formerly? Which is the spot
That was blest in it once, though now it is not?
It is Galilee's growth; it grew at God's will

And broke into bloom upon Nazareth Hill.
    In the Gardens of God, in the daylight divine
    I shall look on thy loveliness, Mother of mine.

[What was its season, then? How long ago?
When was the summer that saw the Bud blow?
Two thousands of years are near upon past
Since its birth, and its bloom, and its breathing its last.]
    In the Gardens of God, in the daylight divine
    I shall keep time with thee, Mother of mine.

Tell me the name now, tell me its name:
The heart guesses easily, is it the same?
Mary, the Virgin, well the heart knows,
She is the Mystery, she is that Rose.
    In the Gardens of God, in the daylight divine
    I shall come home to thee, Mother of mine.

Is Mary that Rose, then? Mary, the Tree?
But the Blossom, the Blossom there, who can it be?
Who can her Rose be? It could be but One:
Christ Jesus, our Lord – her God and her Son.
    In the Gardens of God, in the daylight divine
    Shew my thy Son, Mother, Mother of mine.

[What was the colour of that Blossom bright?
White to begin with, immaculate white.
But what a wild flush on the flakes of it stood,
When the Rose ran in crimsonings down the Crosswood.
    In the Gardens of God, in the daylight divine
    I shall worship the Wounds with thee, Mother of mine.

How many leaves had it? Five they were then,
Five like the senses, and members of men;
Five is the number by nature, but now
They multiply, multiply, who can tell how.
    In the Gardens of God, in the daylight divine
    Make me a leaf in thee, Mother of mine.]

Does it smell sweet, too, in that holy place?
Sweet unto God, and the sweetness is grace;
The breath of it bathes the great heaven above,
In grace that is charity, grace that is love.
    To thy breast, [to thy rest,] to thy glory divine
    Draw me by charity, Mother of mine.

A.M.D.G. (1939)

God's grandeur

The world is charged with the grandeur of God.
    It will flame out, like shining from shook foil;
    It gathers to a greatness, like the ooze of oil
Crushed. Why do men then now not reck his rod?
Generations have trod, have trod, have trod;
    And all is seared with trade; bleared, smeared with toil;
    And wears man's smudge and shares man's smell: the soil
Is bare now, nor can foot feel, being shod.

And for all this, nature is never spent;
    There lives the dearest freshness deep down things;
And though the last lights off the black West went
    Oh, morning, at the brown brink eastward, springs –
Because the Holy Ghost over the bent
    World broods with warm breast and with ah! bright wings.

'Thee, God, I come from'

Thee, God, I come from, to thee go,
All day long I like a fountain flow
From thy hand out, swayed about
Mote-like in thy mighty glow.

What I know of thee I bless,
As acknowledging thy stress
On my being and as seeing
Something of thy holiness.

Once I turned from thee and hid,
Bound on what thou hadst forbid;
Sow the wind I would; I sinned:
I repent of what I did.

Bad I am, but yet thy child.
Father, be thou reconciled.
Spare thou me, since I see
With thy might that thou art mild.

I have life before me still
And thy purpose to fulfil;
Yea a debt to pay thee yet:
Help me, sir, and so I will.

A.M.D.G. (1939)

[But thou bidst, and just thou art,
Me shew mercy from my heart
Towards my brother, every other
Man my mate and counterpart.]

O Deus, ego amo te

O God, I love thee, I love thee –
Not out of hope of heaven for me
Nor fearing not to love and be
   In the everlasting burning.
Thou, thou, my Jesus, after me
   Didst reach thine arms out dying,
For my sake sufferedst nails and lance,
Mocked and marrèd countenance,
   Sorrows passing number,
   Sweat and care and cumber,
Yea and death, and this for me,
   And thou couldst see me sinning:
Then I, why should not I love thee,
Jesu, so much in love with me?
Not for heaven's sake; not to be
Out of hell by loving thee;
Not for any gains I see;
But just the way that thou didst me
I do love and I will love thee:
What must I love thee, Lord, for then?
For being my king and God. Amen.

The soldier

Yes. Whý do we áll, seeing of a soldier, bless him? bless
Our redcoats, our tars? Both these being, the greater part,
But frail clay, nay but foul clay. Here it is: the heart,
Since, proud, it calls the calling manly, gives a guess
That, hopes that, makesbelieve, the men must be no less;
It fancies, feigns, deems, dears the artist after his art;
And fain will find as sterling all as all is smart,
And scarlet wear the spirit of wár thére express.

74]

Mark Christ our King. He knows war, served this soldiering
   through;
He of all can handle a rope best. There he bides in bliss
Now, and séeing somewhere some mán do all that man can do,
For love he leans forth, needs his neck must fall on, kiss,
And cry 'O Christ-done deed! So God-made-flesh does too:
Were I come o'er again' cries Christ 'it should be this'.

Heaven-haven: a nun takes the veil

I have desired to go
   Where springs not fail,
To fields where flies no sharp and sided hail
   And a few lilies blow.

And I have asked to be
   Where no storms come,
Where the green swell is in the havens dumb,
   And out of the swing of the sea.

Les Illuminations Op. 18 (1939)

These settings of Rimbaud, for high voice and string orchestra, were first performed in London on 30 January 1940 by Sophie Wyss and the Boyd Neel Orchestra, conducted by Boyd Neel. They were dedicated 'For Sophie Wyss', to whom Britten wrote '*Les Illuminations*, as I see it, are the visions of heaven that were allowed the poet, and I hope the composer.'

ARTHUR RIMBAUD (tr. Helen Rootham) *Les Illuminations*
Fanfare (from *Parade*)

J'ai seul la clef de cette parade sauvage.   I alone hold the key to this savage parade.

Villes I

Ce sont des villes! C'est un peuple pour qui se sont montés ces Alleghanys et ces Libans de rêve! Des chalets de cristal et de bois se meuvent sur des rails et des poulies invisibles. Les vieux cratères ceints de colosses et de palmiers de cuivre rugissent mélodieusement dans les feux. [Des fêtes amoureuses sonnent sur les canaux pendus derrière les chalets. La chasse des carillons crie dans les gorges. Des corporations de chanteurs géants accourent dans des vêtements et des oriflammes éclatants comme la lumière des cimes. Sur les plateformes au milieu des gouffres les Rolands sonnent leur bravoure. Sur les passerelles de l'abîme et les toits des auberges l'ardeur du ciel pavoise les mâts. L'écroulement des apothéoses rejoint les champs des hauteurs où les centauresses séraphiques évoluent parmi les avalanches. Au-dessus du niveau des plus hautes crêtes, une mer troublée par la naissance éternelle de Vénus, chargée de flottes orphéoniques et de la rumeur des perles et des conques précieuses, – la mer s'assombrit parfois avec des éclats mortels. Sur les versants des moissons de fleurs grandes comme nos armes et nos coupes, mugissent.] Des cortèges de Mabs en robes rousses, opalines, montent des ravines. Là-haut, les pieds dans la cascade et les ronces, les cerfs tettent Diane. Les Bacchantes des banlieues sanglotent et la lune brûle et hurle. Vénus entre dans les cavernes des forgerons et des ermites. Des groupes de beffrois chantent les idées des peuples. Des châteaux bâtis en os sort la musique inconnue.

[Toutes les légendes évoluent et les élans se ruent dans les bourgs.] Le paradis des orages s'effondre. Les sauvages dansent sans cesse la Fête de la Nuit. [Et une heure je suis descendu dans le mouvement d'un boulevard de Bagdad où des compagnies ont chanté la joie du travail nouveau, sous une brise épaisse, circulant sans pouvoir éluder les fabuleux fantômes des monts où l'on a dû se retrouver]

Quels bons bras, quelle belle heure me rendront cette région d'où viennent mes sommeils et mes moindres mouvements?

Towns I
These are towns! It is for the inhabitants of towns that these dream Alleghanies and Lebanons have been raised. Castles of crystal and wood move on rails and invisible pulleys. Old craters, encircled with colossal statues and palms of copper, roar melodiously in their fires. [Festivals of love sound upon the streams which seem to hang in mid-air, behind the chalets. The chimes, in full cry, chase their echoes in the gorges. Multitudes of giant singers flock together, their garments and oriflammes shining like the light on the mountain-tops. On platforms overhanging the gulfs, Rolands proclaim their prowess on horns. On the footbridges of the abyss, and on the roofs of the inns, the burning sky clings to the masts in little flags of shimmering heat. By the falling of the apotheoses the fields are united to the heights where seraphic centauresses wind amongst the avalanches. Above the levels of the highest crests is a sea troubled by the eternal birth of Venus, and covered with choric fleets and the distant murmurs of pearl and rare sinuous shells. Sometimes the sea grows dark with mortal thunders. On the slopes there bellow harvests of flowers as big as our goblets.] Corteges of Queen Mabs in robes red and opaline, climb the ravines. Up there, their hoofs in the cascades and the briars, the stags give Diana suck. Bacchantes of the suburbs weep, and the moon burns and howls. Venus enters the caves of the blacksmiths and hermits. Groups of bell-towers sing aloud the ideas of the people. From castles built of bones proceeds unknown music. [In the boroughs legends are born, and sudden transports spring to life in the streets.] The paradise of the thunders bursts and falls. Savages dance unceasingly the Festival of the Night. [And for one hour I descended into the stir of a Baghdad street where groups of people sang the joy of new work; moving about in a dull breeze, unable to elude the fabulous phantoms of the mountains to which one must return.]

What kindly arms, what good hour, will restore to me those regions from which come my slumbers and the least of my movements?

Phrase

J'ai tendu des cordes de clocher à clocher; des guirlandes de fenêtre à fenêtre; des chaînes d'or d'étoile à étoile, et je danse.

Phrase
I have hung ropes from bell-tower to bell-tower; garlands from window to window; golden chains from star to star – and I dance.

Antique

Gracieux fils de Pan! Autour de ton front couronné de fleurettes et de baies, tes yeux, des boules précieuses, remuent. Tachées de lie brune, tes joues se creusent. Tes crocs luisent. Ta poitrine ressemble à une cithare, des tintements circulent dans tes bras blonds. Ton coeur bat dans ce ventre où dort le double sexe. Promène-toi, la nuit, en mouvant doucement cette cuisse, cette seconde cuisse et cette jambe de gauche.

Antique
Oh, gracious son of Pan! Thine eyes – those precious globes – glance slowly; thy brow is crowned with little flowers and berries. Thy hollow cheeks are spotted with brown lees; thy tusks shine. Thy breast resembles a cithara; tinkling sounds run through thy blond arms. Thy heart beats in that womb where sleeps Hermaphrodite. Walk at night, softly moving this thigh, the other thigh, this left leg.

Royauté

Un beau matin, chez un peuple fort doux, un homme et une femme superbes criaient sur la place publique: 'Mes amis, je veux qu'elle soit reine!' 'Je veux être reine!' Elle riait et tremblait. Il parlait aux amis de révélation, d'épreuve terminée. Ils se pâmaient l'un contre l'autre. En effet, ils furent rois toute une matinée, où les tentures carminées se relevèrent sur les maisons, et tout l'après-midi, où ils s'avancèrent du côté des jardins de palmes.

Royalty
On a beautiful morning, in a country inhabited by a mild and gentle people, a man and woman of proud presence stood in the public square and cried aloud: 'My friends, it is my wish that she should be queen.' 'It is my wish to be queen!' She laughed and trembled. To his friends he spoke of a revelation, of a test concluded. Swooningly they leaned one against the other.
And during one whole morning, whilst the crimson hangings were displayed on the houses, and during the whole afternoon, while they advanced towards the palm gardens, they were indeed kings.

Marine

Les chars d'argent et de cuivre, –
Les proues d'acier et d'argent, –
Battent l'écume, –
Soulèvent les souches des ronces.
Les courants de la lande,
Et les ornières immenses du reflux,
Filent circulairement vers l'est,
Vers les piliers de la forêt, –
Vers les fûts de la jetée,
Dont l'angle est heurté par des tourbillons de lumière.

Chariots of silver and of copper
Prows of steel and of silver
Beat the foam,
Lift the stems of the brambles.
The streams of the barren parts
And the immense tracks of the ebb
Flow circularly towards the east,
Towards the pillars of the forest,
Towards the piles of the jetty,
Against whose angles are hurled whirlpools
    of light.

Les Illuminations Op. 18 (1939)

Being beauteous

Devant une neige, un Etre de beauté de haute taille. Des sifflements de mort et des cercles de musique sourde font monter, s'élargir et trembler comme un spectre ce corps adoré; des blessures écarlates et noires éclatent dans les chairs superbes. Les couleurs propres de la vie se foncent, dansent et se dégagent autour de la vision, sur le chantier. Et les frissons s'élèvent et grondent, et la saveur forcenée de ces effets se chargeant avec les sifflements mortels et les rauques musiques que le monde, loin derrière nous, lance sur notre mère de beauté, – elle recule, elle se dresse. Oh! nos os sont revêtus d'un nouveau corps amoureux.

O la face cendée, l'écusson de crin, les bras de cristal! le canon sur lequel je dois m'abbatre à travers la mêlée des arbres et de l'air léger!

Being beauteous
Against a background of snow is a beautiful Being of majestic stature. Death is all round her, and whistling, dying breaths, and circles of hollow music, cause this adored body to rise, to swell and to tremble like a spectre. Scarlet and black wounds break out on the superb flesh. Colours which belong to life deepen, dance, and separate themselves around the vision, upon the path. Shudders rise and mutter; and the mad savour of all these things, heavy with dying groans and raucous music, is hurled at our Mother of Beauty by the world far behind us. She recoils, she stands erect. Oh rapture. Our bones are covered anew with a body of love.

Ah! The pale ashen face, the mane-like hair, the arms of crystal. And there is the cannon upon which I must cast myself through the noise of trees and light winds.

Parade

Des drôles très solides. Plusieurs ont exploité vos mondes. Sans besoins, et peu pressés de mettre en oeuvre leurs brillantes facultés et leur expérience de vos consciences. Quels hommes mûrs! Des yeux hébétés à la façon de la nuit d'été, rouges et noirs, tricolores, d'acier piqué d'étoiles d'or; des facies déformés, plombés, blêmis, incendiés; des enrouements folâtres! La démarche cruelle des oripeaux! – Il y a quelques jeunes, – [comment regarderaient-ils Chérubin? – pourvus de voix effrayantes et de quelques ressources dangereuses. On les envoie prendre du dos en ville, affublés d'un *luxe* dégoûtant.]

O le plus violent Paradis de la grimace enragée! [Pas de comparaison avec vos Fakirs et les autres bouffonneries scéniques. Dans des costumes improvisés avec le goût du mauvais rêve ils jouent des complaintes, des tragédies de malandrins et de demi-dieux spirituels comme l'histoire ou les religions ne l'ont jamais été.] Chinois, Hottentots, Bohémiens, niais, hyènes, Molochs, vieilles démences, démons sinistres, ils mêlent les tours populaires, maternels, avec les poses et les tendresses bestiales. Ils interpréteraient des pièces nouvelles et des chansons «bonnes filles». Maîtres jongleurs, ils transforment le lieu et les personnes et usent de la comédie magnétique. [Les yeux flambent, le sang chante, les os s'élargissent, les larmes et des filets rouges ruissellent. Leur raillerie ou leur terreur dure une minute, ou des mois entiers.]

J'ai seul la clef de cette parade sauvage.

Parade
These are very sturdy rogues. Many of them have made use of you and your like. Without wants, they are in no hurry to put into action their brilliant faculties and their experience of your consciences. What mature men! Here are sottish eyes out of a midsummer night's dream – red, black, tricoloured; eyes of steel spotted with golden stars; deformed faces, leaden-hued, livid, enflamed; wanton hoarsenesses. They have the ungainly bearing of rag dolls. There are youths among them – [how would they regard Cherubim? – endowed with horrible voices and some dangerous resources. Dressed up with a disgusting richness, they are sent to exhibit themselves in the town.]

It is a violent Paradise of mad grimaces. [Your faquirs and your stage-clowns cannot compare with them. In improvized costumes of a nightmare taste, they play laments, tragedies of criminals and of demi-gods, more spiritual than history or religion has ever been.] Chinese, Hottentots, gypsies, simpletons, hyaenas, Molochs, old insanities, sinister demons, they alternate popular or maternal tricks with bestial poses and caresses. They can interpret modern plays or songs of a simple naivety at will. Master jugglers, they transform places and people, and make use of magnetic comedy. [Eyes flame, blood sings, bones grow bigger, tears and slender red threads trickle down. Their raillery or their terror lasts a minute or months.]

I alone hold the key to this savage parade.

Départ (*Departure*)

Britten wrote to Sophie Wyss that this poem should be sung 'as sweetly as only you know how'.

Assez vu.	Sufficiently seen.
La vision s'est rencontrée à tous les airs.	– The vision has been met in all guises.
Assez eu. Rumeurs des villes, le soir,	Sufficiently heard. – Rumours of the town at night,
et au soleil, et toujours.	in the sunlight, at all times.
	Sufficiently known. – Life's decrees.
Assez connu. Les arrêts de la vie.	Oh Rumours! Oh Vision!
– O Rumeurs et Visions!	Departure in the midst of love and new rumours.
Départ dans l'affection et le bruit neufs.	

Seven Sonnets of Michelangelo Op. 22 (1940)

These settings of sonnets by Michelangelo, for tenor and piano, were first performed on 23 September 1942 at the Wigmore Hall, London, by Pears and Britten. They were dedicated 'To Peter'. Britten wrote that setting these sonnets in Italian is 'pretty brave, but… after Rimbaud in French I feel I can attack anything.'

MICHELANGELO DI LUDOVICO BUONARROTI   (tr. J.A. Symonds)
Seven Sonnets

XVI

Sì come nella penna e nell'inchiostro
è l'alto e 'l basso e 'l mediocre stile,
e ne' marmi l'immagin ricca e vile,
secondo che 'l sa trar l'ingegnio nostro;

  così, signior mie car, nel petto vostro,
quante l'orgoglio è forse ogni atto umile;
ma io sol quel c'a me propio è e simile
ne traggo, come fuor nel viso mostro.

  Chi semina sospir, lacrime e doglie,
(l'umor dal ciel terreste, schietto e solo,
a' vari semi vario si converte),

  però pianto e dolor ne miete e coglie;
chi mira alta beltà con sì gran duolo,
ne ritra' doglie e pene acerbe e certe.

As pen and ink alike serve him who sings
  In high or low or intermediate style;
  As the same stone hath shapes both rich and vile
  To match the fancies that each master brings;
So, my loved lord, within thy bosom springs
  Pride mixed with meekness and kind thoughts that
    smile:
  Whence I draw nought, my sad self to beguile,
  But what my face shows – dark imaginings.
He who for seed sows sorrows, tears, and sighs,
  (The dews that fall from heaven, though pure and
    clear,
From different germs take divers qualities)
Must needs reap grief and garner weeping eyes;
  And he who looks on beauty with sad cheer,
Gains doubtful hope and certain miseries.

XXXI

A che più debb'i' omai l'intensa voglia
sfogar con pianti o con parole meste,
se di tal sorte 'l ciel, che l'alma veste,
tard' o per tempo alcun mai non ne spoglia?

A che 'l cor lass' a più languir m'invoglia,
s'altri pur dee morir? Dunche per queste
luci l'ore del fin fian men moleste;
ch'ogni altro ben val men ch'ogni mia doglia.

Però se 'l colpo ch'io ne rub' e 'nvolo
schifar non posso, almen, s'è destinato,
chi entrerà 'nfra la dolcezza e 'l duolo?

Se vint' e preso i' debb'esser beato,
maraviglia non è se nudo e solo
resto prigion d'un cavalier armato.

Why should I seek to ease intense desire
With still more tears and windy words of grief,
When heaven, or late or soon, sends no relief
To souls whom love hath robed around with fire?
Why need my aching heart to death aspire,
When all must die? Nay, death beyond belief
Unto these eyes would be both sweet and brief,
Since in my sum of woes all joys expire!
Therefore, because I cannot shun the blow
I rather seek, say who must rule my breast,
Gliding between her gladness and her woe?
If only chains and bands can make me blest,
No marvel if alone and bare I go
An arméd Knight's captive and slave confessed.

XXX

Veggio co' be' vostr'occhi un dolce lume
che co' mie ciechi già veder non posso;
porto co' vostri piedi un pondo adosso,
che de' mie zoppi non è giá costume.

Volo con le vostr'ale senza piume;
col vostro ingegno al ciel sempre son mosso;
dal vostro arbitrio son pallido e rosso,
freddo al sol, caldo alle più fredde brume.

Nel voler vostro è sol la voglia mia,
i miei pensier nel vostro cor si fanno,
nel vostro fiato son le mie parole.

Come luna da sé sol par ch'io sia,
ché gli occhi nostri in ciel veder non sanno
se non quel tanto che n'accende il sole.

With your fair eyes a charming sight I see,
For which my own blind eyes would peer in vain;
Stayed by your feet the burden I sustain
Which my lame feet find all too strong for me;
Wingless upon your pinions forth I fly;
Heavenward your spirit stirreth me to strain;
E'en as you will, I blush and blanch again,
Freeze in the sun, burn 'neath a frosty sky.
Your will includes and is the lord of mine;
Life to my thoughts within your heart is given;
My words begin to breathe upon your breath:
Like to the moon am I, that cannot shine
Alone; for lo! our eyes see nought in heaven
Save what the living sun illumineth.

Seven Sonnets of Michelangelo Op. 22 (1940)

LV

Tu sa' ch'i' so, signior mie, che tu sai
:h'i' vengo per goderti più da presso,
: sai ch'i' so che tu sa' ch'i' son desso:
. che più indugio a salutarci omai?

Se vera è la speranza che mi dai,
e vero è 'l gran desio che m'è concesso,
rompasi il mur fra l'uno e l'altra messo,
ché doppia forza hann' i celati guai.

S'i' amo sol di te, signior mie caro,
quel che di te più ami, non ti sdegni,
ché l'un dell'atro spirto s'innamora.

Quel che nel tuo bel volto bramo e 'mparo,
e mal compres' è dagli umani ingegni,
chi 'l vuol sapere convien che prima mora.

Thou knowest, love, I know that thou dost know
That I am here more near to thee to be,
And knowest that I know thou knowest me:
What means it then that we are sundered so?

If they are true, these hopes that from thee flow,
If it is real, this sweet expectancy,
Break down the wall that stands 'twixt me and ┊
For pain in prison pent hath double woe.

Because in thee I love, O my loved lord,
What thou best lovest, be not therefore stern:
Souls burn for souls, spirits to spirits cry!
I seek the splendour in thy fair face stored;
Yet living man that beauty scarce can learn,
And he who fain would find it, first must die.

XXXVIII

Rendete agli occhi mei, o fonte o fiume,
l'onde della non vostra e salda vena,
che più v'innalza e cresce, e con più lena
che non è 'l vostro natural costume.

E tu, folt'aír, che 'l celeste lume
tempri a' trist'occhi, de' sospir mie piena,
rendigli al cor mie lasso e rasserena
tua scura faccia al mie visivo acume.

Renda la terra i passi alle mie piante,
ch'ancor l'erba germugli che gli è tolta,
e 'l suono eco, già sorda a' mie lamenti;

gli sguardi agli occhi miei tuo luce sante,
ch'i' possa altra bellezza un'altra volta
amar, po' che di me non ti contenti.

Give back unto mine eyes, ye fount and rill,
Those streams, not yours, that are so full and
strong,
That swell your springs, and roll your waves along
With force unwonted in your native hill!

And thou, dense air, weighed with my sighs so chill,
That hidest heaven's own light thick mists among,
Give back those sighs to my sad heart, nor wrong
My visual ray with thy dark face of ill!

Let earth give back the footprints that I wore,
That the bare grass I spoiled may sprout again;
And Echo, now grown deaf, my cries return!
Loved eyes, unto mine eyes those looks restore,
And let me woo another not in vain,
Since how to please thee I shall never learn!

XXXII

S'un casto amor, s'una pietà superna,
s'una fortuna infra dua amanti equale,
s'un'aspra sorte all'un dell'altro cale,
s'un spirto, s'un voler duo cor governa;

s'un'anima in duo corpi è facta ecterna,
ambo levando al cielo e con pari ale;
s'Amor d'un colpo e d'un dorato strale
le viscier di duo petti arda e discierna;

s'amar l'un l'altro e nessun se medesmo,
d'un gusto e d'un diletto, a tal mercede
c'a un fin voglia l'uno e l'altro porre:

se mille e mille, non sarien centesmo
a tal nodo d'amore, a tanta fede;
e sol l'isdegnio il può rompere e sciorre.

If love be chaste, if virtue conquer ill,
If fortune bind both lovers in one bond,
If either at the other's grief despond,
If both be governed by one life, one will;
If in two bodies one soul triumph still,
Raising the twin from earth to heaven beyond,
If love with one blow and one golden wand
Have power both smitten breasts to pierce and
thrill;
If each the other love, himself forgoing,
With such delight, such savour, and so well,
That both to one sole end their wills combine;
If thousands of these thoughts, all thought outgoing,
Fail the least part of their firm love to tell:
Say, can mere angry spite this knot untwine?

XXIV

Spirto ben nato, in cu' si spechia e vede
nelle tuo belle membra oneste e care
quante natura e 'l ciel tra no' può fare,
quand'a null'altra suo bell'opra cede:

spirto leggiadro, in cu' si spera e crede
dentro, come di fuor nel viso appare,
amor, pietà, mercè, cose sì rare,
che ma' furn'in beltà con tanta fede;

l'amor mi prende e la beltà mi lega;
la pietà, la mercè con dolci sguardi
ferma speranz'al cor par che ne doni.

Qual uso o qual governo al mondo niega,
qual crudeltà per tempo o qual più tardi,
c'a sì bell'opra morte non perdoni?

Choice soul, in whom, as in a glass, we see,
Mirrored in thy pure form and delicate,
What beauties heaven and nature can create,
The paragon of all their works to be!
Fair soul, in whom love, pity, piety,
Have found a home as from thy outward state
We clearly read, and are so rare and great
That they adorn none other like to thee!
Love takes me captive; beauty binds my soul;
Pity and mercy with their gentle eyes
Wake in my heart a hope that cannot cheat.
What law, what destiny, what fell control,
What cruelty, or late or soon, denies
That death should spare perfection so complete?

Seven Sonnets of Michelangelo Op. 22 (1940)

What's in your mind? (1939/41)

W.H. AUDEN 'What's in your mind?'

What's in your mind, my dove, my coney;
Do thoughts grow like feathers, the dead end of life;
Is it making of love or counting of money,
Or raid on the jewels, the plans of a thief?

Open your eyes, my dearest dallier;
Let hunt with your hands for escaping me;
Go through the motions of exploring the familiar;
Stand on the brink of the warm white day.

Rise with the wind, my great big serpent;
Silence the birds and darken the air;
Change me with terror, alive in a moment;
Strike for the heart and have me there.

Two Songs (1942)

These two songs for voice and piano by Beddoes were first performed on 15 June 1992 at the Aldeburgh Festival by Lucy Shelton and Ian Brown.

THOMAS LOVELL BEDDDOES *Song on the water*

Wild with passion, sorrow-beladen,
    Bend the thought of thy stormy soul
On its home, on its heaven, the loved maiden;
    And peace shall come at her eyes' control.
Even so night's starry rest possesses
    With its gentle spirit these tamed waters,
And bids the wave, with weedy tresses
    Embower the ocean's pavement stilly
    Where the sea-girls lie, the mermaid-daughters,
      Whose eyes, not born to weep,
      More palely-lidded sleep,
    Than in our fields the lily;
      And sighing in their rest
        More sweet than is its breath;
        And quiet as its death
          Upon a lady's breast.

Dirge for Wolfram 'If thou wilt ease'

If thou wilt ease thine heart
Of love and all its smart,
    Then sleep, dear, sleep;
And not a sorrow
    Hang any tear on your eyelashes;
      Lie still and deep,
    Sad soul, until the sea-wave washes
The rim o' th' sun tomorrow,
      In eastern sky.

But wilt thou cure thy heart
Of love and all its smart,
    Then die, dear, die;
'Tis deeper, sweeter,
    Than on a rose bank to lie dreaming
      With folded eye;
    And then alone, amid the beaming
Of love's stars, thou'lt meet her
      In eastern sky.

Hymn to St Cecilia, Op. 27 (1942)

This hymn for five-part chorus and unaccompanied solos was first performed on 22 November 1942 by the BBC Singers, conducted by Leslie Woodgate. It was dedicated 'To Elizabeth Mayer'.

W.H. AUDEN   *Hymn to St Cecilia*

In a garden shady this holy lady
With reverent cadence and subtle psalm,
Like a black swan as death came on
Poured forth her song in perfect calm:
And by ocean's margin this innocent virgin
Constructed an organ to enlarge her prayer,
And notes tremendous from her great engine
Thundered out on the Roman air.

Blonde Aphrodite rose up excited,
Moved to delight by the melody,
White as an orchid she rode quite naked
In an oyster shell on top of the sea;
At sounds so entrancing the angels dancing
Came out of their trance into time again,
And around the wicked in Hell's abysses
The huge flame flickered and eased their pain.

Blessed Cecilia, appear in visions
To all musicians, appear and inspire:
Translated Daughter, come down and startle
Composing mortals with immortal fire.

I cannot grow;
I have no shadow
To run away from,
I only play.

I cannot err;
There is no creature
Whom I belong to,
Whom I could wrong.

I am defeat
When it knows it

Can now do nothing
By suffering.

All you lived through,
Dancing because you
No longer need it
For any deed.

I shall never be
Different.Love me.

Chorus O ear whose creatures cannot wish to fall,
    O calm of spaces unafraid of weight,
    Where Sorrow is herself forgetting all
    The gauchness of her adolescent state,
    Where Hope within the altogether strange
    From every outworn image is released,
    And Dread born whole and normal like a beast
    Into a world of truths that never change:
    Restore our fallen day, O re-arrange.

Solo O dear white children casual as birds,
    Playing among the ruined languages,
    So small beside their large confusing words,
    So gay against the greater silences
    Of dreadful things you did: O hang the head,
    Impetuous child with the tremendous brain,
    O weep, child, weep, O weep away the stain,
    Lost innocence who wished your lover dead,
    Weep for the lives your wishes never led.

Chorus O cry created as the bow of sin
    Is drawn across our trembling violin.

Solo O weep, child, weep, O weep away the stain.

Chorus O law drummed out by hearts against the still
    Long winter of our intellectual will.

Solo That what has been may never be again.

Chorus O flute that throbs with the thanksgiving breath
    Of convalescents on the shores of death.

Solo O bless the freedom that you never chose.

Chorus O trumpets that unguarded children blow
    About the fortress of their inner foe.

Solo O wear your tribulation like a rose.

Cradle song (1942)

This setting, for voice and piano, was first performed on 15 June 1992 at the Aldeburgh Festival by Lucy Shelton and Ian Brown.

LOUIS MACNEICE   *Cradle song for Eleanor* 'Cradle song'

Sleep, my darling, sleep;
 The pity of it all
Is all we compass if
 We watch disaster fall.
Put off your twenty-odd
 Encumbered years and creep
Into the only heaven,
 The robbers' cave of sleep.

The wild grass will whisper,
 Lights of passing cars
Will streak across your dreams
 And fumble at the stars;
Life will tap the window
 Only too soon again,
Life will have her answer –
 Do not ask her when.

When the winsome bubble
 Shivers, when the bough
Breaks, will be the moment
 But not here or now.
Sleep and asleep, forget
 The watchers on the wall
Awake all night who know
 The pity of it all.

A Ceremony of Carols, Op. 28 (1942)

This work for trebles and harp was first performed on 5 December 1942 at Norwich Castle by The Fleet Street Choir and Gwendolen Mason, conducted by T.B. Lawrence. It was dedicated 'For Ursula Nettleship'.

TRAD. *Hodie Christus natus est*

Hodie Christus natus est.	Today Christ was born.
Hodie Salvator apparuit:	Today the Saviour appeared:
Hodie in terra canunt angeli,	Today on earth the angels sing,
Laetantur archangeli:	The archangels rejoice:
Hodie exsultant justi, dicantes	Today the righteous exult, saying
Gloria in excelsis Deo.Alleluia.	Glory to God in the heights. Alleluia.

ANON. (14th century) *Wolcum Yole*

Wolcum be thou hevene king,
Wolcum Yole.
Wolcum, born in one morning,
Wolcum for whom we sall sing.

Wolcum be ye, Stevene and Jon,
Wolcum, innocentes every one,
Wolcum, Thomas marter one,
Wolcum be ye good New Yere,
Wolcum, Twelfthe Day both in fere,
Wolcum, seintes lefe and dere,
Wolcum Yole, wolcum.

Candelmesse,
Quene of bliss,
Wolcum bothe to more and lesse.
Wolcum, wolcum.

Wolcum be ye that are here,
Wolcum Yole.
Wolcum alle and make good cheer,
Wolcum alle another yere,
Wolcum Yole, wolcum.

ANON. (14th century) (tr. Ian Hamnett)   *There is no rose*

There is no rose of such vertu
As is the rose that bare Jesu.
Alleluia.

For in this rose conteinèd was
Heaven and erth in litel space,
a wonderful thing   Res miranda.

By that rose we may well see
There be one God in persons three,
equal in form   Pares forma.

The aungels sungen the shepherds to:
glory to God in the highest   Gloria in excelsis Deo.
let us rejoice   Gaudeamus.

Leave we all this werldly mirth,
And folwè we this joyful birth.
let us go   Transeamus.

ANON. (14th century)   *That yonge child*

That yonge child when it gan weep
With song she lulled him asleep;
That was so sweet a melody
It passed alle minstrelsy.

The nightingale sang also,
Her song is hoarse and nought thereto:
Whoso attendeth to her song
And leaveth the first, then doth he wrong.

JAMES, JOHN AND ROBERT WEDDERBURN   *Balulalow*

O my deare Hert, young Jesus sweit,
Prepare thy creddil in my spreit,
And I sall rock thee to my hert
And never mair from thee depart.

But I sall praise thee evermoir
With sanges sweit unto thy gloir;
The knees of my hert sall I bow
And sing that richt Balulalow.

A Ceremony of Carols, Op. 28 (1942)

ANON. *As dew in Aprille*

> I sing of a maiden

matchless
> That is makèles:
>
> King of all kings

chose
> To her son she ches.

> He came al so stille
> There his moder was,
> As dew in Aprille
> That falleth on the grass.

> He came al so stille
> To his moder's bour,
> As dew in Aprille
> That falleth on the flour.

> He came al so stille
> There his moder lay,
> As dew in Aprille
> That falleth on the spray.

> Moder and maiden
> Was never none but she:
> Well may such a lady
> Goddes moder be.

ROBERT SOUTHWELL   *This little babe*

> This little Babe, so few days old,
> Is come to rifle Satan's fold;
> All hell doth at his presence quake,
> Though he himself for cold do shake;
> For in this weak unarmèd wise
> The gates of hell he will surprise.

> With tears he fights and wins the field,
> His naked breast stands for a shield;
> His battering shot are babish cries,
> His arrows looks of weeping eyes,
> His martial ensigns Cold and Need,
> And feeble Flesh his warrior's steed.

His camp is pitchèd in a stall,
His bulwark but a broken wall;
The crib his trench, hay-stalks his stakes;
Of shepherds he his muster makes;
And thus, as sure his foe to wound,
The angels' trumps alarum sound.

My soul, with Christ join thou in fight;
Stick to the tents that he hath pight.
Within his crib is surest ward;
This little Babe will be thy guard.
If thou wilt foil thy foes with joy,
Then flit not from this heavenly Boy.

ROBERT SOUTHWELL   *In freezing winter night*

Behold, a silly tender babe,
    In freezing winter night,
In homely manger trembling lies –
    Alas, a piteous sight!

The inns are full; no man will yield
    This little pilgrim bed.
But forced he is with silly beasts
    In crib to shroud his head ...

This stable is a Prince's court,
    This crib his chair of state;
The beasts are parcel of his pomp,
    The wooden dish his plate.

The persons in that poor attire
    His royal liveries wear;
The Prince himself is come from heaven;
    This pomp is prizèd there.

With joy approach, O Christian wight,
    Do homage to thy King;
And highly praise his humble pomp,
    Which he from heaven doth bring.

Britten made a somewhat different selection of Southwell's verses for inclusion in
Thy King's Birthday (see pp.15–16).

A Ceremony of Carols, Op. 28 (1942)

WILLIAM CORNYSHE *Spring carol*

Pleasure it is

truly   To hear, iwis,
               The birdes sing.
The deer in the dale,
The sheep in the vale,
          The corn springing;
God's purveyance
For sustenance
          It is for man.
Then we always
To Him give praise,
          And thank Him than,
          And thank Him than.

ANON. (c. 15th century) *Deo gracias*

Adam lay ibounden,
Bounden in a bond;
Four thousand winter
Thought he not too long.

And all was for an appil,
An appil that he tok,
As clerkès finden
Written in their book.

Ne had the appil takè ben,
The appil takè ben,
Ne haddè never our lady
A ben hevenè quene.

Blessèd be the time
That appil takè was.
Therefore we moun singen
Thanks (be) to God   Deo gracias.

Folk Song Arrangements, Vol. 1   British Isles (1943)

For high or medium voice. There is no record of all the folk songs in each volume being performed at a single recital (though all have now been recorded).

W.B. YEATS   *The salley gardens*

Down by the salley gardens my love and I did meet;
She passed the salley gardens with little snow-white feet.
She bid me take love easy, as the leaves grow on the tree;
But I, being young and foolish, with her would not agree.

In the field by the river my love and I did stand,
And on my leaning shoulder she laid her snow-white hand.
She bid me take life easy, as the grass grows on the weirs;
But I was young and foolish, and now am full of tears.

TRAD.   *Little Sir William*

Easter day was a holiday
Of all days in the year,
And all the little schoolfellows went out to play,
But Sir William was not there.

Mamma went to the Jew's wife house †
And knocked at the ring,
Saying, 'Little Sir William if you are there,
Pray let your mother in.'

The Jew's wife opened the door and said,
'He is not here today.
He is with the little schoolfellows out on the green
Playing some pretty play.'

Mamma went to the Boyne water
That is so wide and deep,
Saying, 'Little Sir William if you are there,
Oh pity your mother's weep.'

'How can I pity your weep, mother,
And I so long in pain?
For the little pen knife sticks close to me heart
And the Jew's wife hath me slain.

Go home, go home my mother dear
And prepare my winding sheet,
For tomorrow morning before 8 o'clock,
You with my body shall meet.

And lay my Prayer Book at my head,
And my grammar at my feet,
That all the little schoolfellows as they pass
May read them for my sake.'

† Britten used 'school's' instead of 'Jew's' throughout.

TRAD. *The bonny Earl o' Moray*

Ye Hielands and ye Lowlands,
O where hae ye been?
They hae slain the Earl o' Moray,
And laid him on the green.

He was a braw gallant
And he rade at the ring;
And the bonny Earl o' Moray
He might hae been a King.

O lang will his Lady
Look frae the Castle Doune,
Ere she see the Earl o' Moray
Come soundin' thru the toon.

O wae tae ye, Huntley,
And wherefore did ye sae?
I bade ye bring him wi' you
And forbade ye him to slay.

He was a braw gallant
And he played at the glove;
And the bonnie Earl o' Moray
He was the Queen's love.

O lang...

TRAD. *O can ye sew cushions?*

O can ye sew cushions and can ye sew sheets
And can ye sing ballulow when the bairn greets?
And hie and baw, birdie, and hie and baw lamb,
And hee and baw birdie, my bonnie wee lamb.

Hieo wieo what will I do wi' ye?
Black's the life that I lead wi' ye,
Many o' you, little for to gi' ye,
Hieo wieo what will I do wi' ye?

I've placed my cradle on yon hilly top
And aye as the wind blew my cradle did rock.
O hushaby babie, O baw lilly loo,
And hee and baw birdie, my bonnie wee doo.

TRAD. *The trees they grow so high*

The trees they grow so high and the leaves they do grow green,
And many a cold winter's night my love and I have seen.
Of a cold winter's night, my love, you and I alone have been,
Whilst my bonny boy is young he's agrowing. Growing, growing,
Whilst my bonny boy is young he's agrowing.

O father, dearest father, you've done me great wrong.
You've tied me to a boy when you know he is too young.
O daughter, dearest daughter, if you wait a little while,
A lady you shall be while he's growing. Growing, growing,
A lady you shall be while he's growing.

I'll send your love to college all for a year or two,
And then in the meantime he will do for you;
I'll buy him white ribbons, tie them round his bonny waist
To let the ladies know that he's married. Married, married,
To let the ladies know that he's married.

I went up to the college and I looked over the wall,
Saw four and twenty gentlemen playing at bat and ball.
I called for my true love, but they would not let him come,
All because he was a young boy and growing. Growing, growing,
All because he was a young boy and growing.

At the age of sixteen he was a married man,
And at the age of seventeen he was father to a son,
And at the age of eighteen the grass grew over him,
Cruel death soon put an end to his growing. Growing, growing,
Cruel death soon put an end to his growing.

And now my love is dead and in his grave doth lie.
The green grass grows o'er him so very, very high.
I'll sit and I'll mourn his fate until the day I die,

And I'll watch all o'er his child while he's growing. Growing, growing,
And I'll watch all o'er his child while he's growing.

TRAD. *The ash grove*

Down yonder green valley where streamlets meander,
When twilight is fading I pensively rove,
Or at the bright noontide in solitude wander
Amid the dark shades of the lonely Ash Grove.

'Twas there while the blackbird was joyfully singing,
I first met my dear one, the joy of my heart;
Around us for gladness the bluebells were ringing.
Ah! then little thought I how soon we should part.

Still glows the bright sunshine o'er valley and mountain,
Still warbles the blackbird his note from the tree;
Still trembles the moonbeam on streamlet and fountain,
But what are the beauties of nature to me?

With sorrow, deep sorrow, my bosom is laden,
All day I go mourning in search of my love.
Ye echoes, O tell me, where is the sweet maiden?
She sleeps 'neath the green turf down by the Ash Grove.

TRAD. *Oliver Cromwell*

Oliver Cromwell lay buried and dead,
Hee-haw buried and dead.
There grew an old apple tree over his head,
Hee-haw, over his head.

The apples were ripe and ready to fall;
Hee-haw, ready to fall;
There came an old woman to gather them all,
Hee-haw, gather them all.

Oliver rose and gave her a drop,
Hee-haw, gave her a drop,
Which made the old woman go hippety hop,
Hee-haw, hippety hop.

The saddle and bridle, they lie on the shelf,
Hee-haw, lie on the shelf.
If you want any more you can sing it yourself,
Hee-haw, sing it yourself.

Rejoice in the Lamb, Op. 30 (1943)

This festival cantata, for chorus with treble, alto, tenor and bass solos with organ, was first performed on 21 September 1943 in St Matthew's Church, Northampton. It was composed 'For the Rev. W. Walter Hussey and the choir of St Matthew's Church, Northampton – on the occasion of the 50th anniversary of the consecration of their church, 21 September 1943'.

CHRISTOPHER SMART *Rejoice in the Lamb* (taken from *Jubilate Deo*)

Rejoice in God, O ye Tongues; give the glory to the Lord, and the Lamb.
Nations, and languages, and every Creature, in which is the breath of Life.
Let man and beast appear before him, and magnify his name together.
Let Nimrod, the mighty hunter, bind a Leopard to the altar, and consecrate
his spear to the Lord.
Let Ishmael dedicate a Tyger, and give praise for the liberty in which the
Lord has let him at large.
Let Balaam appear with an Ass, and bless the Lord his people and his crea-
tures for a reward eternal.
Let Daniel come forth with a Lion, and praise God with all his might
through faith in Christ Jesus.
Let Ithamar minister with a Chamois, and bless the name of Him, that
cloatheth the naked.
Let Jakim with the Satyr bless God in the dance.
Let David bless with the Bear – The beginning of victory to the Lord – to
the Lord the perfection of excellence – Hallelujah from the heart of
God, and from the hand of the artist inimitable, and from the echo of
the heavenly harp in sweetness magnifical and mighty.

For I will consider my Cat Jeoffry.
For he is the servant of the Living God, duly and daily serving him.
For at the first glance of the glory of God in the East he worships in his way.
For this is done by wreathing his body seven times round with elegant quick-
ness.
For he knows that God is his Saviour.
For God has blessed him in the variety of his movements.
For there is nothing sweeter than his peace when at rest.
For I am possessed of a cat, surpassing in beauty, from whom I take occasion
to bless Almighty God.

For the Mouse is a creature of great personal valour.

For – this is a true case – Cat takes female mouse – male mouse will not
    depart, but stands threat'ning and daring.

… If you will let her go, I will engage you, as prodigious a creature as you are.

For the Mouse is a creature of great personal valour.

For the Mouse is of an hospitable disposition.

For the flowers are great blessings.

For the flowers have their angels even the words of God's Creation.

For the flower glorifies God and the root parries the adversary.

For there is a language of flowers.

For flowers are peculiarly the poetry of Christ.

For I am under the same accusation with my Saviour –

For they said, he is besides himself.

For the officers of the peace are at variance with me, and the watchman
    smites me with his staff.

For Silly fellow! Silly fellow! is against me and belongeth neither to me nor
    to my family.

For I am in twelve HARDSHIPS but he that was born of a virgin shall
    deliver me out of all.

For H is a spirit and therefore he is God.

For K is king and therefore he is God.

For L is love and therefore he is God.

For M is musick and therefore he is God.

For the instruments are by their rhimes.

For the Shawm rhimes are lawn fawn moon boon and the like.

For the harp rhimes are sing ring string and the like.

For the cymbal rhimes are bell well toll soul and the like.

For the flute rhimes are tooth youth suit mute and the like.

For the Bassoon rhimes are pass class and the like.

For the dulcimer rhimes are grace place beat heat and the like.

For the Clarinet rhimes are clean seen and the like.

For the trumpet rhimes are sound bound soar more and the like.

For the TRUMPET of God is a blessed intelligence and so are all the instru-
    ments in HEAVEN.

For GOD the father Almighty plays upon the HARP of stupendous magni-
    tude and melody.

For at that time malignity ceases and the devils themselves are at peace.

For this time is perceptible to man by a remarkable stillness and serenity of
    soul.

Hallelujah from the heart of God, and from the hand of the artist inimitable,
    and from the echo of the heavenly harp in sweetness magnifical and
    mighty.

Rejoice in the Lamb, Op. 30 (1943)   [101

Serenade, Op. 31 (1943)

This serenade for tenor, horn and strings, was first performed on 15 October 1943 at the Wigmore Hall, London, by Pears, Dennis Brain, and orchestra, conducted by Walter Goehr. It was dedicated 'To Edward Sackville-West'. The lyke-wake dirge was sung in north Yorkshire while carrying a corpse across the moors to the nearest burial ground.

CHARLES COTTON *Evening quatrains* 'Pastoral'

The day's grown old, the fainting sun
Has but a little way to run,
And yet his steeds, with all his skill,
Scarce lug the chariot down the hill.

[With labour spent, and thirst opprest,
Whilst they strain hard to gain the West,
From fetlocks hot drops melted light,
Which turn to meteors in the night.]

The shadows now so long do grow,
That brambles like tall cedars show,
Mole-hills seem mountains, and the ant
Appears a monstrous elephant.

A very little, little flock
Shades thrice the ground that it would stock;
Whilst the small stripling following them,
Appears a mighty Polypheme.

[These being brought into the fold,
And by the thrifty master told,
He thinks his wages are well paid.
Since none are either lost, or stray'd.

Now lowing herds are each-where heard,
farmyard   Chains rattle in the villain's yard,
The cart's on tail set down to rest,
Bearing on high the Cuckold's crest.

The hedge is stripped, the clothes brought in,
Nought's left without should be within,

The bees are hiv'd, and hum their charm,
Whilst every house does seem a swarm.

The cock now to the roost is prest;
For he must call up all the rest;
The sow's fast pegg'd within the sty,
To still her squeaking progeny.

Each one has had his supping mess,
The cheese is put into the press,
The pans and bowls clean scalded all,
Rear'd up against the milk-house wall.]

And now on benches all are sat
In the cool air to sit and chat,
Till Phoebus, dipping in the West,
Shall lead the world the way to rest.

ALFRED, LORD TENNYSON   *Blow, bugle, blow* 'Nocturne'

The splendour falls on castle walls
    And snowy summits old in story:
    The long light shakes across the lakes,
    And the wild cataract leaps in glory.
Blow, bugle, blow, set the wild echoes flying,
Blow, bugle; answer, echoes, dying, dying, dying.

    O hark, O hear! how thin and clear,
      And thinner, clearer, farther going!
    O sweet and far from cliff and scar
      The horns of Elfland faintly blowing!
Blow, let us hear the purple glens replying:
Blow, bugle; answer, echoes, dying, dying, dying.

    O love, they die in yon rich sky,
      They faint on hill or field or river:
    Our echoes roll from soul to soul,
      And grow for ever and for ever.
Blow, bugle, blow, set the wild echoes flying,
And answer, echoes, answer, dying, dying, dying.

WILLIAM BLAKE *The sick rose* 'Elegy'

O Rose, thou art sick!
The invisible worm
That flies in the night,
In the howling storm,

Has found out thy bed
Of crimson joy:
And his dark secret love
Does thy life destroy.

ANON. (15th century) *A lyke-wake dirge*

This ae nighte, this ae nighte,
   – Every nighte and alle,
Fire and fleet and candle-lighte,
   And Christe receive thy saule.

When thou from hence away art past,
   – Every nighte and alle,
To Whinny-muir thou com'st at last;
   And Christe receive thy saule.

If ever thou gavest hosen and shoon,
   – Every night and alle,
Sit thee down and put them on;
   And Christe receive thy saule.

If hosen and shoon thou ne'er gav'st nane
   – Every nighte and alle,
The whinnes sall prick thee to the bare bane;
   And Christe receive thy saule.

From Whinny-muir when thou may'st pass,
   – Every nighte and alle,
To Brig o' Dread thou com'st at last;
   And Christe receive thy saule.

From Brig o' Dread when thou may'st pass,
   – Every nighte and alle,
To Purgatory fire thou com'st at last;
   And Christe receive thy saule.

If ever thou gavest meat or drink,
　 – *Every nighte and alle,*
The fire sall never make thee shrink;
　 And Christe receive thy saule.

If meat or drink thou ne'er gav'st nane,
　 – *Every nighte and alle,*
The fire will burn thee to the bare bane;
　 And Christe receive thy saule.

This ae nighte, this ae nighte,
　 – *Every nighte and alle,*
Fire and fleet and candle-lighte,
　 And Christe receive thy saule.

BEN JONSON　*Hymn to Diana*

Queen and huntress, chaste and fair,
　 Now the sun is laid to sleep,
Seated in thy silver chair,
　 　 State in wonted manner keep:
　 　 　 Hesperus entreats thy light,
　 　 　 Goddess excellently bright.

Earth, let not thy envious shade
　 Dare itself to interpose;
Cynthia's shining orb was made
　 　 Heaven to clear when day did close:
　 　 　 Bless us then with wishèd sight,
　 　 　 Goddess excellently bright.

Lay thy bow of pearl apart,
　 And thy crystal-shining quiver;
Give unto the flying hart
　 　 Space to breathe, how short soever
　 　 　 Thou that mak'st a day of night –
　 　 　 Goddess excellently bright.

JOHN KEATS *To sleep* 'Sonnet'

O soft embalmer of the still midnight!
    Shutting with careful fingers and benign
Our gloom-pleased eyes, embower'd from the light,
    Enshaded in forgetfulness divine;
O soothest Sleep! If so it please thee, close,
    In midst of this thine hymn, my willing eyes,
Or wait the amen, ere thy poppy throws
    Around my bed its lulling charities;
    Then save me, or the passèd day will shine
Upon my pillow, breeding many woes;
Save me from curious conscience, that still lords
    Its strength for darkness, burrowing like a mole;
Turn the key deftly in the oilèd wards,
    And seal the hushèd casket of my soul.

Serenade, Op. 31 (1943)

The Ballad of Little Musgrave and Lady Barnard (1943)

Set for male voices and piano and dedicated to 'Richard Wood and the musicians of Oflag VIIb – Germany – 1943', this ballad was first performed in 1944 at a prisoner-of-war camp at Eichstätt, Germany.

ANON.   *Little Musgrave and Lady Barnard*

[O wow for day!
 And, dear, gin it were day!
 Gin it were day, and I were away –
 For I ha' na lang time to stay.]

As it fell on one holy-day,
 As many be in the year,
When young men and maids together did go
 Their matins and mass to hear,

Little Musgrave came to the church-door –
 The priest was at private mass –
But he had more mind of the fair women
 Than he had of Our Lady's grace.

The one of them was clad in green,
fine cloth   Another was clad in pall,
And then came in my Lord Barnard's wife,
 The fairest among them all.

[She cast an eye on Little Musgrave
 As bright as the summer sun;
And then bethought him Little Musgrave,
 'This lady's heart have I won.']

Quoth she, 'I have loved thee, Little Musgrave,
 Full long and many a day.' –
'So have I loved you, fair ladye,
 Yet never word durst I say.' –

'But I have a bower at Bucklesfordberry,
 Full daintily it is dight;
If thou'lt wend thither, thou Little Musgrave,
lie   Thou's lig in my arms all night.'

[Quoth he, 'I thank thee, fair ladye,
    This kindness thou showest to me;
And whether it be to my weal or woe
    This night I will lodge with thee.']

With that beheard a little tiny page,
    By his lady's coach as he ran.
Says, 'Although I am my lady's foot-page,
    Yet I am Lord Barnard's man.'

Then he's cast off his hose and shoon,
    Set down his feet and ran,
And where the bridges were broken down
    He bent his bow and swam.

'Awake! awake! thou Lord Barnard,
    As thou art a man of life!
Little Musgrave is at Bucklesfordberry
    Along with thy own wedded wife.' –

['If this be true, thou tiny little page,
    This thing thou tellest to me,
Then all the land in Bucklesfordberry
    I freely will give to thee.

'But if it be a lie, thou tiny little page,
    This thing thou tellest to me,
On the highest tree in Bucklesfordberry
    Then hangèd shalt thou be.']

He callèd up his merry men all:
    'Come saddle me my steed;
This night must I go to Bucklesfordberry,
    For I never had greater need.'

But some they whistled, and some they sung,
    And some they thus could say,
Whenever Lord Barnard's horn it blew:
    '*Away, Musgrave, away!*'...

'Methinks I hear the threstle cock,
    Methinks I hear the jay;
Methinks I hear Lord Barnard's horn,
    Away, Musgrave, away!' –

'Lie still, lie still, thou little Musgrave,
    And huggle me from the cold;
'Tis nothing but a shepherd's boy
    A-driving his sheep to the fold.'

By this, Lord Barnard came to his door,
    And lighted a stone upon;
And he's pull'd out three silver keys,
    And open'd the doors each one.

He lifted up the coverlet,
    He lifted up the sheet:
['Dost thou like my bed, Little Musgrave?
    Dost thou find my lady sweet?' –

'I find her sweet,' quoth Little Musgrave,
    'The more 'tis to my pain;
I would gladly give three hundred pounds
    That I were on yonder plain.' –]

'Arise, arise, thou Little Musgrave,
    And put thy clothès on;
It shall ne'er be said in my country
    I have kill'd a naked man.

'I have two swords in one scabbard,
    They are both sharp and clear;
Take you the best, and I the worst,
    We'll end the matter here.'

The first stroke Little Musgrave struck,
    He hurt Lord Barnard sore;
The next stroke that Lord Barnard struck,
    Little Musgrave ne'er struck more.

[With that bespake this fair lady,
    In bed where as she lay:
'Although thou'rt dead, thou Little Musgrave,
    Yet I for thee will pray.

'And wish well to thy soul will I
    So long as I have life;
So will I not for thee, Barnard,
    Although I'm thy wedded wife.'

He cut her paps from off her breast;
    Great pity it was to see
That some drops of this lady's heart's blood
    Ran trickling down her knee.]

'Woe worth you, woe worth, my merry men all,
    You were ne'er born for my good!
Why did you not offer to stay my hand
mad, fierce   When you saw me wax so wood?

'For I have slain the fairest lady
    That ever wore a woman's weed;
Soe I have slain the fairest lady
    That ever did woman's deed.

'A grave, a grave,' Lord Barnard cried,
    'To put these lovers in!
But lay my lady on the upper hand,
    For she comes of nobler kin.'

The Ballad of Little Musgrave and Lady Barnard (1943)

A shepherd's carol (1944)

This carol, for unaccompanied chorus, was written for a BBC programme, *Poet's Christmas*, 1944, and it was first performed at a concert in Holy Trinity Church, London, on 17 October 1962.

W.H. AUDEN   *A shepherd's carol*

finger   *O lift your little pinkie, and touch the winter sky.*
Love's all over the mountains where the beautiful go to die.

If Time were the wicked sheriff, in a horse opera,
I'd pay for riding lessons and take his gun away-O.
O lift...

If I were a Valentino and Fortune were abroad,
I'd hypnotise that iceberg till she kissed me of her own accord-O.

If I'd stacked up the velvet and my crooked rib were dead,
I'd be breeding white canaries and eating crackers in bed-O.

But my cuffs are soiled and fraying. The kitchen clock is slow,
And over the Blue Waters the grass grew long ago.

This Way to the Tomb (1945)

These three songs were composed for Ronald Duncan's masque and anti-masque, *This way to the tomb*, which was first performed on 11 October 1945 at the Mercury Theatre, London, by the Pilgrim Players. In a letter to Duncan, Britten wrote: 'What a one you are! Here I am up to my eyes in opera and spiritual crises & you expect me to drop everything & write you two [later three] songs! Still, maybe I'll have a shot (but *no* promises)...' In Britten's setting, verses two and three of 'Morning' are reversed in order.

RONALD DUNCAN   *This way to the tomb*

Evening

The red fox, the sun,
tears the throat of the evening;
makes the light of the day
bleed into the ocean.

The laced grace of gulls
lift up from the corn fields;
fly across the sunset,
scarlet their silhouette.

The old owl, the moon,
drifts from its loose thatch of clouds,
throws an ivory glance
on an enamelled sea.

Eyes of mice, the stars,
from their privacy of light
peep into the darkness
with the temerity of night.

Morning

Morning is only
A heron rising
With great wings lifting
Day into the sky.

Morning is only
A scarlet stallion
Jumping the ocean,
    Its mane aflame on the sea.

Morning is only
The white plumes of smoke
As the velvet snake
    Night leaves the green valley.

Morning is only
Women bent at the well
Lifting their pails full
    Of their hearts, too heavy.

Night

Night is no more
than a cat which creeps
to the saucer of light
    laps, then sleeps.

Night is no more
than the place waves reach
with their hands of surf
    seeking the beach.

Night is no more
than the hounds of fear
with bloody jowl and bark
    bullying the year.

Night is no more
than my love who lies.
She dreams of a dream,
    lives, then dies.

The Holy Sonnets of John Donne, Op. 35 (1945)

This setting for high voice and piano was first performed on 22 November 1945 at the Wigmore Hall, London, by Pears and Britten. Dedicated 'For Peter'. The cycle was affected by Britten's visit to the Belsen concentration camp, which he found a terrifying experience; according to Christopher Palmer, it 'coloured everything he wrote subsequently'.

JOHN DONNE   *Holy Sonnets*

IV

Oh my blacke Soule! now thou art summoned
By sicknesse, deaths herald, and champion;
Thou art like a pilgrim, which abroad hath done
Treason, and durst not turne to whence hee is fled,
Or like a thiefe, which till deaths doome be read,
Wisheth himselfe delivered from prison;
But damn'd and hal'd to execution,
Wisheth that still he might be imprisoned.
Yet grace, if thou repent, thou canst not lacke;
But who shall give thee that grace to beginne?
Oh make thy selfe with holy mourning blacke,
And red with blushing, as thou art with sinne;
Or wash thee in Christs blood, which hath this might
That being red, it dyes red soules to white.

XIV

Batter my heart, three person'd God; for, you
As yet but knocke, breathe, shine, and seeke to mend;
That I may rise, and stand, o'erthrow mee,'and bend
Your force, to breake, blowe, burn and make me new.
I, like an usurpt towne, to'another due,
Labour to'admit you, but Oh, to no end,
Reason your viceroy in mee, mee should defend,

But is captiv'd, and proves weake or untrue.
Yet dearely' I love you,' and would be loved faine,
But am betroth'd unto your enemie:
Divorce mee,' untie, or breake that knot againe,
Take mee to you, imprison mee, for I
Except you'enthrall mee, never shall be free,
Nor ever chast, except you ravish mee.

III

O might those sighes and teares returne againe
Into my breast and eyes, which I have spent,
That I might in this holy discontent
Mourne with some fruit, as I have mourn'd in vaine;
In mine Idolatry what showres of raine
Mine eyes did waste? what griefs my heart did rent?
That sufferance was my sinne; now I repent;
'Cause I did suffer I must suffer paine.
Th'hydroptique drunkard, and night-scouting thiefe,
The itchy Lecher, and selfe tickling proud
Have the remembrance of past joyes, for reliefe
Of comming ills. To (poore) me is allow'd
No ease; for, long, yet vehement griefe hath beene
Th'effect and cause, the punishment and sinne.

XIX

Oh, to vex me, contraryes meet in one:
Inconstancy unnaturally hath begott
A constant habit; that when I would not
I change in vowes, and in devotione.
As humorous is my contritione
As my prophane Love, and as soone forgott:
As ridlingly distemper'd, cold and hott,
As praying, as mute; as infinite, as none.
I durst not view heaven yesterday; and to day
In prayers, and flattering speaches I court God:
To morrow I quake with true feare of his rod.
So my devout fitts come and go away
Like a fantastique Ague: save that here
Those are my best dayes, when I shake with feare.

XIII

What if this present were the worlds last night?
Marke in my heart, O Soule, where thou dost dwell,
The picture of Christ crucified, and tell
Whether that countenance can thee affright,
Teares in his eyes quench the amazing light,
Blood fills his frownes, which from his pierc'd head fell.
And can that tongue adjudge thee unto hell,
Which pray'd forgiveness for his foes fierce spight?
No, no; but as in my idolatrie
I said to all my profane mistresses,
Beauty, of pitty, foulnesse onely is
A signe of rigour: so I say to thee,
To wicked spirits are horrid shapes assign'd,
This beauteous forme assures a pitious minde.

XVII

Since she whom I lov'd hath payd her last debt
To Nature, and to hers, and my good is dead,
And her Soule early into heaven ravished,
Wholly on heavenly things my mind is sett.
Here the admyring her my mind did whett
To seeke thee God; so streames do shew their head;
But although I have found thee, and thou my thirst hast fed,
A holy thirsty dropsy melts mee yett.
But why should I begg more Love, when as thou
Dost wooe my soule for hers; offring all thine:
And dost not only feare least I allow
My Love to Saints and Angels things divine,
But in thy tender jealosy dost doubt
Least the World, Fleshe, yea Devill putt thee out.

VII

At the round earths imagin'd corners, blow
Your trumpets, Angells, and arise, arise
From death, you numberlesse infinities
Of soules, and to your scattred bodies goe,
All whom the flood did, and fire shall o'erthrow,
All whom warre, dearth, age, agues, tyrannies,

The Holy Sonnets of John Donne, Op. 35 (1945)

Despaire, law, chance, hath slaine, and you whose eyes,
Shall behold God, and never tast deaths woe.
But let them sleepe, Lord, and mee mourne a space,
For, if above all these, my sinnes abound,
'Tis late to aske abundance of thy grace,
When wee are there; here on this lowly ground,
Teach mee how to repent; for that's as good
As if thou'hadst seal'd my pardon, with thy blood.

I

Thou hast made me, And shall thy worke decay?
Repaire me now, for now mine end doth haste,
I runne to death, and death meets me as fast,
And all my pleasures are like yesterday;
I dare not move my dimme eyes any way,
Despaire behind, and death before doth cast
Such terrour, and my feeble flesh doth waste
By sinne in it, which it t'wards hell doth weigh;
Onely thou art above, and when towards thee
By thy leave I can looke, I rise againe;
But our old subtle foe so tempteth me,
That not one houre my selfe I can sustaine;
Thy Grace may wing me to prevent his art,
And thou like Adamant draw mine iron heart.

X

Death be not proud, though some have called thee
Mighty and dreadfull, for, thou art not soe,
For, those, whom thou think'st, thou dost overthrow,
Die not, poore death, nor yet canst thou kill mee.
From rest and sleepe, which but thy pictures bee,
Much pleasure, then from thee, much more must flow,
And soonest our best men with thee doe goe,
Rest of their bones, and soules deliverie.
Thou art slave to Fate, Chance, kings, and desperate men,
And dost with poyson, warre, and sicknesse dwell,
And poppie, or charmes, can make us sleepe as well,
And better than thy stroake; why swell'st thou then?
One short sleepe past, wee wake eternally,
And death shall be no more; death, thou shalt die.

Birthday song for Erwin (1945)

Erwin Stein, one of Britten's musical 'fathers', worked for Boosey & Hawkes, Britten's publishers. This birthday song was first performed for him privately by Pears and Britten on his birthday; and in public on 22 November 1988 by Christopher Hobkirk and Rosalind Jones at the Royal College of Music, to commemorate the 75th anniversary of Britten's birth.

RONALD DUNCAN *Birthday song for Erwin*

> See how the sun
> Strikes the bronze gong of earth,
> Making the linnet lift
> Like sparks of sound
> Rising to the echo!
>
> For on this day a man was born:
> Music his element,
> And friendship his echo.

Folk Song Arrangements, Vol. 2 France (1946)

For high or medium voice.

TRAD. *La Noël passée* (tr. Boris Ford) (*Last Christmas*)

La Noël passée,
Povret orphelin,
Ma goule affamée
N'avait plus de pain.
M'en fus sous fenêstre
Du bon Roi Henri
Et lui dis, 'Mon Maistre,
Oyez bien ceci.'
  Prenez vos musettes,
  Et vos épinettes.
  Jésus, cette nuit,
  S'est fait tout petit.

En cette nuitée,
Au vieux temps jadis,
Naquit en Judée
Un de mes amis.
Avait pour couchette
Une crêche en bois,
Et dans la povreté
Des ramas de pois.

Et de sa chambrette,
Oyant mon réit,
Avecque amourette
Le bon Roy sourit,
Prit en sa cassette
Deux écus dorés;
De sa main doucette
Me les a donnés.

Disant, 'Petit ange,
Je suis moult content;
Afin si tu manges
Voilà de l'argent.
Pour la doulce France
Et son Roy Henri
Prie avecque instance
Ton petit amy.'

Last Christmas,
A poor orphan,
My famished mouth
Had no more bread.
I went under the window
Of the good King Henry
And said to him, 'My Master,
Please listen to this.'
Take your pipe
And your spinet.
Jesus, this night,
Is new born.

On this night,
In olden times,
Was born in Judea
One of my friends.
He had for his crib
A wooden manger,
And in poverty
Only a pile of peas.

And from his chamber,
Hearing my story,
With love
The good King smiled,
Took from his casket
Two golden crowns
And with his gentle hand
Gave them to me.

He said, 'Little angel,
I am very pleased;
So that you may eat
Here is money.
For sweet France
And her King Henry
May you pray earnestly
To your little friend.'

TRAD. *Voici le printemps* (*Here is spring*)

Voici le printemps qui passe:
'Bonjour, tisserand, bonjour.
Ami, cède moi ta place,
J'en ai besoin pour un jour.
C'est moi qui fait ta toilette
Des bois, des près et des fleurs.
Donne moi vite ta navette,
Tu sais qu'on m'attend ailleurs.'

Here is spring passing by:
'Good day, weaver, good day.
My friend, let me have your place,
I need it for one day.
It is I who dresses you
With woods, and fields and flowers.
Give me your shuttle quickly,
You know that I'm needed elsewhere.'

Voici le printemps qui passe:
'Bonjour, peintre, bonjour.
Ta main s'obstine et se lasse
A faire semblant du jour.
Donne vite ta palette,
Ta palette et ton pinceau.
Tu va voir le ciel en fête
Rajeunir dans mon tableau.'

Here is spring passing by:
'Good day, painter, good day.
Your hand is persistent, and is weary
With making a likeness of the day.
Give me your pallet quickly,
Your pallet and your brush.
You will see the festive sky
Rejuvenated in my picture.'

Voici le printemps qui passe:
'Bonjour, fillettes, bonjour.
Donnez vos fuseaux, de grace,
Que je travaille à mon tour.
J'ai promis sous les charmilles
Ma laine aux nids d'alentours.
Je vous dirai, jeunes filles,
Où se niche aussi l'amour.'

Here is spring passing by:
'Good day, lasses, good day.
Kindly give me your spindles,
That I may take my turn at working.
I promised to give my wool for the nests
In the hedges roundabout.
And I'll tell you, young girls,
Where love is also nesting.'

TRAD. *Fileuse* (*The Spinster*)

Lorsque j'étais jeunette
Je gardais les moutons,
Tirouli, tiroula, tirouli, touroulou,
Tirouli, rouli, roule.
N'étais jamais seulette
A songer par les monts.
Tirouli...
Mais d'autres bergerettes
Avec moi devisaient.
Parfois de sa musette
Un berger nous charmait.
Il nous faisait des rondes,
Jolies rondes d'amour.
Mais me voilà vieille,
Reste seule toujours.

When I was a young girl
I looked after my sheep.
Tirouli, tiroula, tirouli, touroulou,
Tirouli, rouli, roule.
I was never lonely
And dreaming on the mountains.
Tirouli...

But other young shepherdesses
Chatted with me.
Now and then a shepherd
Charmed us with his pipe.

He danced rounds with us,
Gay dances of love.
But here I am now, old
And alone all my days.

TRAD.   *Le roi s'en va-t-en chasse* (*The king is gone a-hunting*)

Le roi s'en va-t'en chasse
Dans le bois des Bourbons
Dans le bois des Bourbons;,
Mon aimable bergère,
Dans le bois des Bourbons,
Bergère Nanon.

The king is gone a-hunting
In the wood of the Bourbons
In the wood of the Bourbons,
My lovely shepherdess,
In the wood of the Bourbons,
My shepherdess Nanon.

Ne trouve rien en chasse,
Ni cailles, ni pigeons,

He catches nothing while hunting,
Neither quails nor pigeons,

Rencontre une bergère
Qui dormit dans les joncs,

He meets a shepherdess
Sleeping among the rushes,

'Voulez vous être reine
Dedans mes beaux donjons?'

'Will you be my queen
In my beautiful castle?'

'Vous aurez des carrosses
Et de l'or à foison,

'You will have carriages
And gold in abundance,

'Et cour de grandes dames,
De ducs et de barons,'

And a court of noble ladies,
And of dukes and barons,'

'Merci, merci, beau Sire,
Mais j'aime un pauv' garçon
Mais j'aime un pauv' garçon
Qui aime sa bergère,
Mais j'aime un pauv' garçon
Qui aime Nanon.'

'I thank you, good Sir,
But I love a poor lad
But I love a poor lad
Who loves his shepherdess,
But I love a poor lad
Who loves Nanon.'

TRAD.   *La belle est au jardin d'amour* (*The beautiful girl is in the garden of love*)

La belle est au jardin d'amour,
Il y a un mois ou cinq semaines,
Lari-don-don, lari-don-daine.
Son père la cherche partout.
Son amoureux qui est en peine.

The beautiful girl is in the garden of love
For a month or five weeks.
Hey derry down, hey derry ding.
Her father is looking for her everywhere.
Her lover is in distress.

'Berger, berger, n'as tu point vu
Passer ici celle que j'aime?'

'Shepherd, shepherd, have you not seen
The girl I love passing this way?'

'Elle est là-bas dans ce vallon,
A un oiseau conte ses peines.'

'She's down there in the vale,
Telling her sorrows to a bird.'

TRAD.   *Il est quelqu'un sur terre* (*There is someone on the earth*)

Il est quelqu'un sur terre,
Va mon rouet,
Docile tourne, va ton train,
Et dis, tous bas, ton doux refrain:
Il est quelqu'un sur terre
Vers qui mes rêves vont.

There is someone on the earth,
Turn my little wheel,
Turn gently, keep spinning,
And say, quietly, your soft refrain:
There is someone on the earth
To whom my dreams go out.

Il est dans la vallée,
Il est dans la vallée,
Un moulin près du pont.

L'Amour y moud sa graine,
L'amour y moud sa graine
Tant que le jour est long.

La nuit vers les étoiles,
La nuit vers les étoiles
Soupire sa chanson.

La rou' s'y est brisé,
La rou' s'y est brisé,
Finie est ma chanson.

He is in the valley,
He is in the valley,
At a mill by the bridge.

There love grinds his corn,
There love grinds his corn,
All the day long.

Towards the stars, night
Towards the stars, night
Whispers her song.

There the little wheel is broken,
There the little wheel is broken,
That is the end of my song.

TRAD.   *Eho! Eho!*

Eho! Eho! Eho!
Les agneaux vont aux plaines,
Eho! Eho! Eho!
Et les loups vont aux bois.
Tant qu'aux bords des fontaines
Ou dans les frais ruisseaux
Les blancs moutons s'y baignent,
Y dansant au préau.

Mais quelq'-fois par vingtaine
Y s'éloign' des troupeaux,
Pour aller sous les chênes,
Aux herbages nouveaux.

Et les ombres lointaines
Leur-z'y cach'leurs bourreaux,
Malgré leurs plaintes vaines
Les loups mang'les agneaux.

T'es mon agneau, ma reine.
Le grand'vill' c'est le bois,
Par ainsi Madeleine
T'en va pas loin de moi.

Eho! Eho! Eho!
The lambs are going to the plains,
Eho! Eho! Eho!
And the wolves are going to the woods.
By the brink of the fountains
Or in the fresh brooks,
There the white sheep are bathing,
And dancing in the yard.

But sometimes about twenty of them
Stray far from the flock,
To wander under the oak trees
To new pastures.

And the distant shadows
Conceal their executioners from them,
And in spite of their vain lament
The wolves eat the lambs.

You are my lamb, my queen.
The great town is the wood,
And so, Madeleine,
Do not stray far from me.

TRAD. *Quand j'étais chez mon père (When I lived with my father)*

Quand j'étais chez mon père,
Apprenti pastouriau,
Il m'a mis dans la lande
Pour garder les troupiaux.
  Troupiaux, troupiaux,
  Je n'en avais guère,
  Troupiaux, troupiaux
  Je n'en avais biaux.
Mais je ne'en avais guère,
Je n'avais qu'trois agneaux;
Et le loup de la plaine
Mange le plus biau.

Il était si vorace
N'a laissé que la piau,
N'a laissé que la queue,
Pour mettre à mon chapiau.

Mais des os de la bête
Me fis un chalumiau
Pour jour à la fête,
A la fêt' du hamiaux.

Pour fair' danser l'village
Dessous le grand ormiau,
Et les jeun's et les vieilles,
Les pieds dans les sabots.

When I lived with my father
I was a shepherd-boy,
He sent me out to the heath
To look after the flocks.
  Flocks, flocks,
  I had only a few,
  Flocks, flocks,
  I had no beautiful ones.

But I hardly had any,
I had only three lambs;
And the wolf from the plain
Ate the most beautiful of them.

It was so voracious
It only left the hide,
Only left the tail
To put on my hat.

But from the bones of the animal
I made a pipe
To play at the fair,
At the fair in the hamlet.

To make the village dance
Under the great elm,
Both the young and the old,
With their feet in clogs.

Canticle I: My beloved is mine, Op. 40 (1947)

This Canticle was written for the Dick Shepherd Memorial Concert on 1
November 1947, when it was performed by Pears and Britten.

FRANCIS QUARLES *Ev'n like two little bank-dividing brooks*
'My beloved is mine'

*My beloved is mine, and I am his; he feedeth among
the lilies* (Canticles ii.16)

Ev'n like two little bank-dividing brooks
    That wash the pebbles with their wanton streams,
And having ranged and searched a thousand nooks,
    Meet both at length in silver-breasted Thames,
      Where in a greater current they conjoin,
So I my best beloved's am; so he is mine.

Ev'n so we met, and after long pursuit,
    Ev'n so we joined; we both became entire.
No need for either to renew a suit,
    For I was flax, and he was flames of fire.
      Our firm-united souls did more than twine;
So I my best beloved's am; so he is mine.

If all those glitt'ring monarchs that command
    The servile quarters of this earthly ball
Should tender, in exchange, their shares of land,
    I would not change my fortunes for them all;
      Their wealth is but a counter to my coin;
The world's but theirs; but my beloved's mine.

[Nay more, if the fair Thespian ladies all
    Should heap together their diviner treasure,
That treasure should be deemed a price too small
    To buy a minute's lease of half my pleasure.
      'Tis not the sacred wealth of all the Nine
Can buy my heart from him, or his from being mine.]

Nor time, nor place, nor chance, nor death can bow
My least desires unto the least remove;
He's firmly mine by oath†, I his by vow;
He's mine by faith, and I am his by love;
He's mine by water, I am his by wine;
Thus I my best beloved's am; thus he is mine.

He is my altar; I, his holy place;
I am his guest, and he my living food;
I'm his by penitence, he mine by grace;
I'm his by purchase, he is mine by blood!
He's my supporting elm, and I his vine;
Thus I my best beloved's am; thus he is mine.

He gives me wealth, I give him all my vows;
I give him songs, he gives me length of days;
With wreaths of grace he crowns my conq'ring brows,‡
And I his temples with a crown of praise,
Which he accepts as an everlasting sign
That I my best beloved's am, that he is mine.

† Britten has 'blood' instead of 'oath'
‡ and 'longing' instead of 'conq'ring'.

A Charm of Lullabies, Op. 41 (1947)

This 'charm', for mezzo-spoprano and piano, was first performed on 3 January 1948 at the Hague by Nancy Evans and Felix de Nobel. In the setting included in *A Charm*, verse 3 of 'A cradle song' is omitted. But all five verses were included in a previous setting as a duet, in 1938.

WILLIAM BLAKE   *A cradle song*

Sleep! sleep! beauty bright,
Dreaming o'er the joys of night;
Sleep! sleep! in thy sleep
Little sorrows sit and weep.

Sweet Babe, in thy face
Soft desires I can trace,
Secret joys and secret smiles,
Little pretty infant wiles.

[As thy softest limbs I feel,
Smiles as of the morning steal
O'er thy cheek, and o'er thy breast
Where thy little heart does rest.]

O! the cunning wiles that creep
In thy little heart asleep.
When thy little heart does wake
Then the dreadful lightnings break,

From thy cheek and from thy eye,
O'er the youthful harvests nigh.
Infant wiles and infant smiles
Heaven and Earth of peace beguiles.

ROBERT BURNS   *The Highland balou*

lullaby

Hee-balou, my sweet wee Donald,
Picture o' the great Clanronald
Brawlie kens our wanton Chief
Wha gat my young Highland thief.

blessings on thy pretty throat   Leeze me on thy bonie craigie
nag   An thou live, thou'll steal a naigie,

Travel the country thro' and thro',
And bring hame a Carlisle cow.

succeed

rogues

then

Thro' the Lawlands, o'er the Border,
Weel, my babie may thou furder
Herry the louns o' the laigh Countrie,
Syne to the Highlands hame o me.

ROBERT GREENE   *Sephestia's lullaby*

Weep not, my wanton, smile upon my knee;
When thou art old there's grief enough for thee.
Mother's wag, pretty boy,
Father's sorrow, father's joy;
When thy father first did see
Such a boy by him and me,
He was glad, I was woe;
Fortune changèd made him so,
When he left his pretty boy,
Last his sorrow, first his joy.

[Streaming tears that never stint,
Like pearl-drops from a flint,
Fell by course from his eyes,
That one another's place supplies;
Thus he grieved in every part,
Tears of blood fell from his heart,
When he left his pretty boy,
Father's sorrow, father's joy.]

The wanton smiled, father wept,
Mother cried, baby leapt;
More he crowèd, more we cried,
Nature could not sorrow hide:
He must go, he must kiss
Child and mother, baby bliss,
For he left his pretty boy,
Father's sorrow, father's joy.
Weep not,...

THOMAS RANDOLPH *A charm* (from *The Jealous Lovers*)

Quiet, sleep! or I will make
Erinnys whip thee with a snake,
And cruel Rhadamanthus take
Thy body to the boiling lake,
Where fire and brimstone never slake;
Thy heart shall burn, thy head shall ache,
And every joint about thee quake;
And therefore dare not yet to wake!

Quiet, sleep! or thou shalt see
The horrid hags of Tartary,
Whose tresses ugly serpents be,
And Cerberus shall bark at thee,
And all the Furies that are three –
The worst is call'd Tisiphone, –
Shall lash thee to eternity;
And therefore sleep thou peacefully.

JOHN PHILLIPS *The nurse's song* (from *The Play of Patient Grissell*)

Lullaby baby, lullaby baby,
Thy nurse will tend thee as duly as may be.
Be still, my sweet sweeting, no longer do cry;
Sing lullaby baby, lullaby baby.
Let dolours be fleeting, I fancy thee, I,
To rock and to lull thee I will not delay me.
Lullaby baby,...

[What creature now living would hasten thy woe?
Sing lullaby, lullaby, lullaby baby.
See for thy relieving the time I bestow,
To dance and to prance thee as prettily as may be.
Lullaby baby,...

The gods be thy shield and comfort in need!
Sing lullaby, lullaby, lullaby baby.
They give thee good fortune and well for to speed,
And this to desire I will not delay me.
Lullaby baby,...

A Charm of Lullabies, Op. 41 (1947)

Folk Song Arrangements, Vol. 3 British Isles (1947)

For high or medium voice.

TRAD. *The plough boy*

A flaxen-headed cowboy, as simple as may be,
And next a merry plough-boy, I whistled o'er the lea;
But now a saucy footman I strut in worstead lace,
And soon I'll be a butler, and whey my jolly face.
When steward I'm promoted I'll snip the tradesmen's bill,
My master's coffers empty, my pockets for to fill.
When lolling in my chariot so great a man I'll be,
  So great a man, so great a man, so great a man I'll be,
  You'll forget the little plough-boy who whistled o'er the lea.

I'll buy votes at elections, and when I've made the pelf,
I'll stand poll for the parliament, and then vote in myself.
Whatever's good for me, sir, I never will oppose;
When all my ayes are sold off, why then I'll sell my noes.
I'll joke, harangue and paragraph, with speeches charm the ear,
And when I'm tired on my legs, then I'll sit down a peer.
In court or city honour so great a man I'll be.
  So great a man,...

ANON. *There's none to soothe*

There's none to soothe my soul to rest,
There's none my load of grief to share
Or wake to joy this lonely breast,
Or light the gloom of dark despair.

The voice of joy no more can cheer,
The look of love no more can warm
Since mute for aye's that voice so dear,
And closed that eye alone could charm.

TRAD. *Sweet Polly Oliver*

As sweet Polly Oliver lay musing in bed,
A sudden strange fancy came into her head.

'Nor father nor mother shall make me false prove,
I'll list as a soldier, and follow my love.'

So early next morning she softly arose,
And dressed herself up in her dead brother's clothes.
She cut her hair close, and she stained her face brown,
And went for a soldier to fair London Town.

Then up spoke the sergeant one day at his drill.
'Now who's good for nursing? A captain he's ill.'
'I'm ready,' said Polly, to nurse him she's gone,
And finds it's her true love all wasted and wan.

The first week the doctor kept shaking his head,
'No nursing, young fellow, can save him,' he said.
But when Polly Oliver had nursed him back to life
He said, 'You have cherished him as if you were his wife.'

O then Polly Oliver, she burst into tears
And told the good doctor her hopes and her fears;
And very shortly after, for better or worse,
The captain took joyfully his pretty soldier nurse.

TRAD.   *The miller of Dee*

There was a jolly miller once lived on the river Dee;
He worked and sung from morn till night, no lark
   more blithe than he.
And this the burden of his song for ever used to be,
'I care for nobody, no, not I, since nobody cares for me.

I love my mill, she is to me like parent, child and wife,
I would not change my station for any other in life.
Then push, push, push the bowl, my boys, and pass
   it round to me,
The longer we sit here and drink, the merrier we shall be.'

So sang the jolly miller who lived on the river Dee,
He worked and sung from morn till night, no lark
   more blithe than he.
And this the burden of his song for ever used to be,
'I care for nobody, no, not I; since nobody cares for me,
I care for nobody, no, not I, since nobody cares for me.'

TRAD. *The foggy, foggy dew*

When I was a bachelor I lived all alone,
And worked at the weaver's trade,
And the only, only thing that I ever did wrong,
Was to woo a fair young maid.
I wooed her in the winter time,
And in the summer too;
And the only, only thing I did that was wrong
Was to keep her from the foggy, foggy dew.

One night she came to my bedside
When I lay fast asleep.
She laid her head upon my bed
And she began to weep.
She sighed, she cried, she damn near died,
She said, 'What shall I do?'
So I hauled her into bed and I covered up her head,
Just to keep her from the foggy, foggy dew.

Oh I am a bachelor and I live with my son,
And we work at the weaver's trade.
And ev'ry single time that I look into his eyes,
He reminds me of the fair young maid.
He reminds me of the winter time,
And of the summer too,
And of the many, many times that I held her in my arms
Just to keep her from the foggy, foggy dew.

TRAD. *O Waly, Waly*

The water is wide, I cannot get o'er,
And neither have I wings to fly.
Give me a boat that will carry two,
And both shall row, my love and I.

O down in the meadows the other day,
A-gathering flowers both fine and gay,
A-gathering flowers both red and blue,
I little thought what love can do.

I leaned my back up against some oak
Thinking that he was a trusty tree;
But first he bended, and then he broke;
And so did my false love to me.

A ship there is, and she sails the sea,
She's loaded deep as deep can be,
But not so deep as the love I'm in:
I know not if I sink or swim.

O, love is handsome and love is fine,
And love's a jewel while it is new,
But when it is old, it groweth cold,
And fades away like morning dew.

TRAD.   *Come you not from Newcastle?*

Come you not from Newcastle?
Come you not there away?
O met you not my true love,
Riding on a bonny bay?

Why should I not love my love?
Why should my love not love me?
Why should I not speed after him,
Since love to all is free?

Saint Nicolas, Op. 42 (1948)

This cantata, for tenor solo, chorus, semi-chorus, four boy singers, piano duet, percussion and string orchestra, was first performed on 5 June 1948 at the Aldeburgh Festival by Peter Pears and the Aldeburgh Festival Chorus, conducted by Leslie Woodgate. 'This Cantata was written for performance at the centenary celebrations of Lancing College, Sussex, on 24 July 1948.' It was Britten's first big work for amateurs. Carpenter quotes him as saying that 'amateurs have been an important force in the shaping of our musical tradition ... There is something very fresh and unrestrained in the quality of the music produced by amateurs.'

ERIC CROZIER *Saint Nicolas*

I

INTRODUCTION

Chorus Our eyes are blinded by the holiness you bear.
   The bishop's robe, the mitre and the cross of gold
   Obscure the simple man within the Saint.
   Strip off your glory, Nicolas, and speak!

Nicolas Across the tremendous bridge of sixteen hundred years
   I come to stand in worship with you, as I stood
   Among my faithful congregation long ago.

All who knelt beside me then are gone.
   Their name is dust, their tombs are grass and clay,
   Yet still their shining seed of Faith survives –

In you! It weathers time, it springs again
   In you! With you it stands like forest oak
   Or withers with the grasses underfoot.

Preserve the living Faith for which your fathers fought!
   For Faith was won by centuries of sacrifice
   And many martyrs died that you might worship God.

Chorus Help us, LORD! to find the hidden road
   That leads from love to greater Love, from faith
   To greater Faith. Strengthen us, O LORD!
   Screw up our strength to serve Thee with simplicity.

2

THE BIRTH OF NICOLAS

Women Nicolas was born in answer to prayer
    And leaping from his mother's womb he cried
                      God be Glorified!

Swaddling-bands and crib awaited him there
    But Nicolas clapped both his hands and cried
                      God be Glorified!

Innocent and joyful, naked and fair
    He came in pride on earth to abide
                      God be Glorified!

Water rippled *Welcome*! in the bath-tub by his side.
    He dived in open-eyed: he swam: he cried
                      God be Glorified!

When he went to Church at Christmastide
    He climbed up to the font to be baptised
                      God be Glorified!

Pilgrims came to kneel and pray by his side.
    He grew in grace! his name was sanctified
                      God be Glorified!

Nicolas grew in innocence and pride:
    His glory spread a rainbow round the countryside.
    'Nicolas will be a Saint!' the neighbours cried.
                      God be Glorified!

3

NICOLAS DEVOTES HIMSELF TO GOD

Nicolas My parents died. All too soon
    I left the tranquil beauty of their home
    And knew the wider world of man.
    Poor man! I found him solitary, racked
    By doubt: born, bred doomed to die
    In everlasting fear of everlasting death:
    The foolish toy of time, the darling of decay –
    Hopeless, faithless, defying God.

Heartsick, in hope to mask
    The twisted face of poverty,
    I sold my lands to feed the poor.

I gave my goods to charity
But Love demanded more.

Heartsick, I cast away
All things that could distract my mind
From full devotion to His will.
I thrust my happiness behind
But Love desired more still.

Heartsick, I called on God
To purge my angry soul, to be
My only Master, friend and guide.
I begged for sweet humility
And Love was satisfied.

4
HE JOURNEYS TO PALESTINE

Men Nicolas sailed for Palestine
Across the sunlit seas.
The South West Wind blew soft and fair,
Seagulls hovered through the air,
And spices scented the breeze.

Everyone felt that land was near:
All dangers now were past:
Except for one who knelt in prayer,
Fingers clasped and head quite bare,
Alone by the mizzenmast.

The sailors jeered at Nicolas,
Who paid them no regard,
Until the hour of sunset came
When up he stood and stopped their game
Of staking coins on cards.

Nicolas spoke and prophesied
A tempest far ahead
The sailors scorned his words of fear
Since sky and stars shone bright and clear
So *'Nonsense!'* all they said.

Darkness was soon on top of them,
But still the South Wind blew.
The Captain went below to sleep

And left the helmsman there to keep
  His course with one of the crew.

Nicolas swore he'd punish them
  For mocking at the Lord.
The wind arose, the thunder roared,
Lightning split the waves that poured
  In wild cascades on board.

Waterspouts rose in majesty
  Until the ship was tossed
Abaft, aback, astern, abeam,
Lit by lightning's livid gleam
  And all aboard cried '*LOST!*'

The Storm Lightning hisses through the night
  Blinding sight with living light!

    Winds and tempests howl their cry
    Of battle through the raging sky!

    Waves repeat their angry roar,
    Fall and spring again once more!

    Thunder rends the sky asunder
    With its savage shouts of wonder!

      Lightning, Thunder, Tempest, Ocean
      Praise their God with voice and motion!

Men (*Shouting above The Storm*) spare us! Save us! Saviour!
  Man the pumps! Lifeboats! Lower away!
  Axes! Shorten sail! Reef her! Heave to – !
  Let her run before the wind!
  Pray to God! Kneel and pray! Pray!

Chorus Nicolas waited patiently
    Till they were on their knees:
  Then down he knelt in thankfulness
  Begging God their ship to bless
    And make the storm to cease.

Nicolas O God! we are all weak, sinful, foolish men.
  We pray from fear and from necessity – at death, in sickness
  or private loss. Without the prick of fear our conscience
  sleeps, forgetful of Thy Grace.

Help us, O God! to see more clearly. Tame our stubborn
hearts. Teach us to ask for less and offer more in gratitude
to Thee.

Pity our simplicity, for we are truly pitiable in Thy sight.

Men Amen.

Nicolas The winds and waves lay down to rest,
　　The sky was clear and calm.
　The ship sailed onward without harm
　And all creation sang a psalm
　　Of loving thankfulness.

　　Beneath the stars the sailors slept
　　　Exhausted by their fear, while I
　　Knelt down for love of God on high
　　And saw His angels in the sky
　　　Smile down at me – and wept.

5

NICOLAS COMES TO MYRA AND IS CHOSEN BISHOP

Chorus Come, stranger sent from God! Come, man of God!
　　Stand foremost in our Church, and serve this diocese
　　As Bishop Nicolas, our shield, our strength, our peace!

Nicolas I, Nicolas, Bishop of Myra and its diocese, shall with the
　　unfailing grace of God defend His faithful servants, comfort
　　the widow and fatherless, and fulfil His will for this most
　　blessed Church.

All Amen!

Choirs Place the mitre on your head to show your mastery of men!
　　Take the golden robe that covers you with Christ's authority!
　　Wear the fine dalmatic woven with the cross of faith!
　　Bear the crozier as a staff and comfort to your flock!
　　Set the ring upon your hand in sacramental sign of wedlock with
　　　thy God!

　　Serve the Faith and spurn His enemies!

A hymn for choirs and congregation All people that on earth do dwell,
　　Sing to the Lord with cheerful voice!
　　Him serve with fear, His praise forth tell,
　　　Come ye before Him and rejoice.

Saint Nicolas, Op. 42 (1948)　　　　　　　　　　　　　　　[137

O enter then His gates with praise,
    Approach with joy His courts unto;
Praise, laud and bless His name always,
    For it is seemly so to do.

For why? the Lord our God is good:
    His mercy is for ever sure;
His truth at all times firmly stood,
    And shall from age to age endure.

6
NICOLAS FROM PRISON

Nicolas Persecution sprang upon our Church
    And stilled its voice. Eight barren years
    It stifled under Roman rule:
    And I lay bound, condemned to celebrate
    My lonely sacrament with prison bread,
    While wolves ran loose among my flock.

O man! the world is set for you as for a king!
    Paradise is yours in loveliness.
The stars shine down for you, for you the angels sing,
    Yet you prefer your wilderness.

You hug the rack of self, embrace the lash of sin,
    Pour your treasures out to pay distress.
You build your temples fair without and foul within:
    You cultivate your wilderness.

Yet Christ is yours. Yours! For you he lived and died.
    God in mercy gave his Son to bless
You all, to bring you life – and Him you crucified
    To desecrate your wilderness.

Turn, turn, turn away from sin! Ah! bow
    Down your hard and stubborn hearts! Confess
Yourselves to Him in penitence, and humbly vow
    Your lives to Him, to Holiness.

7
NICOLAS AND THE PICKLED BOYS

Travellers Famine tracks us down the lanes,
    Hunger holds our horses' reins,

Winter heaps the roads with snow
O we have far to go!

Starving beggars howl their cry,
Snarl to see us spurring by.
Times are bad and travel slow
O we have far to go!

Mothers We mourn our boys, our missing sons!
We sorrow for three little ones!
Timothy, Mark and John
Are gone! Are gone! Are gone!

Travellers Landlord, take this piece of gold!
Bring us food before the cold
Makes our pangs of hunger grow!
O we have far to go!

Mothers Day by day we seek to find
Some trace of them – but oh! unkind! –
Timothy, Mark and John
Are gone! Are gone! Are gone!

Travellers Let us share this dish of meat.
Come, my friends, sit down and eat!
Join us, Bishop, for we know
That you have far to go!

Mothers Mary meek and Mother mild
Who lost thy Jesus as a child,
Our Timothy, Mark and John
Are gone! Are gone! Are gone!

Travellers Come, your Grace, don't eat so slow!
Take some meat...

Nicolas O do not taste!
O do not feed
On sin! But haste
To save three souls in need!

The mother's cry
Is sad and weak.
Within these walls they lie
Whom mothers sadly seek.

Saint Nicolas, Op. 42 (1948)   [139

Timothy, Mark and John,
Put your fleshly garments on!
Come from dark oblivion!...

Travellers See! three boys spring back to life,
  Who, slaughtered by the butcher's knife,
  Lay salted down! – and entering,
  Hand-in-hand they stand and sing
  ALLELUIA! to their King!

Small Boys (*Entering*) Alleluia! Alleluia! Alleluia!

All Alleluia!

8

HIS PIETY AND MARVELLOUS WORKS

Chorus For forty years our Nicolas,
  Our Prince of men, our shepherd and
  Our gentle guide, walked by our side.

We turned to him at birth and death,
In time of famine and distress,
In all our grief, to bring relief.

He led us from the valleys to
The pleasant hills of grace. He fought
To fold us in from mortal sin.

O! he was prodigal of love!
A spendthrift in devotion to
Us all – and blessed as he caressed.

We keep his memory alive
In legends that our children and
Their children's children treasure still.

Choirs A captive at the heathen court
    Wept sorely all alone.
    'O Nicolas is here, my son!
    And he will bring you home!'

  Three daughters of a nobleman
      Were doomed to shameful sin,
  Till our good Bishop ransomed them
      By throwing purses in.

Saint Nicolas, Op. 42 (1948)

'Fill, fill my sack with corn!' he said:
  'We die from lack of food!'
And from that single sack he fed
  A hungry multitude.

The gates were barred, the black flag flew,
  Three men knelt by the block.
But Nicolas burst in like flame
  And stayed the axe's shock.

'O Help us, good Nicolas!
  Our ship is full of foam!'
He walked across the waves to them
  And led them safely home.

He sat among the Bishops who
  Were summoned to Nicaea:
Then rising with the wrath of God
  Boxed Arius's ear!

He threatened Constantine the Great
  With bell and book and ban:
Till Constantine confessed his sins
  Like any common man.

Chorus Let the legend that we tell
  Praise him, with our prayers as well.

9

THE DEATH OF NICOLAS

Nicolas DEATH, I hear thy summons and I come
  In haste, for my short life is done;
  And oh! my soul is faint with love
  For Him who waits for me above.

LORD, I come to life, to final birth.
  I leave the misery of earth
  For Light, by Thy eternal grace,
  Where I shall greet Thee face to face.

CHRIST, receive my soul with tenderness,
  For in my last of life I bless
  Thy name, who lived and died for me,
  And dying, yield my soul to Thee.

Chorus LORD, now lettest thou Thy servant depart in peace,
    according to Thy word.
For mine eyes have seen Thy salvation
Which Thou hast prepared before the face of all people
To be a light to lighten the Gentiles and to be the glory of
    Thy people Israel.

Glory be to the Father, and to the Son, and to the Holy Ghost!
As it was in the beginning, is now, and ever shall be: world
    without end.
Amen.

A HYMN FOR CHOIRS AND CONGREGATION

God moves in a mysterious way
    His wonders to perform;
He plants His footsteps in the sea,
    And rides upon the storm.

Deep in unfathomable mines
    Of never-failing skill
He treasures up His bright designs
    And works His sovereign will.

Ye fearful saints, fresh courage take,
    The clouds ye so much dread
Are big with mercy, and shall break
    In blessings on your head.

Spring Symphony, Op. 44 (1949)

This symphony is scored for soprano, alto and tenor solos, chorus, boys' choir and orchestra. It was first performed on 14 July 1949, at the Holland Festival at Amsterdam, by Jo Vincent, Kathleen Ferrier, Pears, the Dutch Radio Chorus and the Concertgebouw Orchestra, conducted by Eduard van Beinum. It was dedicated 'For Serge Koussevitzky and the Boston Symphony Orchestra'.

ANON. (17th century)   *Song*   'Shine out, fair Sun' (from *The Masque of the Twelve Months*)

Shine out, fair Sun, with all your heat,
  Show all your thousand-coloured light!
Black Winter freezes to his seat;
  The grey wolf howls, he does so bite;
Crookt Age on three knees creeps the street;
  The boneless fish close quaking lies
And eats for cold his aching feet;
  The stars in icicles arise:
Shine out, and make this winter night
Our beauty's Spring, our Prince of Light!

EDMUND SPENSER   *The merry cuckoo*

The merry Cuckoo, messenger of Spring,
His trumpet shrill hath thrice already sounded;
That warns all lovers wait upon their king,
Who now is coming forth with garlands crownèd.
With noise whereof the quire of birds resounded
Their anthems sweet devisèd of Love's praise;
That all the woods their echoes back rebounded,
As if they knew the meaning of their lays.
But 'mongst them all which did Love's honour raise,
No word was heard of her that most it ought:
But she his precept idly disobeys,
And doth his idle message set at nought.
Therefore, O Love, unless she turn to thee
Ere Cuckoo end, let her a rebel be!

THOMAS NASHE 'Spring, the sweet Spring'

Spring, the sweet Spring, is the year's pleasant king;
  Then blooms each thing, then maids dance in a ring,
Cold doth not sting, the pretty birds do sing –
  Cuckoo, jug-jug, pu-we, to-witta-woo!

The palm and May make country houses gay,
Lambs frisk and play, the shepherds pipe all day,
And we hear aye birds tune this merry lay –
  Cuckoo, jug-jug, pu-we, to-witta-woo!

The fields breathe sweet, the daisies kiss our feet,
Young lovers meet, old wives a-sunning sit,
In every street these tunes our ears do greet –
  Cuckoo, jug-jug, pu-we, to-witta-woo!
    Spring, the sweet Spring!

GEORGE PEELE AND JOHN CLARE *The impatient maid* 'The driving boy'

When as the rye reach'd to the chin,
And chop cherry, chop cherry ripe within,
Strawberries swimming in the cream,
And schoolboys playing in the stream;
Then O, then O, then O, my true love said,
Till that time come again
She could not live a maid!

JOHN MILTON *Song. – On May morning* 'The morning star'

Now the bright morning star, day's harbinger,
Comes dancing from the East, and leads with her
The flow'ry May, who from her green lap throws
The yellow cowslip, and the pale primrose.
  Hail, bounteous May, that dost inspire
  Mirth and youth and warm desire;
  Woods and groves are of thy dressing,
  Hill and dale doth boast thy blessing.
Thus we salute thee with our early song,
And welcome thee, and wish thee long.

Spring Symphony, Op. 44 (1949)

ROBERT HERRICK   *To violets* 'Welcome, maids of honour'

Welcome, maids of honour,
   You do bring
   In the spring,
And wait upon her.

She has virgins many,
   Fresh and fair;
   Yet you are
More sweet than any.

You're the maiden posies,
   And so graced
   To be placed
'Fore damask roses.

Yet though thus respected,
   By-and-by
   Ye do lie,
Poor girls, neglected.

HENRY VAUGHAN   *The Shower* (II) 'Waters above'

Waters above! eternal springs!
The dew, that silvers the *Dove's* wings!
O welcome, welcome to the sad:
Give dry dust drink; drink that makes glad!
Many fair *evenings*, many *flowers*
Sweetened with rich and gentle showers
Have I enjoyed, and down have run
Many a fine and shining *sun*;
But never till this happy hour
Was blest with such an *Evening-shower*!

W.H. AUDEN   'Out on the lawn'

Out on the lawn I lie in bed,
Vega conspicuous overhead
   In the windless nights of June;
Forests of green have done complete
The day's activity; my feet
   Point to the rising moon.

[Lucky, this point in time and space
Is chosen as my working place;
 Where the sexy airs of summer,
The bathing hours and the bare arms,
The leisured drives through a land of farms,
 Are good to the newcomer.

Equal with colleagues in a ring
I sit on each calm evening,
 Enchanted as the flowers
The opening light draws out of hiding
From leaves with all its dove-like pleading
 Its logic and its powers.

That later we, though parted then
May still recall these evenings when
 Fear gave his watch no look;
The lion griefs loped from the shade
And on our knees their muzzles laid,
 And Death put down his book.

Moreover, eyes in which I learn
That I am glad to look, return
 My glances every day;
And when the birds and rising sun
Waken me, I shall speak with one
 Who has not gone away.]

Now North and South and East and West
Those I love lie down to rest;
 The moon looks on them all:
The healers and the brilliant talkers,
The eccentrics and the silent walkers,
 The dumpy and the tall.

[She climbs the European sky;
Churches and power stations lie
 Alike among earth's fixtures:
Into the galleries she peers,
And blankly as an orphan stares
 Upon the marvellous pictures.]

To gravity attentive, she
Can notice nothing here; though we
 Whom hunger cannot move,

From gardens where we feel secure
Look up, and with a sigh endure
  The tyrannies of love:

And, gentle, do not care to know,
Where Poland draws her Eastern bow,
  What violence is done;
Nor ask what doubtful act allows
Our freedom in this English house,
  Our picnics in the sun.

[The creepered wall stands up to hide
The gathering multitudes outside
  Whose glances hunger worsens;
Concealing from their wretchedness
Our metaphysical distress,
  Our kindness to ten persons.

And now no path on which we move
But shows already traces of
  Intentions not our own,
Thoroughly able to achieve
What our excitement could conceive,
  But our hands left alone.

For what by nature and by training
We loved, has little strength remaining:
  Though we would gladly give
The Oxford colleges, Big Ben,
And all the birds in Wicken Fen,
  It has no wish to live.

Soon through the dykes of our content
The crumpling flood will force a rent,
  And, taller than a tree,
Hold sudden death before our eyes
Whose river-dreams long hid the size
  And vigours of the sea.

But when the waters make retreat
And through the black mud first the wheat
  In shy green stalks appears;
When stranded monsters gasping lie,
And sounds of riveting terrify
  Their whorled unsubtle ears:

Spring Symphony, Op. 44 (1949)   [147

May this for which we dread to lose
Our privacy, need no excuse
    But to that strength belong;
As through a child's rash happy cries
The drowned voice of his parents rise
    In unlamenting song.

After discharges of alarm,
All unpredicted may it calm
    The pulse of nervous nations;
Forgive the murderer in his glass,
Tough in its patience to surpass
    The tigress her swift motions.]

RICHARD BARNFIELD   *The teares of an affectionate shepheard sicke for love:*
Or the complaint of Daphnis for the love of Ganimede
'When will my May come'†

v.15   [… Oh would to God he would but pitty mee,
    That love him more than any mortall wight;
    Then he and I with love would soone agree,
    That now cannot abide his Sutors sight.
        O would to God (so I might have my fee)
        My lips were honey, and thy mouth a Bee.

Then shouldst thou sucke my sweete and my faire flower
    That now is ripe, and full of honey-berries:
    Then would I leade thee to my pleasant Bower
    Fild full of Grapes, of Mulberries, and Cherries;
        Then shouldst thou be my Waspe or else my Bee,
        I would thy hive, and thou my honey bee.

I would put amber Bracelets on thy wrests,
    Crownets of Pearle about thy naked Armes:
    And when thou sitst at swilling *Bacchus* feasts
    My lips with charmes should save thee from all harmes:
        And when in sleepe thou tookst thy chiefest Pleasure,
        Mine eyes should gaze upon thine eye-lids Treasure.

And every Morne by dawning of the day,
When Phoebus; riseth with a blushing face,
Silvanus; Chappel-Clarkes shall chaunt a Lay,
And play thee hunts-up in thy resting place:

† Britten's text is made up of v.38, ll. 1 & 2; v.28; v.20; v.34, in that order.

My Coote thy Chamber, my bosome thy Bed;
Shall be appointed for thy sleepy head...]

v.20 And when it pleaseth thee to walke abroad,
(Abroad into the fields to take fresh ayre:)
The Meades with *Floras* treasure should be strowde,
(The mantled meaddowes, and the fields so fayre.)
    And by a silver Well (with golden sands)
    Ile sit me downe, and wash thine yvory hands.

[And in the sweltring heate of summer time,
I would make Cabinets for thee (my Love:)
Sweet-smelling Arbours made of Eglantine
Should be thy shrine, and I would be thy Dove.
    Coole Cabinets of fresh greene Laurell boughs
    Should shadow us, ore-set with thicke-set Eughes.

Or if thou list to bathe thy naked limbs,
Within the Christall of a Pearle-bright brooke,
Paved with dainty pibbles to the brims;
Or cleare, wherein thyselfe thy selfe mayst looke;
    Weele goes to *Ladon* whose still trickling noyse,
    Will lull these fast asleepe amids thy joyes.

Or if thou goe unto the River side,
To angle for the sweet fresh-water fish:
Arm'd with thy implements that will abide
(Thy rod, hooke, line) to take a dainty dish;
    Thy rods shall be of cane, thy lines of silke,
    Thy hooks of silver, and thy bayts of milke.

Or if thou lov'st to heare sweet Melodie,
Or pipe a Round upon an Oaten Reede,
Or make thy selfe glad with some myrthfull glee,
Or play them Musicke whilst thy flocke doth feede;
    To *Pans* owne Pipe Ile helpe my lovely Lad,
    (*Pans* golden Pype) which he of *Syrinx* had.

Or if thou dar'st to climbe the highest Trees
For Apples, Cherries, Medlars, Peares, or Plumbs,
Nuts, Walnuts, Filbeards, Chest-nuts, Ceruices,
The hoary Peach, when snowy winter comes;
    I have fine Orchards full of mellowed frute;
    Which I will give thee to obtain my sute.

Not proud *Alcynous* himselfe can vaunt,
Of goodlier Orchards or of braver Trees

Than I have planted; yet thou wilt not graunt
My simple sute; but like the honey Bees
   Thou suckst the flowre till all the sweet be gone;
   And lov'st mee for my Coyne till I have none.

Leave *Guendolen* (sweet hart) though she be faire
Yet is she light; not light in vertue shining;
But light in her bahaviour, to impaire
Her honour in her Chastities declining;
   Trust not her teares, for they can watonnize,
   When teares in pearle are trickling from her eyes.]

v.28   If thou wilt come and dwell with me at home;
My sheep-cote shall be strowed with new greene rushes;
Weele haunt the trembling Prickets as they rome
About the fields, along the hauthorne bushes;
   I have a pie-bald Curre to hunt the Hare:
   So we will live with daintie forrest fare…

v.34   But if thou wilt not pittie my Complaint,
My Teares, nor Vowes, nor Oathes, made to thy Beautie:
What shall I doo? But languish, die, or faint,
Since thou dost scorne my Teares, and my Soules Duetie:
   And Teares contemned, Vowes and Oaths must faile;
   For where Teares cannot, nothing can prevaile.

[Compare the love of faire Queene Guendolin;
With mine, and thu shalt see how she doth love thee;
I love thee for thy qualities divine,
But she doth love another Swaine above thee:
   I love thee for thy gifts, She for hir pleasure;
   I for thy Vertue, She for Beauties treasure.

And alwaies (I am sure) it cannot last,
But sometimes Nature will denie those dimples:
Instead of Beautie (when thy Blossom's past)
Thy face will be deformed, full of wrinckles:
   Then She that lov'd thee for thy Beauties sake,
   When Age drawes on, thy love will soone forsake.

But I that lov'd thee for thy gifts divine,
In the December of thy Beauties waning,
Will still admire (with joy) those lovely eine,
That now behold me with their beauties baning:
   Though Januarie will never come againe,
   Yet April yeres will come in showers of raine.]

Spring Symphony, Op. 44 (1949)

v.38　When will my May come, that I may embrace thee?
　　　When will the hower be of my soules joying?
　　　[Why dost thou seeke in mirthe still to disgrace mee?
　　　Whose mirth's my health, whose griefe's my harts annoying.
　　　　　Thy bane my bale, thy blisse my blessednes,
　　　　　Thy ill my hell, thy weale my welfare is.

Thus doo I honour thee that love thee so,
And love thee so, that so doo honour thee
Much more than anie mortall man doth know,
Or can discerne by Love or Jealozie:
　　　But if that thou disdainst my loving ever;
　　　Oh happie I, if I have loved never. *Finis.*]

GEORGE PEELE　'Fair and fair'

Œnone　Fair and fair, and twice so fair,
　　　　　As fair as any may be;
　　　　The fairest shepherd on our green,
　　　　　A love for any lady.
Paris　Fair and fair, and twice so fair,
　　　　　As fair as any may be;
　　　　Thy love is fair, for thee alone
　　　　And for no other lady.
Œnone　My love is fair, my love is gay.
　　　　　As fresh as bin the flowers in May,
　　　　And of my love my roundelay,
　　　　　My merry, merry, merry roundelay,
　　　　Concludes with Cupid's curse,
　　　　　'They that do change old love for new,
　　　　Pray gods they change for worse!'
Ambo simul　They that do change old love for new
　　　　　Pray gods they change for worse!
Œnone　Fair and fair, and twice so fair,
　　　　　As fair as any may be;
　　　　The fairest shepherd on our green.
　　　　　A love for any lady.
Paris　Fair and fair, and twice so fair,
　　　　　As fair as any may be;
　　　　Thy love is fair for thee alone
　　　　And for no other lady.

Spring Symphony, Op. 44 (1949)　　　　　　　　　　　[151

Œnone   My love can pipe, my love can sing,
        My love can many a pretty thing,
        And of his lovely praises ring
        My merry, merry, merry roundelays.
            Amen to Cupid's curse, –
            'They that do change old love for new
            Pray gods they change for worse.'
Ambo simul They that do change old love for new
        Pray gods they change for worse.

WILLIAM BLAKE   *Spring* 'Sound the flute'

            Sound the Flute!
            Now it's mute.
            Birds delight
            Day and Night;
            Nightingale
            In the dale,
            Lark in Sky,
            Merrily,
    Merrily, Merrily, to welcome in the Year.

            Little Boy,
            Full of joy;
            Little Girl,
            Sweet and small;
            Cock does crow,
            So do you;
            Merry voice,
            Infant noise,
    Merrily, Merrily, to welcome in the Year.

            Little Lamb,
            Here I am;
            Come and lick
            My white neck;
            Let me pull
            Your soft Wool;
            Let me kiss
            Your soft face:
    Merrily, Merrily, we welcome in the Year.

Spring Symphony, Op. 44 (1949)

'London, to thee I do present' (from *The Knight of the Burning Pestle* IV.v)

Enter RALPH, *dressed as a May-lord*

Ralph London, to thee I do present the merry month of May;
 Let each true subject be content to hear me what I say:
 [For from the top of Conduit-Head, as plainly may appear,
 I will both tell my name to you, and wherefore I came here.
 My name is Ralph, by due descent, though not ignoble I,
 Yet far inferior to the flock of gracious grocery:
 And by the common counsel of my fellows in the Strand,]
 With gilded staff, and crossed scarf, the May lord here I stand.
 Rejoice, oh, English hearts, rejoice, rejoice, oh, lovers dear;
 Rejoice, oh, city, town, and country, rejoice eke every shere!
 For now the fragrant flowers do spring and sprout in seemly sort,
 The little birds do sit and sing, the lambs do make fine sport;
 And now the burchin-tree doth bud, that makes the schoolboy cry,
 The morris rings, while hobby-horse doth foot it featuously;
 The lords and ladies now abroad, for their disport and play,
 Do kiss sometimes upon the grass, and sometimes in the hay.
 Now butter with a leaf of sage is good to purge the blood,
 Fly Venus and phlebotomy, for they are neither good!
 Now little fish on tender stone begin to cast their bellies,
 And sluggish snails, that erst were mew'd, do creep out of their shellies.
 The rumbling rivers now do warm, for little boys to paddle;
 The sturdy steed now goes to grass, and up they hang his saddle.
 The heavy hart, the bellowing buck, the rascal, and the pricket,
 Are now among the yeoman's pease, and leave the fearful thicket.
 And be like them, oh, you, I say, of this same noble town,
 And lift aloft your velvet heads, and slipping off your gown,
 With bells on legs, and napkins clean, unto your shoulders tied,
 With scarfs and garters as you please, and 'Hey for our town!' cried.
 March out and shew your willing minds, by twenty and by twenty,
 To Hogsdon, or to Newington, where ale and cakes are plenty!
 And let it ne'er be said for shame, that we the youths of London,
 Lay thrumming of our caps at home, and left our custom undone.
 Up then, I say, both young and old, both man and maid a-Maying,
 With drums and guns that bounce aloud, and merry tabor playing!†
 Which to prolong, God save our king, and send his country peace,
 And root out treason from the land! and so, my friends, I cease. *Exit.*

†Between ll. 34 and 35 Britten inserts the three verses of 'Sumer is icumen in'.

ANON. (c. 1250?) *Sumer is icumen in*

Sumer is icumen in,
loud   Lhude sing cuccu.
Groweth sed, and bloweth med,
         And springeth the wude nu –
             Sing cuccu.

ewe   Awe bleteth after lomb,
lows   Llouth after calve cu;
leaps, turns about   Bulluc sterteth, bucke verteth,
merry   Murie sing cucu.

Cuccu, cuccu, well singes thu, cuccu:
cease   Ne swike thu naver nu;
Sing cuccu, nu, sing cuccu,
         Sing cuccu, sing cuccu, nu.

Spring Symphony, Op. 44 (1949)

A wedding anthem (Amo Ergo Sum), Op. 46 (1949)

This anthem, for soprano and tenor solos, choir and organ, was written for the wedding of the Earl and Countess of Harewood. It was first performed on 29 September 1949 in St Mark's Church, North Audley Street, London, by Joan Cross, Pears, and St Mark's Choir, conducted by Britten.

RONALD DUNCAN (tr. Ian Hamnett)   *A wedding anthem*

Now let us sing gaily
   Ave Maria!
And may the Holy Virgin
Who was the Mother of Jesus
Grant that these two children
May live together happily
   For Faith releases Gaiety
     As Marriage does true Chastity!
     Ave Maria!

See how the scarlet sun
   Overthrows the heavy night
And where black shadows hung
There reveals a rose, a rose so pure and white,
     Thus did Jesus bring
     To the blind world of man
That faith which is their sight
And Love that is their light.

As mountain streams
   find one another
Till they are both merged
   there – in a broad, peaceful river
As it flows to the sea
   and in it
   are lost forever,
So those who love
   seek one another
But when they are joined
   here – to Christ's Love, oh so tender
Though their years may be brief

             yet through Him
         they love forever.

         These two are not two
         Love has made them one
I love therefore I am   Amo Ergo Sum!
         And by its mystery
         Each is no less but more
             Amo Ergo Sum!
         For to love is to be
         And in loving Him, I love Thee
             Amo Ergo Sum!

         Per Vitam Domini
             Spes nobis cantavit,
         Per fidem Domini
             Lux diem novavit,
         Per mortem Domini
             Mors mortem fugavit,
         Amen!

Through the Lord's life, hope has sung to us; Through the faith of (in) the
Lord, light has renewed the day; Through the Lord's death, death has put
death to flight.

A wedding anthem (Amo Ergo Sum), Op. 46 (1949)

Five Flower Songs, Op. 47 (1950)

These songs, for unaccompanied chorus, were dedicated 'To Leonard and Dorothy Elmhirst on the occasion of their twenty-fifth Wedding Anniversary – 3 April 1950.' 'Marsh flowers' is made up of ten lines (1–4, 7–10, 13–14) from *The Borough* by Crabbe: Letter XVIII, 'The Poor and their Dwellings', interspersed with four lines (5–6, 11–12) from Tale X, 'The Lover's Journey'.

ROBERT HERRICK *To daffodils*

> Fair daffodils, we weep to see
>   You haste away so soon;
> As yet the early-rising sun
>   Has not attain'd his noon.
>   Stay, stay
>   Until the hasting day
>   Has run
>   But to evensong;
> And, having pray'd together, we
>   Will go with you along.
>
> We have short time to stay, as you,
>   We have as short a spring;
> As quick a growth to meet decay,
>   As you, or anything.
>   We die
>   As your hours do, and dry
>   Away
> Like to the summer's rain;
> Or as the pearls of morning's dew;
>   Ne'er to be found again.

HERRICK *The succession of the four sweet months* 'First, April, she with mellow showers'

> First, April, she with mellow showers
> Opens the way for early flowers;
> Then after her comes smiling May,
> In a more rich and sweet array;

Next enters June, and brings us more
Gems, than those two, that went before:
Then (lastly) July comes, and she
More wealth brings in, than all those three.

GEORGE CRABBE   'Marsh flowers'

Here the strong mallow strikes her slimy root,
Here the dull nightshade hangs her deadly fruit:
On hills of dust the henbane's faded green,
And pencil'd flower of sickly scent is seen;
Here on its wiry stem, in rigid bloom,
Grows the salt lavender that lacks perfume;
At the wall's base the fiery nettle springs,
With fruit globose and fierce with poison'd stings;
In ev'ry chink delights the fern to grow,
With glossy leaf and tawny bloom below;
The few dull flowers that o'er the place are spread
Partake the nature of their fenny bed;
These, with our sea-weeds, rolling up and down,
Form the contracted Flora of our town.

The poor and their dwellings

[... Lo! yonder shed; observe its garden-ground,
With the low paling, form'd of wreck around:
There dwells a fisher;...
    Here our reformers come not; none object
To paths polluted, or upbraid neglect;...
    There, fed by food they love, to rankest size,
Around the dwelling docks and wormwood rise;]
Here the strong mallow strikes her slimy root,
Here the dull night-shade hangs her deadly fruit;
On hills of dust the henbane's faded green,
And pencil'd flower of sickly scent is seen:
At the wall's base the fiery nettle springs,
With fruit globose and fierce with poison'd stings;
[Above (the growth of many a year) is spread
The yellow level of the stone-crop's bed;]
In every chink delights the fern to grow,
With glossy leaf and tawny blooms below:

Five Flower Songs, Op. 47 (1950)

These, with our sea-weeds, rolling up and down,
Form the contracted Flora of the town.
　　[Say, wilt thou more of scenes so sordid know?
Then will I lead thee down the dusty row;
By the warm alley and the long close lane, –
There mark the fractured door and paper'd pane,
Where flags the noon-tide air, and, as we pass,
We fear to breathe the putrefying mass:…]

The lover's journey

[… Fair was the morning, and the month was June,
When rose a lover; love awakens soon;
Brief his repose, yet much he dreamt the while
Of that day's meeting, and his Laura's smile;
Fancy and love that name assign'd to her,
Call'd Susan in the parish-register;
And he no more was John – his Laura gave
The name Orlando to her faithful slave.
　　Bright shone the glory of the rising day,
When the fond traveller took his favourite way;
He mounted gaily, felt his bosom light,
And all he saw was pleasing in his sight.
　　'Ye hours of expectation, quickly fly,
And bring on hours of blest reality;
When I shall Laura see, beside her stand,
Hear her sweet voice, and press her yielded hand.'…
　　On rode Orlando, counting all the while
The miles he pass'd and every coming mile;
Like all attracted things, he quicker flies,
The place approaching where th' attraction lies;
When next appear'd a *dam* – so call the place –
Where lies a road confined in narrow space;
A work of labour, for on either side
Is level fen, a prospect wild and wide,
With dikes on either hand by ocean's self supplied:
Far on the right the distant sea is seen,
And salt the springs that feed the marsh between;
Beneath an ancient bridge, the straiten'd flood
Rolls through its sloping banks of slimy mud;
Near it a sunken boat resists the tide,
That frets and hurries to th' opposing side;

The rushes sharp, that on the borders grow,
Bend their brown flow'rets to the stream below,
Impure in all its course, in all its progress slow:
Here a grave Flora scarcely deigns to bloom;
Nor wears a rosy blush, nor sheds perfume;]
The few dull flowers that o'er the place are spread
Partake the nature of their fenny bed;
Here on its wiry stem, in rigid bloom,
Grows the salt lavender that lacks perfume;
[Here the dwarf sallows creep, the septfoil harsh,
And the soft slimy mallow of the marsh;
Low on the ear the distant billows sound,
And just in view appears their stony bound;
No hedge nor tree conceals the glowing sun,
Birds, save a wat'ry tribe, the district shun,
Nor chirp among the reeds where bitter waters run.
    'Various as beauteous, Nature, is thy face,'
Exclaim'd Orlando: 'all that grows has grace;
All are appropriate – bog, and marsh, and fen,
Are only poor to undiscerning men;
Here may the nice and curious eye explore
How Nature's hand adorns the rushy moor;
Here the rare moss in secret shade is found,
Here the sweet myrtle of the shaking ground;
Beauties are these that from the view retire,
But well repay th' attention they require;
For these my Laura will her home forsake,
And all the pleasures they afford partake.'...]

JOHN CLARE   *The evening primrose*

When once the sun sinks in the west,
And dewdrops pearl the evening's breast;
Almost as pale as moonbeams are,
Or its companionable star,
The evening primrose opes anew
Its delicate blossoms to the dew;
And, hermit-like, shunning the light,
Wastes its fair bloom upon the night,
Who, blindfold to its fond caresses,
Knows not the beauty he possesses;
Thus it blooms on while night is by;

When day looks out with open eye,
Bashed at the gaze it cannot shun,
It faints and withers and is gone.

ANON.　*The ballad of green broom*

There was an old man lived out in the wood,
　His trade was a-cutting of Broom, green Broom;
He had but one son without thrift, without good,
　Who lay in his bed till 'twas noon, bright noon.

The old man awoke, one morning and spoke,
　He swore he would fire the room, that room,
If his John would not rise and open his eyes,
　And away to the wood to cut Broom, green Broom.

So Johnny arose, and he slipped on his clothes,
　And away to the wood to cut Broom, green Broom,
He sharpened his knives, for once he contrives
　To cut a great bundle of Broom, green Broom.

When Johnny passed under a lady's fine house,
　Passed under a lady's fine room, fine room,
She called to her maid, 'Go fetch me,' she said,
　'Go fetch me the boy that sells Broom, green Broom.'

When Johnny came in to the lady's fine house,
　And stood in the lady's fine room, fine room;
'Young Johnny,' she said, 'Will you give up your trade,
　And marry a lady in bloom, full bloom?'

Johnny gave his consent, and to church they both went,
　And he wedded the lady in bloom, full bloom,
At market and fair, all folks do declare,
　There is none like the Boy that sold Broom, green Broom.

Canticle II: Abraham and Isaac, Op. 51 (1952)

This Canticle, for alto and tenor voices and piano, was first performed in Nottingham on 21 January 1952 by Kathleen Ferrier, Pears and Britten. It was dedicated 'For Kathleen Ferrier and Peter Pears'. The text is taken from the *Histories of Lot and Abraham*, the fourth of the Chester Miracle Plays, acted by the 'Barbers and the Waxe Chaundlers'. Britten changed the sequence of a few utterances. In this, one of Britten's most inspired works, the voices of God and the Expositor are sung by the alto and tenor in homophony.

ANON. (15th century)   *The sacrifice of Isaac*

l.209   ... GOD. Abraham, my servante, Abraham.
[ABRAHAM Loe, Lorde, all readye heare I am.]

GOD   Take, Isaake, thy sonne by name,
        That thou loveste the best of all,
      And in sacrifice offer hym to me
      Uppon that hyll their besides thee.
      Abraham, I will that soe it be,
        For oughte that maye befalle.

ABRAHAM [My] Lorde, to thee is myne intente
      Ever to be obediente.
      That sonne that thou to me hast sente,
        Offer I will to thee,
      [And fulfill thy comaundemente,
      With hartie will, as I am kente.
      Highe God, Lorde omnipotente,]
        Thy byddinge done shalbe.
      [My meanye and my children eichone
      Lenges at home, bouth all and one,
      Save Isaake, my sonne, with me shall gone
        To an hill heare besyde.]

Heare Abraham, torninge hym to his sonne Isaake, saith:
      Make thee readye, my deare darlinge,
      For we must doe a littill thinge.
      This woode doe on thy backe it bringe,
        We maye no longer abyde.
      A sworde and fier that I will take;
      [*Heare Abraham taketh a sworde and fier.*]

For sacrifice me behoves to make:
Godes byddinge will I not forsake,
    But ever obediente be.

Heare Isaake speaketh to his father, and taketh a burne of stickes
    and beareth after his father, and saieth:

ISAAKE Father, I am all readye
    To doe your byddinge moste mekelye,

willing   And to beare this woode full beane am I,
    As you comaunded me.

[ABRAHAM O Isaake, my darlinge deare,
    My blessinge nowe I geve thee heare,
    Take up this faggote with good cheare,
        And on thy backe it bringe.
    And fier with us I will take.

ISAAKE Your byddinge I will not forsake;
    Father, I will never slake
        To fulfill your byddinge.]

Heare they goe bouth to the place to doe sacriffice.

ABRAHAM Now, Isaake sonne, goe we our waie
    To yender mounte, yf that we maye.

ISAAKE My deare father, I will asaye
    To follow you full fayne.

Abraham, beinge mynded to sleye his sonne Isaake, leiftes up his
    hands, and saith fowlowinge.

ABRAHAM O! my harte will breake in three,
    To heare thy wordes I have pittye;
    As thou wylte, Lorde, so muste yt be,
        To thee I wilbe bayne.
    Laye downe thy faggote, my owne sonne deare.

ISAAKE All readye, father, loe yt is heare.
    But whye make you sucke heavye cheare?
        Are you anye thinge adreade?
    Father, yf yt be your will,
    Wher is the beaste that we shall kill?

ABRAHAM Therof, sonne, is non upon this hill,
    [That I see here in this steade.

Isaake, fearinge leste his ffather woulde slaye him, saith:]

ISAAKE Father, I am full soar affearde
   To see you beare that drawn swerde:
   [I hope for all myddel-earde
      You will not slaye your childe.

Abraham comfortes his sonne, and saieth:

ABRAHAM Dreede thee not, my childe, I reade;
   Our Lorde will sende of his godheade
   Some manner of beaste into this steade,
      Either tame or wilde.

ISAAKE Father, tell me or I goe
   Wheither I shalbe harmede or noe.

ABRAHAM Ah! deare God! that me is woe!
   Thou breakes my harte in sunder.

ISAAKE Father, tell me of this case,
   Why you your sorde drawne hase.
   And beares yt nacked in this place,
      Theirof I have greate wonder.]

ABRAHAM saake, sonne, peace, I praie thee,
   Thou breakes my harte even in three.

hide   ISAAKE I praye you, father, leane nothinge from me,
   But tell me what you thinke.

ABRAHAM Ah! Isaake, Isaake, I muste thee kille!

ISAAKE Alas, father, is that your will,
   Your owine childe for to spill
      Upon this hilles brinke?
   Yf I have treasspasede in anye degree,
   With a yarde you maye beate me;
   Put up your sorde, yf your wil be,
      For I am but a childe.

[ABRAHAM O, my deare sonne, I am sorye
   To doe to thee this greate anoye:
   Godes commaundmente doe muste I,
      His workes are ever full mylde.]

ISAAKE Woulde God my mother were here with me!
   Shee woulde kneele downe upon her knee,
   Prainge you, father, if yt may be,
      For to save my liffe.

Canticle II: Abraham and Isaac, Op. 51 (1952)

ABRAHAM [O! comelye creature, but I thee kille,
I greve my God, and that full ylle;
I maye not worke againste his will,
    But ever obediente be.]
O! Isaake, sonne, to thee I saie,
God hath commaunded me to daye
Sacrifice, this is no naye,
    To make of thy bodye.

ISAAKE Is yt Godes will I shalbe slayne?

ABRAHAM Yea, sonne, it is not for to leane;
[To his byddinge I wilbe bayne,
    And ever to hym pleasinge.
    But that I do this dilfull deede,
My Lorde will not quite me in my nede.

ISAAKE Marye, father, God forbydde,
    But you doe your offeringe!
Father, at home your sonnes you shall fynde,
That you must love by course of kinde;
Be I onste out of your mynde,
    Your sorowe maie sone cease;
But yet you muste do Godes byddinge.
Father, tell my mother for no thinge.

Here Abraham wrynges his handes, and saith:

ABRAHAM For sorowe I maie my handes wringe,
    Thy mother I can not please.
Ho! Isaake, Isaake, blessed muste thou be!
Allmoste my witte I lose for thee;
The blood of thy bodye so free
    I am full lothe to sheede.]

Here Isaake askinge his father blessinge one his knyes, and saith:

ISAAKE Father, seinge you muste nedes doe soe,
    Let it passe lightlie, and over goe;
Kneeling on my kneeyes towe,
    Your blessinge on me spreade.

ABRAHAM My blessinge deere son, give I thee
And thy mothers with hart free;
The blessing of the Trinitie
    My deare sone, on thee lighte.

[ISAAKE Father, I praye you hyde my eyne
    That I see not the sorde so keyne,
    Your strocke, father, woulde I not seene,
rail   Leste I againste yt grylle.

ABRAHAM My deare sonne Issake, speake no more,
    Thy wordes makes my harte full sore.

ISAAKE O deare father, wherefore! wherefore!
    Seinge I muste nedes be dead,
Of on thinge I will you praie,
Seithen I muste dye the death to daie,
As few strockes as you may well maie,
    When you smyte of my heade.

ABRAHAM Thy meekness, childe, makes me affraye;
    My songe maybe be wayle-a-waie.

ISAAKE O dere father, doe awaye, do awaye
    Your makeinge so moche mone!
Nowe, trewly, father, this talkinge
Doth but make longe taryeinge.
I praye you, come and make endinge,
    And let me hense be gone.]

*Hence Isaake riseth and cometh to his father, and he taketh hym,
and byndeth and laieth hym upon the alter to sacrifice hymn,
and saith:*

ABRAHAM Come heither, my childe, thou arte soe sweete,
     Thou must be bounde both hande and feete.

ISAAKE Father [we muste no more meete
    Be oughte that I maie see;
But] doe with me then as you will,
I muste obaye, and that is skille,
Godes commaundmente to fulfill,
    For nedes soe must yt be.
[Upon the porpose that you have sette you,
For south, father, I will not let you,
But ever more to you bowe,
    While that ever I maie.]
Father, greete well my brethren yinge,
And praye my mother of her blessinge,
I come noe more under her wynge,
    Fare well for ever and aye;

166]   Canticle II: Abraham and Isaac, Op. 51 (1952)

[But father! crye you mercye,
For all that ever I have trespassed to thee,
Forgeven, father, that it maybe be
    Untell domesdaie.

ABRAHAM My deare sonne, let be thy mones!
My childe, thou greved me never ones;
Blessed be thou bodye and bones,
    And I forgeve thee heare!
Nowe, my deere sonne, here shalt thou lye,
Unto my worke nowe must I hie;
I hade as leeve my selfe to die,
    As thou, my darlinge deare.

ISAAKE Father, if you be to me kinde,
Aboute my head a carschaffe bynde,
And let me lightlie out of your mynde,
    And sone that I were speede.]

*Here Abraham doth kisse his sonne Isaake, and byndes a
charschaffe about his heade.*

ABRAHAM Fare well, my sweete sonne of grace!
    [*Here let Isaake kneele downe and speake.*]

ISAAKE I praye you, father, torne downe my face
    [A litill while, while you have space.]
    For I am sore adreade.

ABRAHAM To doe this deed I am sorye.

[ISAAKE Yea, Lorde, to thee I call and crye,
Of my soule thou have mercye,
    Hartelye I thee praie!]

ABRAHAM Lorde, [I would fayne worke thy will,
This young innocente that lieth so still.]
Full loth were me hym to kille,
    [By anye maner a waye.

ISAAKE My deare father, I thee praye,
Let me take my clothes awaie,
For sheedinge blude on them to daye
    At my laste endinge.

ABRAHAM Harte, yf thou wouldest borst in three,
Thou shalt never master me;

I will no longer let for thee;
  My God I maye not greeve.]

ISAAKE A! mercye, father, why tarye you soe?
  [Smyte of my head, and let me goe.
  I pray you rydd me of my woe,
    For nowe I take my leve.

ABRAHAM Ah, sonne! my harte will breake in three,
  To heare thee speake such wordes to me.]
  Jesu! on me thou have pittye,
    That I have moste in mynde.

ISAAKE Nowe father, I see that I shall dye:
  Almightie God in magistie!
  My soule I offer unto thee;
    [*Lorde, to yt be kinde.*]

*Here let Abraham take and bynde his sonne Isaake upon the
alter; let hym make a signe as though he woulde cut of his head
with his sorde; [then let the angell come and take the sworde by
the end and state it, sainge:]*

ANGELLUS Abraham, my servante dere.†

[ABRAHAM Loe. Lorde, I am all readye here!]

ANGELLUS Laye not thy sworde in noe manere
  On Isake, thy deare darlinge;
  [And do to him no anoye.]
  For thou dredes God [me], wel wote I,
  That of thy sonne has no mercye,
    To fulfill his byddinge.

[SECUNDUS ANGELLUS And for hys byddinge thou dose aye,
  And spareste nether for feare nor fraye,
  To doe thy sonne to death to daie,
    Isake, to theee full deare:
  Therefore, God hathe sent by me, in faye!
  A lambe, that is bouth good and gaye,
  Into thou place as thou se may,
    Lo, have hym righte here.]

ABRAHAM Ah! Lorde of heaven, and kinge of blesse,
  Thy byddinge shalbe done, i-wysse!
  Sacrafice here sente me is,
    And all, Lorde through thy grace.

    † Britten replaces the Angel by God.

Canticle II: Abraham and Isaac, Op. 51 (1952)

lamb

A horned weither here I see,
Amonge the breyers tyed is he,
To thee offred shall he be
Anon righte in this place.

Then let Abraham take the lambe and kille hym, [and let God saie:]

[GOD Abraham, by my selfe I sweare,
For thou haste bene obediente ever,
And spared not thy sonne to teare,
To fulfill my byddinge,
Thou shalbe blessed, that pleased me,
Thy seed I shall so multiplie,
As starres and sande so manye het I,
Of thy bodye cominge.
Of enemyes thou shalte have power,
And thy bloode also in feare,
Thou haste bene meke and bonere,
To do as I thee bade;
And of all nacions, leve thou me,
Blessed ever more shalt thou be,
Through frute that shall come of thee,
And saved be through thy seede.

EXPOSITOR Lordinges, the significacioun
Of this deed of devocion,

find out

And you will, you witten mone,
May torne you to moche good.
This deed you see done here in this place,
In example of Jesu done it was,
That for to wynne mankindes grace
Was sacrifised on the roode.
By Abraham I maie understande
The father of heaven, that can fand
With his sonnes bloode to breake that bande,
That the devill had broughte us to.
By Isaake understande I maie
Jesu, that was obedient aye,
His fathers will to worke alwaie,
And death for to confounde.
Here let the doctor knele downe, and saie:]

Expositor Such obedience grante us, O Lorde!
Ever to thy moste holye worde,
That in the same we maie accorde
As this Abraham was bayne;
And then al togaither shall we
That worthy kinge in heaven see,
And dwell with hym in greate glorye
    For ever and ever, amen.
        [*Here the messinger maketh an ende.*

Make rombe, lordinges, and geve us waye,
And let Balacke come in and plaie,
And Balame that well can saie,
    To tell you of prophescie.
That Lorde that died on Good Frydaie,
He save you all bouth nighte and daie!
Fare well, my lordinges; I goe my waie,
    I maye no longer abyde.

Winter Words, Op. 52 (1953)

This setting of lyrics and ballads by Thomas Hardy, for high voice and piano, were first performed on 8 October 1953 at the Leeds Festival at Harewood House, by Pears and Britten. It was dedicated 'To John and Myfanwy Piper'. Britten referred to 'These great words, sad and wise.'

THOMAS HARDY *At day-close in November* 'Winter words'

The ten hours' light is abating,
    And a late bird wings across,
Where the pines, like waltzers waiting,
    Give their black heads a toss.

Beech leaves, that yellow the noon-time,
    Float past like specks in the eye;
I set every tree in my June time,
    And now they obscure the sky.

And the children who ramble through here
    Conceive that there never has been
A time when no tall trees grew here,
    A time when none will be seen.

Midnight on the Great Western

In the third-class seat sat the journeying boy,
    And the roof-lamp's oily flame
Played down on his listless form and face,
Bewrapt past knowing to what he was going,
    Or whence he came.

In the band of his hat the journeying boy
    Had a ticket stuck; and a string
Around his neck bore the key of his box,
That twinkled gleams of the lamp's sad beams
    Like a living thing.

What past can be yours, O journeying boy
    Towards a world unknown,
Who calmly, as if incurious quite
On all at stake, can undertake
    This plunge alone?

Knows your soul a sphere, O journeying boy,
    Our rude realms far above,
Whence with spacious vision you mark and mete
This region of sin that you find you in,
    But are not of?

Wagtail and the baby

A baby watched a ford, whereto
    A wagtail came for drinking;
A blaring bull went wading through,
    The wagtail showed no shrinking.

A stallion splashed his way across,
    The birdie nearly sinking;
He gave his plumes a twitch and toss,
    And held his own unblinking.

Next saw the baby round the spot
    A mongrel slowly slinking;
The wagtail gazed, but faltered not
    In dip and sip and prinking.

A perfect gentleman then neared;
    The wagtail, in a winking,
With terror rose and disappeared;
    The baby fell a-thinking.

The little old table

Creak, little wood thing, creak,
When I touch you with elbow or knee;
That is the way you speak
Of one who gave you to me!

You, little table, she brought –
Brought me with her own hand,
As she looked at me with a thought
That I did not understand.

– Whoever owns it anon,
And hears it, will never know
What a history hangs upon
This creak from long ago.

The choirmaster's burial

He often would ask us
That, when he died,
After playing so many
To their last rest,
If out of us any
Should here abide,
And it would not task us,
We would with our lutes
Play over him
By his grave-brim
The psalm he liked best –
The one whose sense suits
'Mount Ephraim' –
And perhaps we should seem
To him, in Death's dream,
Like the seraphim.

As soon as I knew
That his spirit was gone
I thought this his due,
And spoke thereupon.
'I think,' said the vicar,
'A read service quicker
Than viols out-of-doors
In these frosts and hoars.
That old-fashioned way
Requires a fine day,
And it seems to me
It had better not be.'

Hence, that afternoon,
Though never knew he
That his wish could not be,
To get through it faster
They buried the master
Without any tune.

But 'twas said that, when
At the dead of next night
The vicar looked out,
There struck on his ken
Thronged roundabout,
Where the frost was graying
The headstoned grass,
A band all in white
Like the saints in church-glass,
Singing and playing
The ancient stave
By the choirmaster's grave.

Such the tenor man told
When he had grown old.

Proud songsters

The thrushes sing as the sun is going,
    And the finches whistle in ones and pairs,
And as it gets dark loud nightingales
        In bushes
Pipe, as they can when April wears,
    As if all Time were theirs.

These are brand-new birds of twelve-months' growing,
    Which a year ago, or less than twain,
No finches were, nor nightingales,
        Nor thrushes,
But only particles of grain,
    And earth, and air, and rain.

At the railway station, Upway

'There is not much that I can do,
    For I've no money that's quite my own!'
    Spoke up the pitying child –
A little boy with a violin
At the station before the train came in, –
'But I can play my fiddle to you,
And a nice one 'tis, and good in tone!'

The man in the handcuffs smiled;
The constable looked, and he smiled, too,
    As the fiddle began to twang;
And the man in the handcuffs suddenly sang
        With grimful glee:
        'This life so free
        Is the thing for me!'
And the constable smiled, and said no word,
As if unconscious of what he heard;
And so they went on till the train came in –
The convict, and boy with the violin.

Before life and after

A time there was – as one may guess
And as, indeed, earth's testimonies tell –
    Before the birth of consciousness,
        When all went well.

None suffered sickness, love, or loss,
None knew regret, starved hope, or heart-burnings;
    None cared whatever crash or cross
        Brought wrack to things.

If something ceased, no tongue bewailed,
If something winced and waned, no heart was wrung;
    If brightness dimmed, and dark prevailed,
        No sense was stung.

But the disease of feeling germed,
And primal rightness took the tinct of wrong;
    Ere nescience shall be reaffirmed
        How long, how long?

If it's ever spring again (1953)

When Britten was setting the poems by Hardy that made up the cycle *Winter Words*, he also set a few other Hardy poems which he never published. Among these was this nostalgic poem, which was first performed on 22 November 1983 at the Wigmore Hall, London, by Neil Mackie and Iain Burnside, at a celebration for the seventieth anniversary of Britten's birth.

THOMAS HARDY *If it's ever spring again*

If it's ever spring again,
        Spring again,
I shall go where went I when
Down the moor-cock splashed, and hen,
Seeing me not, amid their flounder,
Standing with my arm around her;
If it's ever spring again,
        Spring again,
I shall go where went I then.

If it's ever summer-time,
        Summer-time,
With the hay crop at the prime,
And the cuckoos – two – in rhyme,
As they used to be, or seemed to,
We shall do as long we've dreamed to,
If it's ever summer-time,
        Summer-time,
With the hay, and bees achime.

Canticle III: Still falls the rain, Op. 55 (1954)

This Canticle, for tenor, horn and piano, was first performed on 28 January 1955 at the Wigmore Hall, London, by Pears, Dennis Brain and Britten. It was dedicated 'To the memory of Noel Mewton-Wood'.

EDITH SITWELL   *Still falls the rain*
The Raids, 1940.   *Night and Dawn*

Still falls the Rain –
Dark as the world of man, black as our loss –
Blind as the nineteen hundred and forty nails
Upon the Cross.

Still falls the Rain
With a sound like the pulse of the heart that is changed to
    the hammer-beat
In the Potter's Field, and the sound of the impious feet

On the Tomb:
       Still falls the Rain
In the Field of Blood where the small hopes breed and
    the human brain
Nurtures its greed, that worm with the brow of Cain.

Still falls the Rain
At the feet of the Starved Man hung upon the Cross.
Christ that each day, each night, nails there, have mercy on us –
On Dives and on Lazarus:
Under the Rain the sore and the gold are as one.

Still Falls the Rain –
Still falls the Blood from the Starved Man's wounded Side:
He bears in His Heart all wounds, – those of the light that died,
The last faint spark
In the self-murdered heart, the wounds of
    the sad uncomprehending dark,
The wounds of the baited bear, –
The blind and weeping bear whom the keepers beat
On his helpless flesh… the tears of the hunted hare.

Still falls the Rain –
Then – O Ile leape up to my God: who pulles me doune –
See, see where Christ's blood streames in the firmament:
It flows from the Brow we nailed upon the tree
Deep to the dying, to the thirsting heart
That holds the fires of the world, – dark-smirched with pain
As Caesar's laurel crown.

Then sounds the voice of One who like the heart of man
Was once a child who among beasts has lain –
'Still do I love, still shed my innocent light, my Blood, for thee.'

Canticle III: Still falls the rain, Op. 55 (1954)   [177

Song (1956)

After hearing the first performance of *Canticle III*, a setting of her poem 'Still falls the rain', Edith Sitwell was so moved and 'haunted' that she agreed to Britten setting more of her work, including this song. It was first performed the following year, on 21 June 1956, together with *Canticle III*, by Pears, Dennis Brain (horn) and Britten in Aldeburgh Parish Church in a programme of music and readings entitled 'The Heart of the Matter'.

EDITH SITWELL *Song*

We are the darkness in the heat of the day,
The rootless flowers in the air, the coolness: we are the water
Lying upon the leaves before Death, our sun,
And its vast heat has drunken us… Beauty's daughter,
The heart of the rose, and we are one.

We are the summer's children, the breath of evening, the days
When all may be hoped for – we are the unreturning
Smile of the lost one, seen through the summer leaves –
That sun and its false light scorning.

Hymn to St Peter, Op. 56a (1955)

This hymn, for choir and organ, was written for the Quincentenary of St Peter Mancroft, Norwich, and was first performed there on 20 November 1955.

Hymn to St Peter From the *Gradual of the Feast of St Peter and St Paul*

Thou shalt make them princes over all the earth.
They shall remember thy name, O Lord.
Instead of thy fathers, sons are born to thee:
Therefore shall the people praise thee, Alleluia.
Tu es Petrus, et super hanc petram
aedificamus Ecclesiam meam. Alleluia.
Thou art Peter. And upon this rock
I will build my church. Alleluia.

Antiphon, Op. 56b (1956)

This Antiphon, set for choir (with optional soloists: three boys) and organ, for the centenary of St Michael's College, Tenbury, was first performed at the centenary service on 29 September 1956.

GEORGE HERBERT *Antiphon*

Cho. Praised be the God of Love,
   Men Here below,
   Angels And here above:
Cho. Who has dealt his mercies so,
   Angels To his friend,
   Men And to his foe;

Cho. That both grace and glory tend
   Angels Us of old,
   Men And us in th'end.
Cho. The great Shepherd of the fold
   Angels Us did make,
   Men For us was sold.

Cho. He our foes in pieces brake:
   Angels Him we touch;
   Men And him we take.
Cho. Wherefore since that he is such,
   Angels We adore,
   Men And we do crouch.

Cho. Lord, thy praises should be more.
   Men We have none,
   Angels And we no store.
Cho. Praised be the God alone,
   Who hath made of two folds one.

The holly and the ivy (1957)

This carol for unaccompanied chorus was dedicated 'For June Gordon and the Haddo House Choral Society, 1957'.

TRAD.   *The holly and the ivy*

The holly and the ivy
Are trees that's both well known;
Of all the trees that grows in woods,
The holly bears the crown.
> *The rising of the sun,*
> *The running of the deer,*
> *The playing of the merry harp,*
> *Sweet singing in the choir.*

The holly bears a blossom
As white as any flower;
And Mary bore sweet Jesus Christ
To be our sweet Saviour.

The holly bears a colour
As green as any tree;
And Mary bore her sweet Jesus Christ
To set poor sinners free.

The holly bears a berry
As red as any blood,
And Mary bore sweet Jesus Christ
To do poor sinners good.

The holly bears a prickle
As sharp as any thorn;
And Mary bore sweet Jesus Christ
At Christmas day in the morn.

The holly bears a bark
As bitter as any gall,
And Mary bore sweet Jesus Christ
For to redeem us all.

The holly and the ivy
Are trees that's both well known,
Of all the trees that grows in woods
The holly bears the crown.

Songs from the Chinese, Op. 58 (1957)

These songs for high voice and guitar were first performed on 17 June 1958 at the Aldeburgh Festival, at Great Glemham House, by Pears and Julian Bream (who edited the guitar part).

CHINESE POEMS   (tr. Arthur Waley)
The big chariot from *The Book of Songs*

> Don't help-on the big chariot;
> You will only make yourself dusty.
> Don't think about the sorrows of the world;
> You will only make yourself wretched.
>
> Don't help-on the big chariot;
> You won't be able to see for dust.
> Don't think about the sorrows of the world;
> Or you will never escape from your despair.
>
> Don't help-on the big chariot;
> You'll be stifled with dust.
> Don't think about the sorrows of the world;
> You will only load yourself with care.

PO CHÜ-I   *The old lute*

> Of cord and cassia-wood is the lute compounded;
> Within it lie ancient melodies.
> Ancient melodies – weak and savourless,
> Not appealing to present men's taste.
> Light and colour are faded from the jade stops;
> Dust has covered the rose-red strings.
> Decay and ruin came to it long ago,
> But the sound that is left is still cold and clear.
> I do not refuse to play it, if you want me to;
> But even if I play, people will not listen.
>
> *
>
> How did it come to be neglected so?
> Because of the Ch'iang flute and the zithern of Ch'in.

WU-TI   *The autumn wind*

Autumn wind rises; white clouds fly.
Grass and trees wither; geese go south.
Orchids, all in bloom; chrysanthemums smell sweet.
I think of my lovely lady; I never can forget.
Floating-pagoda boat crosses Fên River;
Across the mid-stream white waves rise.
Flute and drum keep time to sound of rowers' song;
Amidst revel and feasting sad thoughts come;
Youth's years how few, age how sure!

LU YU   *The herd-boy*

In the southern village the boy who minds the ox
With his naked feet stands on the ox's back.
Through the hole in his coat the river wind blows;
Through his broken hat the mountain rain pours.
On the long dyke he seemed to be far away;
In the narrow lane suddenly we were face to face.

*

The boy is home and the ox is back in its stall;
And a dark smoke oozes through the thatched roof.

PO CHÜ-I   *Poems in depression, at Wei village* 'Depression'

I

[I hug my pillow and do not speak a word;
In my empty room no sound stirs.
Who knows that, all day a-bed,
I am not ill and am not even asleep?]

II

Turned to jade are the boy's rosy cheeks;
To his sick temples the frost of winter clings...
Do not wonder that my body sinks to decay;
Though my limbs are old, my heart is older yet.

Songs from the Chinese, Op. 58 (1957)

Dance song   from *The Book of Songs*

The unicorn's hoofs!
The duke's sons throng.
Alas for the unicorn!

The unicorn's brow!
The duke's kinsmen throng.
Alas for the unicorn!

The unicorn's horn!
The duke's clansmen throng.
Alas for the unicorn!

Nocturne, Op. 60 (1958)

This work, for tenor, seven obbligato instruments and string orchestra, was first performed on 16 October 1958 at the Leeds Centenary Festival in the Leeds Town Hall by Pears and the BBC Symphony Orchestra, conducted by Rudolph Schwarz. It was dedicated 'To Alma Mahler'.

PERCY BYSSHE SHELLEY   'On a poet's lips I slept'
(ii. 164–71 from *Prometheus Unbound*)

Fourth Spirit

On a poet's lips I slept
Dreaming like a love-adept
In the sound his breathing kept;
Nor seeks nor finds he mortal blisses,
But feeds on the aëreal kisses
Of shapes that haunt thought's wildernesses.
He will watch from dawn till gloom
The lake-reflected sun illume
The yellow bees in the ivy-bloom,
Nor heed nor see, what things they be:
But from these create he can
Forms more real than living man,
Nurslings of immortality!
[One of these awakened me,
And I sped to succour thee.]

ALFRED, LORD TENNYSON   *The Kraken*

Below the thunders of the upper deep;
Far, far beneath in the abysmal sea,
His ancient, dreamless, uninvaded sleep
The Kraken sleepeth: faintest sunlights flee
About his shadowy sides: above him swell
Huge sponges of millennial growth and height;
And far away into the sickly light,
From many a wondrous grot and secret cell
Unnumber'd and enormous polypi
Winnow with giant arms the slumbering green.

There hath he lain for ages and will lie
Battening upon huge seaworms in his sleep,
Until the latter fire shall heat the deep;
Then once by men and angels to be seen,
In roaring he shall rise and on the surface die.

SAMUEL TAYLOR COLERDGE   *The wanderings of Cain*

Encinctured with a twine of leaves,
That leafy twine his only dress!
A lovely Boy was plucking fruits,
By moonlight, in a wilderness.
The moon was bright, the air was free,
And fruits and flowers together grew
On many a shrub and many a tree:
And all put on a gentle hue,
Hanging in the shadowy air
Like a picture rich and rare.
It was a climate where, they say,
The night is more beloved than day.
But who that beauteous Boy beguiled,
That beauteous Boy to linger here?
Alone, by night, a little child,
In place so silent and so wild –
Has he no friend, no loving mother near?

THOMAS MIDDLETON   *'Midnight's bell goes ting, ting, ting'*
(from *Blurt, Master Constable*)

Midnight's bell goes ting, ting, ting, ting, ting,
Then dogs do howl, and not a bird does sing
But the nightingale, and she cries twit, twit, twit;
Owls then on every bough do sit;
Ravens croak on chimneys' tops;
The cricket in the chamber hops;
The nibbling mouse is not asleep,
But he goes peep, peep, peep, peep, peep;
    And the cats cry mew, mew, mew,
    And still the cats cry mew, mew, mew.

Nocturne, Op. 60 (1958)   [185

'But that night, When on my bed I lay'
(ll. 1–82 from *The Prelude*, Book X)

[It was a beautiful and silent day
That overspread the countenance of earth,
Then fading, with unusual quietness,
When from the Loire I parted, and through scenes
Of vineyard, orchard, meadow-ground and tilth,
Calm waters, gleams of sun, and breathless trees
Towards the fierce Metropolis turn'd my steps
Their homeward way to England. From his Throne
The King had fallen; the congregated Host,
Dire cloud upon the front of which was written
The tender mercies of the dismal wind
That bore it, on the Plains of Liberty
Had burst innocuously, say more, the swarm
That came elate and jocund, like a Band
Of Eastern Hunters, to enfold in ring
Narrowing itself by moments and reduce
To the last punctual spot of their despair
A race of victims, so they seem'd, *themselves*
Had shrunk from sight of their own task, and fled
In terror; desolation and dismay
Remained for them whose fancies had grown rank
With evil expectations, confidence
And perfect triumph to the better cause.
The State, as if to stamp the final seal
On her security, and to the world
Shew what she was, a high and fearless soul,
Or rather in a spirit of thanks to those
Who had stirr'd up her slackening faculties
To a new transition, had assumed with joy
The body and the venerable name
Of a Republic: lamentable crimes
'Tis true had gone before this hour, the work
Of massacre, in which the senseless sword
Was pray'd to as a judge; but these were past,
Earth free from them for ever, as was thought,
Ephemeral monsters, to be seen but once;
Things that could only shew themselves and die.

This was the time in which enflam'd with hope,
To Paris I returned. Again I rang'd
More eagerly than I had done before
Through the wide City, and in progress pass'd
The Prison where the unhappy Monarch lay,
Associate with his Children and his Wife
In bondage; and the Palace lately storm'd
With roar of cannon, and a numerous Host.
I cross'd (a blank and empty area then)
The Square of the Carousel, few weeks back
Heap'd up with dead and dying, upon these
And other sights looking as doth a man
Upon a volume whose contents he knows
Are memorable, but from him lock'd up,
Being written in a tongue he cannot read,
So that he questions the mute leaves with pain
And half upbraids their silence.] But that night
When on my bed I lay, I was most mov'd
And felt most deeply in what world I was;
[My room was high and lonely near the roof
Of a large Mansion or Hotel, a spot
That would have pleas'd me in more quiet times,
Nor was it wholly without pleasure then.]
With unextinguish'd taper I kept watch,
Reading at intervals; the fear gone by
Press'd on me almost like a fear to come;
I thought of those September Massacres,
Divided from me by a little month,
And felt and touch'd them, a substantial dread;
The rest was conjured up from tragic fictions,
And mournful Calendars of true history,
Remembrances and dim admonishments.
'The horse is taught his manage, and the wind
Of heaven wheels round and treads in his own steps,
Year follows year, the tide returns again,
Day follows day, all things have second birth;
The earthquake is not satisfied at once.'
And in such way I wrought upon myself,
Until I seem'd to hear a voice that cried,
To the whole City, 'Sleep no more.' [To this
Add comments of a calmer mind, from which
I could not gather full security,

Nocturne, Op. 60 (1958)   [187

But at the best it seem'd a place of fear
Unfit for the repose which night requires,
Defenceless as a wood where tigers roam…

WILFRED OWEN   *The kind ghosts*

She sleeps on soft, last breaths; but no ghost looms
Out of the stillness of her palace wall,
Her wall of boys on boys and dooms on dooms.

She dreams of golden gardens and sweet glooms,
Not marvelling why her roses never fall
Nor what red mouths were torn to make their blooms.

The shades keep down which well might roam her hall.
Quiet their blood lies in her crimson rooms
And she is not afraid of their footfall.

They move not from her tapestries, their pall,
Nor pace her terraces, their hecatombs,
Lest aught she be disturbed, or grieved at all.

JOHN KEATS   *Sleep and Poetry*
'What is more gentle'

[As I lay in my bed slepe full unmete
Was unto me, but why that I ne might
Rest I ne wist, for there n'as erthly wight
(As I suppose) had more of hertis ese
Than I, for I n'ad sicknesses nor disease.
                    – *Chaucer.*]

What is more gentle than a wind in summer?
What is more soothing than the pretty hummer
That stays one moment in an open flower,
And buzzes cheerily from bower to bower?
What is more tranquil than a musk-rose blowing
In a green island, far from all men's knowing?
More healthful than the leafiness of dales?
More secret than a nest of nightingales?
More serene than Cordelia's countenance?
More full of visions than a high romance?
What, but thee, Sleep? Soft closer of our eyes!
Low murmurer of tender lullabies!
Light hoverer around our happy pillows!

Wreather of poppy buds, and weeping willows!
Silent entangler of a beauty's tresses!
Most happy listener! when the morning blesses
Thee for enlivening all the cheerful eyes
That glance so brightly at the new sun-rise.

[But what is higher beyond thought than thee?
Fresher than berries of a mountain-tree?
More strange, more beautiful, more smooth, more regal,
Than wings of swans, than doves, than dim-seen eagle?
What is it? And to what shall I compare it?
It has a glory, and nought else can share it:
The thought thereof is awful, sweet, and holy,
Chasing away all worldliness and folly:
Coming sometimes like fearful claps of thunder;
Or the low rumblings earth's regions under;
And sometimes like a gentle whispering
Of all the secrets of some wondrous thing
That breathes about us in the vacant air;
So that we look around with prying stare,
Perhaps to see shapes of light, aërial limning;
And catch soft floatings from a faint-heard hymning;
To see the laurel-wreath, on high suspended,
That is to crown our name when life is ended.
Sometimes it gives a glory to the voice,
And from the heart up-springs rejoice! rejoice!
Sounds which will reach the Framer of all things,
And die away in ardent mutterings.

No one who once the glorious sun has seen,
And all the clouds, and felt his bosom clean
For his great Maker's presence, but must know
What 'tis I mean, and feel his being glow:
Therefore no insult will I give his spirit,
By telling what he sees from native merit.

O Poesy! for thee I hold my pen,
That am not yet a glorious denizen
Of thy wide heaven – should I rather kneel
Upon some mountain-top until I feel
A glowing splendour round about me hung,
And echo back the voice of thine own tongue?
O Poesy! for thee I grasp my pen,
That am not yet a glorious denizen

Of thy wide heaven; yet, to my ardent prayer,
Yield from thy sanctuary some clear air,
Smoothed for intoxication by the breath
Of flowering bays, that I may die a death
Of luxury, and my young spirit follow
The morning sunbeams to the great Apollo,
Like a fresh sacrifice; or, if I can bear
The o'erwhelming sweets, 'twill bring me to the fair
Visions of all places: a bowery nook
Will be elysium – an eternal book
Whence I may copy many a lovely saying
About the leaves, and flowers – about the playing
Of nymphs in woods and fountains; and the shade
Keeping a silence round a sleeping maid;
And many a verse from so strange influence
That we must ever wonder how, and whence
It came. Also imaginings will hover
Round my fire-side, and haply there discover
Vistas of solemn beauty, where I'd wander
In happy silence, like the clear Meander
Through its lone vales; and where I found a spot
Of awfuller shade, or an enchanted grot,
Or a green hill o'erspread with chequer'd dress
Of flowers, and fearful from its loveliness,
Write on my tablets all that was permitted,
All that was for our human senses fitted.
Then the events of this wide world I'd seize
Like a strong giant, and my spirit tease,
Till at his shoulders it should proudly see
Wings to find out an immortality…

WILLIAM SHAKESPEARE   *Sonnet 43: When most I wink*

When most I wink, then do mine eyes best see,
For all the day they view things unrespected;
But when I sleep, in dreams they look on thee,
And darkly bright are bright in dark directed:
Then thou whose shadow shadows doth make bright,
How would thy shadow's form form happy show
To the clear day with thy much clearer light,
When to unseeing eyes thy shade shines so!

Nocturne, Op. 60 (1958)

How would, I say, mine eyes be blessèd made
By looking on thee in the living day,
When in dead night thy fair imperfect shade
Through heavy sleep on sightless eyes doth stay!
    All days are nights to see till I see thee,
      And nights bright days when dreams do show thee me.

Nocturne, Op. 60 (1958)

Sechs Hölderlin-Fragmente, Op. 61 (1958)
Six Hölderlin Fragments

These settings of six Hölderlin poems, for voice and piano, were first performed on 20 November 1958, at Schloss Wolfsgarten, by Pears and Britten. They were dedicated to 'Meinem Freund, dem Prinzen von Hessen und bei Rhein, zum fünfzigsten Geburtstag'.

SECHS HÖLDERLIN-FRAGMENTE
JOHANN CHRISTIAN FRIEDRICH HÖLDERLIN
(tr. Elizabeth Mayer and Peter Pears)

Menschenbeifall (The applause of men)

Ist nicht heilig mein Herz, schöneren Lebens voll,
Seit ich liebe? Warum achtetet ihr mich mehr,
   Da ich stolzer und wilder,
   Wortereicher und leerer war?

Ach! der Menge gefällt, was auf den Marktplatz taugt,
Und es ehret der Knecht nur den Gewaltsamen;
   An das Göttliche glauben
   Die allein, die es selber sind.

Love has hallowed my heart, filled it
   with fairer life,
Filled it with beauty. Why then did
   you esteem me more,
   In my arrogant wilderness,
   Rich in empty resounding words?

Ah! the masses delight in ev'ry cheap
   device,
And the servile obey nought but a
   tyranny;
   They acknowledge the godlike –
   Only they, who themselves are gods.

Die Heimat (Home)

Froh kehrt der Schiffer heim an den stillen Strom
Von fernen Inseln, wo er geerntet hat.
   Wohl möcht auch ich zur Heimat wieder;
   Aber was hab ich, wie Leid, geerntet?

Ihr holden Ufer, die ihr mich auferzogt,
Stillt ihr der Liebe Leiden? ach gebt ihr mir,
   Ihr Wälder meiner Kindheit! wann ich
   Komme, die Ruhe noch einmal wieder?

With joy the fisher steers into quiet port
From distant islands, where he has harvested.
   So too would I be turning homewards;
   Ah, but what have I, save grief, for
   harvest?

Ye blessed shores, the guardians of my youth,
Can you not ease my longing? Then give me
   back,
   You forests of my childhood, at my
   Coming, that peace which once you
   gave me!

Sokrates und Alcibiades (*Socrates and Alcibiades*)

Warum huldigest du, heiliger Sokrates,
Diesem Jünglinge stets? kennest du Grössers nicht?
   Warum siehet mit Liebe,
     Wie auf Götter, dein Aug' auf ihn?

Wer das Tiefste gedacht, liebt das Lebendigste,
Hohe Tugend versteht, wer in die Welt geblickt,
   Und es neigen die Weisen
     Oft am Ende zu Schönem sich.

And why favourest thou, holy Socrates,
Such a stripling as this? Know'st
   thou no higher things?
   And why gazest upon him
   Like an immortal, with eyes of love?

Who most deeply enquires, loves what is
   liveliest,
And true Virtue perceives, who has
   observed the world,
   And at moments the sages
   Must be yielding to Beauty itself.

Die Jugend (*Youth*)

Da ich ein Knabe war,
Rettet' ein Gott mich oft
Vom Geschrei und der Ruthe der Menschen,
Da spielt' ich sicher und gut
Mit den Blumen des Hains,
Und die Lüftchen des Himmels
Spielten mit mir.

When I was still a boy
I was saved by a god
From the noise and the bruises of mankind.
I played securely and free
With the flowers of the fields,
And the breezes of heaven
Sported with me.

Und wie du das Herz
Der Pflanzen erfreust,
Wenn sie entgegen dir
Die zarten Arme streken,
So hast du mein Herz erfreut
Vater Helios! Und, wie Endymion,
War ich dein Liebling,
Heilege Luna!

And as you delight
The hearts of the flowers
When they incline to you,
Their tender arms outstretching,
So you filled my heart with joy,
Father Helios! And, like Endymion,
I was your darling,
Heavenly Luna!

O all ihr treuen
Freundlichen Götter!
Dass ihr wüsstet,
Wie euch meine Seele geliebt!

O all you friendly
Faithful Immortals!
Could I tell you
How belov'd you were to my heart!

[Zwar damals ruft ich noch nicht
Euch mit Nahmen, auch ihr
Nanntet mich nie, wie die Menschen sich nennen,
Als kennten sie sich.

[Though then I did not yet call
You by your names, and you
Never named me, as men name each other,
As though they knew each other.

Doch kannt' ich euch besser
Als ich je die Menschen gekannt,
Ich verstand die Stille des A´thers,
Der Menschen Worte verstand ich nie.]

Yet I knew you better
Than I ever knew men;
I understood the stillness of the ether,
But human words I never understood.]

Sechs Hölderlin-Fragmente, Op. 61 (1958)

Mich erzog der Wohllaut
Des sa´uselnden Hains
Und lieben lernt' ich
Unter den Blumen.
Im Arme der Götter wuchs ich gross.

I was taught the songs
Of the whispering trees
And amid the flowers
I learnt the art of love.
The arms of the gods made me a man.

Hälfte des Lebens (*The middle of life*)

Mit gelben Birnen hänget
Und voll mit wilden Rosen
Das Land in den See,
Ihr holden Schwäne,
Und trunken von Küssen
Tunkt ihr das Haupt
Ins heilignüchterne Wasser.

With golden fruit it hangs there
And full of wild roses
The land into the lake,
Ye gentle swans
And drunken with kissing
Dip your heads
Into the pure hallowed water.

Weh mir, wo nehm' ich, wenn
Es Winter ist, die Blumen, und wo
Den Sonnenschein
Und Schatten der Erde?
Die Mauern stehn
Sprachlos und kalt, im Winde
Klirren die Fahnen.

Alas! where are they, in
The winter time, the flowers, and where
The shining sun
And shadows of the Earth?
The walls stand there
Speechless and cold; the wind sets
Weather-vanes clatt'ring.

Die Linien des Lebens (*Lines of life*)

Die Linien des Lebens sind verschieden,
Wie Wege sind, und wie der Berge Grenzen.
Was hier wir sind, kann dort ein Gott ergänzen,
Mit Harmonien und ew'gem Lohn und Frieden.

Each line of life is different from another,
As rivers are, or like the mountain ranges.
What we are here is there by God completed
With harmony, reward and peace eternal.

Sechs Hölderlin-Fragmente, Op. 61 (1958)

Um Mitternacht (1959/60)

This setting, for voice and piano, was first performed on 15 June 1992 at the Aldeburgh Festival by Lucy Shelton and Ian Brown.

JOHANN WOLFGANG VON GOETHE   (tr. David Luke)
Um Mitternacht

Um Mitternacht ging ich, nicht eben gerne,
Klein, kleiner Knabe, jenen Kirchhof hin
Zu Vaters Haus, des Pfarrers; Stern am Sterne,
Sie leuchteten doch alle gar zu schön;
     Um Mitternacht.

Wenn ich dann ferner, in des Lebens Weite
Zur Liebsten musste, musste, weil sie zog,
Gestirn und Nordschein über mir im Streite,
Ich gehend, kommend Seligkeiten sog;
     Um Mitternacht.

Bis dann zuletzt des vollen Mondes Helle
So klar und deutlich mir ins Finstere drang,
Auch der Gedanke willig, sinnig, schnelle
Sich ums Vergangne wie ums Künftige schlang;
     Um Mitternacht.

At midnight I would walk, rather
unwillingly, as a very little boy, along past that
churchyard to father's, to the parson's house;
star upon star, how beautifully
they all shone,
     at midnight.

Then, later, far back in life, when I was
going to my beloved, drawn by her
compulsion, the stars and the northern lights
would be at war above me, and as I went and as
I came I sucked in happiness with every breath –
     at midnight.

Until at last the full moon's radiance
penetrated my darkness so clearly and
painfully, and thought willingly,
meaningfully, swiftly embraced the past and
the future;
     at midnight.

A Midsummer Night's Dream, Op. 64 (1960)

The opera in three acts was first performed on 11 June 1960 in the Jubilee Hall at the Aldeburgh Festival by The English Opera Group conducted by Britten. It was 'Dedicated to Stephen Reiss'. The libretto was adapted from Shakespeare's play by Britten and Pears. Britten referred to 'the tremendous challenge' of setting Shakespeare's 'heavenly words', and this anthology includes some of the most 'heavenly' of the play's lyrics. Britten starts with Act II, and one fairy becomes four.

WILLIAM SHAKESPEARE   *'Over hill, over dale'*

> [*Puck* How now, spirit! whither wander you?]
> *Fairy* Over hill, over dale.
>   Thorough bush, thorough briar,
>   Over park, over pale,
>   Thorough flood, thorough fire,
>   I do wander every where,
>   Swifter than the moonës sphere:
>   And I serve the Fairy Queen,
>   To dew her orbs upon the green.
>   The cowslips tall her pensioners be,
>   In their gold coats spots you see:
>   Those be rubies, fairy favours:
>   In those freckles live their savours.
>   I must go seek some dewdrops here,
>   And hang a pearl in every cowslip's ear.

(II. i. 1–16)

'Either I mistake your shape'

> *Fairy* Either I mistake your shape and making quite,
>   Or else you are that shrewd and knavish sprite
>   Called Robin Goodfellow. Are not you he
>   That frights the maidens of the villagery,
>   Skim milk, and sometimes labour in the quern,
>   And bootless make the breathless housewife churn,
>   And sometimes make the drink to bear no barm,
>   Mislead night-wanderers, laughing at their harm?
>   Those that Hobgoblin call you and sweet Puck,
>   You do their work, and they shall have good luck.

(II. i. 32–41)

A Midsummer Night's Dream, Op. 64 (1960)

'These are the forgeries of jealousy'

Titania† [These are the forgeries of jealousy:
And never, since the middle summer's spring,
Met we on hill, in dale, forest, or mead,
By pavéd fountain, or by rushy brook,
Or in the beachéd margent of the sea,
To dance our ringlets to the whistling wind,
But with thy brawls thou hast disturbed our sport.]
Therefore the winds, [piping to us in vain,
As in revenge,] have sucked up from the sea
Contagious fogs: [which falling in the land,
Hath every pelting river made so proud
That they have overborne their continents.]
The ox hath therefore stretched his yoke in vain,
[The ploughman lost his sweat, and the green corn
Hath rotted ere his youth attained a beard;]
The fold stands empty in the drownéd field,
And crows are fatted with the murrion flock;
[The nine men's morris is filled up with mud,
And the quaint mazes in the wanton green
For lack of tread are undistinguishable.
The human mortals want their winter cheer;
No night is now with hymn or carol blest;
Therefore the moon, the governess of floods,
Pale in her anger, washes all the air,
That rheumatic diseases do abound.
And through this distemperature we see]
The seasons alter: [hoary-headed frosts
Fall in the fresh lap of the crimson rose,
And on old Hiems' thin and icy crown
An odorous chaplet of sweet summer buds
Is, as in mockery, set.] The spring, the summer,
The chiding autumn, angry winter change
Their wonted liveries; and the mazéd world,
By their increase, now knows not which is which.

(II. i. 81–114)

†Britten turns this into an exchange between Titania and Oberon.

'I know a bank'

Oberon I know a bank where the wild thyme blows,
Where oxlips and the nodding violet grows,
Quite over-canopied with luscious woodbine,
With sweet musk-roses, and with eglantine:
There sleeps Titania sometime of the night,
Lulled in these flowers with dances and delight;
And there the snake throws her enamelled skin,
Weed wide enough to wrap a fairy in.
And with the juice of this I'll streak her eyes,
And make her full of hateful fantasies.

(II. i. 249–58)

'You spotted snakes'

Fairies You spotted snakes, with double tongue,
Thorny hedgehogs, be not seen;
Newts and blind-worms do no wrong,
Come not near our Fairy Queen.

Philomele, with melody,
Sing in our sweet lullaby,
Lulla, lulla, lullaby,
Lulla, lulla, lullaby,
Never harm,
Nor spell, nor charm,
Come our lovely lady nigh.
So good night, with lullaby.

Fairy Weaving spiders come not here:
Hence you long-legged spinners, hence:
Beetles black approach not near:
Worm nor snail do no offence.

Philomele, with melody,
Sing in our sweet lullaby,
Lulla, lulla, lullaby,
Lulla, lulla, lullaby,
Never harm,
Nor spell, nor charm,
Come our lovely lady nigh.
So good night, with lullaby. [*Titania sleeps*

(II. ii. 9–32)

A Midsummer Night's Dream, Op. 64 (1960)

'Be kind and courteous'

Titania Be kind and courteous to this gentleman;
    Hop in his walks and gambol in his eyes;
    Feed him with apricocks and dewberries,
    With purple grapes, green figs, and mulberries;
    The honey-bags steal from the humble-bees,
    And for night-tapers crop their waxen thighs,
    And light them at the fiery glow-worm's eyes,
    To have my love to bed and to arise;
    [And pluck the wings from painted butterflies,
    To fan the moonbeams from his sleeping eyes.]
    Nod to him, elves, and do him courtesies.

(III. i. 155–65)

'Now the hungry lion roars'

Puck Now the hungry lion roars,
  And the wolf behowls the moon;
 Whilst the heavy ploughman snores,
  All with weary task fordone.
 Now the wasted brands do glow,
  Whilst the screech-owl, screeching loud,
 Puts the wretch that lies in woe
  In remembrance of a shroud.
 Now it is the time of night,
  That the graves, all gaping wide,
 Every one lets forth his sprite,
  In the church-way paths to glide.
 And we fairies, that do run
  By the triple Hecate's team
 From the presence of the sun,
  Following darkness like a dream,
 Now are frolic. Not a mouse
 Shall disturb this hallowed house.
 I am sent with broom before,
 To sweep the dust behind the door.

(V. i. 369–88)

'Now, until the break of day'

Fairies† Now, until the break of day,
    Through this house each fairy stray.
    To the best bride-bed will we:
    Which by us shall bléssed be:
    And the issue, there create
    Ever shall be fortunate:
    So shall all the couples three
    Ever true in loving be:
    [And the blots of Nature's hand
    Shall not in their issue stand.
    Never mole, hare-lip, nor scar,
    Nor mark prodigious, such as are
    Despiséd in nativity,
    Shall upon their children be.]
    With this field-dew consecrate,
    Every fairy take his gait,
    And each several chamber bless,
    Through this palace, with sweet peace;
    And the owner of it blest
    Ever shall in safety rest.
    Trip away,
    Make no stay,
    Meet me all by break of day.

(V. i. 399–421)

†Britten gives the lines to Oberon.

'If we shadows have offended'
Epilogue

Puck If we shadows have offended,
    Think but this, and all is mended,
    That you have but slumb'red here
    While these visions did appear.
    [And this weak and idle theme,
    No more yielding but a dream,]
    Gentles, do not reprehend.
    If you pardon, we will mend.

         A Midsummer Night's Dream, Op. 64 (1960)

[And, as I am an honest Puck,
If we have unearnéd luck
Now to 'scape the serpent's tongue,
We will make amends, ere long:]
Else the Puck a liar call.
So, good night unto you all.
Give me your hands, if we be friends,
And Robin shall restore amends.

(V. i. 422–37)

Folk Song Arrangements, Vol. 4 (1960)
Moore's Irish melodies

For voice and piano.

THOMAS MOORE *Avenging and bright*

Avenging and bright falls the swift sword of Erin
On him whom the brave sons of Usna betrayed.
For every fond eye which he wakened a tear in,
A drop from his heart-wounds shall weep o'er her blade.

By the red cloud which hung over Connor's dark dwelling.
When Ulad's three champions lay sleeping in gore,
By the billows of war which so often high swelling
Have wafted these heroes to victory's shore.

We swear to avenge them, no joy shall be tasted,
The harp shall be silent, the maiden unwed,
Our halls shall be mute and our fields shall lie wasted
Till vengeance be wreaked on the murderer's head.

Yes, monarch, though sweet are our home recollections,
Though sweet are the tears that from tenderness fall;
Though sweet are our friendships, our hopes and affections,
Revenge on a tyrant is sweetest of all.

The humming of the ban 'Sail on, sail on'

Sail on, sail on, thou fearless bark,
Wherever blows the welcome wind;
It cannot lead to scenes more dark,
More sad than those we leave behind.
Each smiling billow seems to say,
'Though death beneath our surface be,
Less cold are we, less false than they
Whose smiling wrecked thy hopes and thee.

Sail on, sail on, through endless space,
Through calm, through tempest, stop no more;
The stormiest sea's a resting place
To him who leaves such hearts on shore.

Or if some desert land we meet
Where never yet false hearted men
Profaned a world that else were sweet,
Then rest thee, bark, but hopes and thee.

The wren 'How sweet the answer'

How sweet the answer Echo makes
    To music at night,
When, roused by lute or horn, she wakes
And far away, o'er lawns and lakes,
    Goes answering light.

Yet love hath echoes truer far,
    And far more sweet,
Than e'er beneath the moonlight's star
Of horn, or lute, or soft guitar
    The songs repeat.

'Tis when the sigh, in youth sincere,
    And only then –
The sigh, that's breathed for one to hear,
Is by that one, that only dear,
    Breathed back again,
    Again, again, again, again.

The minstrel boy

The minstrel boy to the war is gone
In the ranks of death you'll find him;
His father's sword he has girded on,
And his wild harp slung behind him.
'Land of song,' said the warrior bard,
'Though all the world betrays thee,
One sword, at least, thy rights shall guard,
One faithful harp shall praise thee.'

The minstrel fell, but the foeman's chain
Could not bring that proud soul under;
The harp he loved ne'er spoke again,
For he tore its chords asunder;
And said, 'No chain shall sully thee,
Thou soul of love and brav'ry.

Thy songs were made for the pure and free,
They shall never sound in slav'ry.'

Molly, my dear   'At the mid hour of night'

At the mid hour of night when stars are weeping, I fly
To the lone vale we loved when life shone warm in thine eye;
And I think that if spirits can steal from the region of air
To visit past scenes of delight, thou wilt come to me there
And tell me our love is remembered e'en in the sky.

Then I'll sing the wild song, which once 'twas rapture to hear,
When our voices, both mingling, breathed like one on the ear,
And as echo far off through the vale my sad orison rolls,
I think, Oh my love, 'tis thy voice from the kingdom of souls
Faintly answering still the notes which once were so dear.

The summer is coming   'Rich and rare'

Rich and rare were the gems she wore,
And a bright gold ring on her wand she bore;
But O her beauty was far beyond
Her sparkling gems and her snow white wand.

'Lady, dost thou not fear to stray,
So lone and lovely, through this bleak way?
Are Erin's sons so good or so cold
As not to be tempted by woman or gold?'

'Sir Knight, I feel not the least alarm;
No son of Erin will offer me harm;
For though they love woman and golden store,
Sir Knight, they love honour and virtue more.'

On she went, and her maiden smile
In safety lighted her round the green isle;
And blest was she who relied
Upon Erin's honour and Erin's pride.

Kate Tyrrel   'Dear harp of my country'

Dear harp of my country, in darkness I found thee,
The cold chain of silence had hung o'er thee long;
When proudly, my own island harp, I unbound thee,
And gave all thy chords to light, freedom and song.

The warm lay of love and the light tone of gladness
Have wakened thy fondest, thy liveliest thrill;
But so oft has thou echoed the deep sigh of sadness
That e'en in thy mirth it will steal from thee still.

Dear harp of my country, farewell to thy numbers,
This sweet wreath of song is the last we shall twine,
Go, sleep with the sunshine of fame on thy slumbers
Till touched by some hand less unworthy than mine.
If the pulse of the patriot, soldier or lover,
Have throbbed at our lay, 'tis *thy* glory alone;
I was but as the wind, passing heedlessly over,
And all the wild sweetness I waked was thy own.

Oft in the stilly night

Oft in the stilly night ere slumber's chain has bound me,
Fond memory brings the light of other days around me:
The smiles, the tears of boyhood's years,
The words of love then spoken;
The eyes that shone, now dimmed and gone,
The cheerful hearts now broken.
Thus in the stilly night ere slumber's chain has bound me,
Sad memory brings the light of other days around me.

When I remember all the friends, so linked together,
I've seen around me fall like leaves in wintry weather,
I feel like one who treads alone
Some banquet hall deserted,
Whose lights are fled, whose garlands dead,
And all but he departed.

Groves of Blarney   'The last rose of summer'

'Tis the last rose of summer, left blooming alone;
All her lovely companions are faded and gone;
No flower of her kindred, no rosebud is nigh
To reflect back her blushes, or give sigh for sigh.

I'll not leave thee, thou lone one, to pine on the stem;
Since the lovely are sleeping, go, sleep thou with them;
Thus kindly I scatter thy leaves o'er the bed
Where thy mates of the garden lie senseless and dead.

So soon may I follow when friendships decay,
And from love's shining circle the gems drop away.
When true hearts lie withered, and fond ones are flown,
Oh who would inhabit this bleak world alone?

Planxty Sudley   'O the sight entrancing'

> *O the sight entrancing,*
> *When morning's beam is glancing*
> *O'er files arrayed with helm and blade,*
> *And plumes in the gay wind dancing.*
> When hearts are all high beating,
> And the trumpet's voice repeating
> That song whose breath may lead to death,
> But never to retreating.
> Then if a cloud comes over
> The brow of sire or lover,
> Think 'tis the shade by victory made,
> Whose wings right over us hover.
> > *O the sight…*

> Yet 'tis not helm or feather,
> For ask yon despot whether
> His plumèd bands could bring such hands
> And hearts as ours together.
> Leave pomps to those who need 'em,
> Adorn but man with freedom,
> And proud he braves the gaudiest slaves
> That crawl where monarchs lead 'em.
> The sword may pierce the beaver,
> Stone walls in time may sever,
> 'Tis mind alone, worth steel and stone,
> That keeps men free for ever.
> > *O the sight…*

Jubilate Deo (1961)

This setting of Psalm 100 for choir and organ was first performed on 8 October 1961 in Leeds Parish Church, together with *Te Deum* (1935). It was 'Written for St George's Chapel, Windsor, at the request of H.R.H. The Duke of Edinburgh'.

THE BOOK OF COMMON PRAYER *Jubilate Deo: Psalm* 100

O be joyful in the Lord, all ye lands: serve the Lord with gladness, and come before his presence with a song.

Be ye sure that the Lord he is God: it is he that hath made us, and not we ourselves; we are his people, and the sheep of his pasture.

O go your way into his gates with thanksgiving, and into his courts with praise: be thankful unto him, and speak good of his name.

For the Lord is gracious, his mercy is everlasting: and his truth endureth from generation to generation.

Glory be to the Father, and to the Son, and to the Holy Ghost; As it was in the beginning, is now, and ever shall be: world without end. AMEN.

Folk Song Arrangements, Vol. 5   British Isles (1961)

For voice and piano.

TRAD.   *The brisk young widow*

In Chester town there lived a brisk young widow,
For beauty and fine clothes none could excel her,
    She was proper stout and tall,
    Her fingers long and small,
    She's a comely dame withal,
She's a brisk young widow.

A lover soon there came, a brisk young farmer,
With his hat turned up all round, seeking to gain her.
    'My dear, for love of you
    This wide world I'd go through,
    If you will but prove true
You shall wed a farmer.'

Says she, 'I'm not for you nor no such fellow,
I'm for a lively lad with lands and riches,
    'Tis not your hogs and yowes
    Can maintain furbelows,
    My silk and satin clothes
Are all my glory.'

'O madam don't be coy, for all your glory,
For fear of another day and another story.
    If the world on you should frown
    Your top-knot must come down
    To a Lindsey-woolsey gown.
Where is then your glory?'

At last there came that way a sooty collier,
With his hat bent down all round, he soon did gain her.
    Whereat the farmer swore,
    'The widow's mazed, I'm sure.
    I'll never court no more
A brisk young widow.'

HENRY CAREY *Sally in our alley*

Of all the girls that are so smart
There's none like pretty Sally;
She is the darling of my heart
And lives in our alley.
There's ne'er a lady in the land
That's half so sweet as Sally.
  She is the darling of my heart
  And lives in our alley.

Of all the days within the week,
I dearly love but one day,
And that's the day that comes between
A Saturday and Monday,
For then I'm dressed all in my best
To walk abroad with Sally.

When she is by I leave my work,
I love her so sincerely;
My master comes like any Turk
And bangs me most severely.
But let him bang his bellyful
I'll bear it all for Sally.

My master carries me to church
And often am I blamèd
Because I leave him in the lurch
As soon as text is namèd;
I leave the church in sermon-time
And slink away to Sally.

My master and the neighbours all
Make game of me and Sally,
And but for her I'd better be
A slave and row a galley.
But when my seven long years are out,
O then I'll marry Sally.
  O then we'll wed and then we'll bed,
  But not in our alley.

TRAD. *The Lincolnshire poacher*

When I was bound apprentice in famous Lincolnshire,
Full well I served my master for more than seven year
Till I took up to poaching, as you will quickly hear.
  O 'tis my delight on a shining night
  In the season of the year.

As me and my companions were setting of a snare
'Twas there we spied the game-keeper, for him we did not care,
For we can wrestle and fight, my boys, and jump o'er any where.

As me and my companions were setting four or five
And taking on 'em up again, we caught a hare alive;
We took the hare alive, my boys, and through the woods did steer.

I threw him on my shoulder and then we trudgèd home,
We took him to a neighbour's house and sold him for a crown,
We sold him for a crown, my boys, but I did not tell you where.

Success to every gentleman that lives in Lincolnshire,
Success to every poacher that wants to sell a hare,
Bad luck to every game-keeper that will not sell his deer.

TRAD. *Early one morning*

Early one morning, just as the sun was rising,
I heard a maid singing in the valley below,
'O don't deceive me, O never leave me,
How could you use a poor maiden so?

'O gay is the garland, fresh are the roses
I've culled from the garden to bind on thy brow.
O don't deceive me, O do not leave me,
How could you use a poor maiden so?

'Remember the vows that you made to your Mary,
Remember the bow'r where you vowed to be true.
O don't deceive me, O never leave me,
How could you use a poor maiden so?'

Thus sung the poor maiden, her sorrow bewailing,
Thus sung the poor maid in the valley below,
'O don't deceive me, O do not leave me,
How could you use a poor maiden so?'

ROBERT BURNS   *Ca' the yowes*

ewes, hillocks	*Ca' the yowes to the knowes,*
	Ca' them where the heather growes,
stream rolls	*Ca' them where the burnie rowes,*
	My bonnie dearie.

thrush   Hark the mavis evening sang,
Sounden Clouden's woods amang,
Then afolding let us gang,
    My bonnie dearie.

We'll gang down by Clouden side,
Through the hazels spreading wide
O'er the waves that sweetly glide
    To the moon sae clearly.

Fair and lovely as thou art,
Thou has stol'n my very heart;
I can die but canna part,
    My bonnie dearie.

Ca' the yowes...

Fancie (1961)

WILLIAM SHAKESPEARE *'Tell me where is Fancie bred'*
'Fancie' *(from The Merchant of Venice* III. ii*)*

> Tell me where is Fancie bred,
> Or in the heart or in the head?
> How begot, how nourishèd?
> Replie, replie!
> It is engendered in the eyes,
> With gazing fed; and Fancy dies
> In the cradle where it lies.
> Let us all ring Fancie's knell:
> Ile begin it:
> *Ding, dong, bell.*
> *Ding, dong, bell.*

Folk Song Arrangements, Vol. 6   England (1961)

For voice and piano. In 'The sailor and the soldier', Britten changed 'King' to 'Queen' throughout. This volume of folk songs included 'Bonny at morn' as the penultimate song, which Britten also included in *Eight Folk Song Arrangements* (see p.281).

TRAD.   *I will give my love an apple*

I will give my love an apple without e'er a core,
I will give my love a house without e'er a door,
I will give my love a palace wherein she may be,
And she may unlock it without any key.

My head is the apple without e'er a core,
My mind is the house without e'er a door,
My heart is the palace wherein she may be,
And she may unlock it without any key.

TRAD.   *Sailor-boy*

We go walking on the green grass, thus, thus, thus.
Come all you pretty fair maids,
Come walk along with us.
So pretty and so fair
As you take yourself to be,
I'll choose you for a partner,
Come walk along with me.

I would not be a blacksmith
That smuts his nose and chin,
I'd rather be a sailor boy
That sails through the wind.
Sailor boy, sailor boy,
Sailor boy for me,
If ever I get married
A sailor's wife she'll be.

TRAD. *Master Kilby*

In the heat of the day
When the sun shines so freely,
Then I met Master Kilby
So fine and so gay.

Then I pulled off my hat
And I bowed to the ground,
And I said: 'Master Kilby,
Pray where are you bound?'

'I am bound for the West,
There in hopes to find rest,
And in Nancy's soft bosom
I will build a new nest.

'And if I was the master
Of ten thousand pound,
All in gay gold and silver,
Or in King William's crown,

'I would part with it all
With my own heart so freely
And it's all for the sake
Of my charming Nancy.

'She's the fairest of girls,
She's the joyest of my own heart,
She's painted like waxwork
In every part.

'I would part with it all
With my own heart so freely
But it's all for the sake
Of my charming Nancy.

'She's the fairest of girls,
She's the joyest of my own heart,
She's painted like waxwork
In every part.

['Then I gives her more kisses,
It was on the sea-shore,
But still she lay asking,
Lay asking for more.']

TRAD.　*The sailor and the soldier* 'The soldier and the sailor'

As the soldier and the sailor was a-walking one day,
Said the soldier to the sailor: 'I've a mind for to pray.'
'Pray on then,' said the sailor, 'pray on once again,
And whatever you do pray for, I will answer: Amen.'

[The first thing they came to was an old hollow tree
Said the sailor to the soldier: 'This my pulpit shall be.'
'Pray on,' said the soldier, 'pray on once again,
And pray for whatever thou wilt, I will answer: Amen.']

'Now the first thing I'll pray for, I'll pray for our King
That he have peace and plenty all the days of his reign,
And where he got one man I wish he had ten,
And never never want an army.' Said the soldier: 'Amen.'

'The next thing I'll pray for, I'll pray for the King
That he have peace and plenty all the days of his reign,
And where he got one ship I wish he had ten,
And never never want for navy.' Said the soldier: 'Amen.'

'The next thing I'll pray for is a pot of good beer,
For good liquors were sent our spirits to cheer,
And where we got one pot I wish we had ten,
And never never want for liquor.' Said the soldier: 'Amen.'

TRAD.　*The shooting of his dear*

O come all you young fellows that carry a gun,
I'd have you get home by the light of the sun,
For young Jimmy was a fowler and a-fowling alone,
When he shot his own true love in the room of a swan.

Then home went young Jimmy with his dog and his gun,
Saying, 'Uncle, dear uncle, have you heard what I've done?
Cursèd be that old gunsmith that made my old gun,
For I've shot my own true love in the room of a swan.'

Then out came bold uncle with his locks hanging grey,
Saying, 'Jimmy, dear Jimmy, don't you go away,
Don't you leave your own country till the trial come on,
For you never will be hangèd for the shooting of a swan.'

So the trial came on and pretty Polly did appear,
Saying, 'Uncle, dear uncle, let Jimmy go clear,
For my apron was bound round me and he took me for a swan,
And his poor heart lay bleeding for Polly his own.'

War Requiem, Op. 66 (1961)

This work, for soprano, tenor and baritone solos, chorus and boys' choir, orchestra and chamber orchestra, and organ, was first performed on 30 May 1962 at the festival to celebrate the re-consecration of St Michael's Cathedral, Coventry. The performers were Heather Harper (in place of Galina Vishnevskaya, who was refused a visa to come to England), Pears, Dietrich Fischer-Dieskau, with the Coventry Festival Chorus and the boys of Holy Trinity, Leamington, and Holy Trinity, Stratford, the City of Birmingham Symphony Orchestra conducted by Meredith Davies, and the Melos Ensemble conducted by Britten. In his invitation to Fischer-Dieskau to take part, Britten referred to 'these magnificent poems, full of the hate of destruction'.

The work was dedicated 'In loving memory of Roger Burney, Sub-Lieutenant RNVR, Piers Dunkerley, Captain Royal Marines, David Gill, Ordinary Seaman, Royal Navy, Michael Halliday, Lieutenant, RNZNVR'.

Missa pro defunctis   (Mass for the dead: English text of the Requiem Mass according to the English Missal.)

WILFRED OWEN   POEMS

My subject is War, and the pity of War.
The Poetry is in the pity.
All a poet can do today is warn.

I. REQUIEM AETERNAM

Requiem aeternam dona eis, Domine:	Rest eternal grant unto them, O Lord:
et lux perpetua luceat eis.	and let light eternal shine upon them.
Te decet hymnus, Deus in Sion:	Thou, O God, art praised in Sion;
et tibi reddetur votum in Jerusalem;	and unto Thee shall the vow be performed in Jerusalem;
exaudi orationem meam, ad te omnis caro veniet.	Thou who hearest the prayer, unto Thee shall all flesh come.

Anthem for doomed youth

What passing-bells for these who die as cattle?
Only the monstrous anger of the guns.
Only the stuttering rifles' rapid rattle
Can patter out their hasty orisons.
No mockeries for them from prayers or bells,
Nor any voice of mourning save the choirs, –
The shrill, demented choirs of wailing shells;
And bugles calling for them from sad shires.

What candles may be held to speed them all?
Not in the hands of boys, but in their eyes
Shall shine the holy glimmers of good-byes.
The pallor of girls' brows shall be their pall;
Their flowers the tenderness of silent minds,
And each slow dusk a drawing-down of blinds.

Kyrie eleison. Christe eleison.
Kyrie eleison.

Lord have mercy upon us. Christ have mercy upon us.
Lord have mercy upon us.

II. DIES IRAE

Dies irae, dies illa,
Solvet saeclum in favilla:
Teste David cum Sibylla.
Quantus tremor est futurus,
Quando Judex est venturus,
Cuncta stricte discussurus!
Tuba mirum spargens sonum
Per sepulchra regionum,
Coget omnes ante thronum.
Mors stupebit et natura,
Cum resurget creatura,
Judicanti responsura.

Day of wrath and doom impending,
Heaven and earth in ashes ending!
David's words with Sibyl's blending!
Oh, what fear man's bosom rendeth
when from heaven the judge descendeth,
on whose sentence all dependeth!
Wondrous sound the trumpet flingeth,
through earth's sepulchres it ringeth,
all before the throne it bringeth.
Death is struck and nature quaking,
all creation is awaking,
to its judge an answer making.

Voices

Bugles sang, saddening the evening air,
And bugles answered, sorrowful to hear.

Voices of boys were by the river-side.
Sleep mothered them; and left the twilight sad.
The shadow of the morrow weighed on men.

War Requiem, Op. 66 (1961)

[217

Voices of old despondency resigned,
Bowed by the shadow of the morrow, slept.

[†dying tone
Of receding voices that will not return.
The wailing of the high far-travelling shells
And the deep cursing of the provoking†

The monstrous anger of our taciturn guns.
The majesty of the insults of their mouths.]

†missing words.

Liber scriptus proferetur,	Lo! the book exactly worded,
In quo totum continetur,	wherein all hath been recorded;
Unde mundus judicetur.	thence shall judgement be awarded.
Judex ergo cum sedebit	When the judge his seat attaineth,
Quidquid latet, apparebit:	and each hidden deed arraigneth,
Nil inultum remanebit.	nothing unavenged remaineth.
Quid sum miser tunc dicturus?	What shall I, frail man, be pleading?
Quem patronum rogaturus,	Who for me be interceding,
Cum vix justus sit securus?	when the just are mercy needing?
Rex tremendae majestatis,	King of majesty tremendous,
Qui salvandos salvae gratis,	who dost free salvation send us.
Salva me, fons pietatis.	Fount of pity, then befriend us!

The next war

War's a joke for me and you,
While we know such dreams are true.
SASSOON;

Out there, we've walked quite friendly up to Death;
    Sat down and eaten with him, cool and bland, –
    Pardoned his spilling mess-tins in our hand.
We've sniffed the green thick odour of his breath, –
Our eyes wept, but our courage didn't writhe.
    He's spat at us with bullets and he's coughed
    Shrapnel. We chorussed when he sang aloft;
We whistled while he shaved us with his scythe.

Oh, Death was never enemy of ours!
    We laughed at him, we leagued with him, old chum.
No soldier's paid to kick against his powers.
    We laughed, knowing that better men would come,
And greater wars; when each proud fighter brags
He wars on Death – for Life; not men – for flags.

War Requiem, Op. 66 (1961)

Recordare Jesu pie,
Quod sum causa tuae viae:
Ne me perdas illa die.
Quaerens me, sedisti lassus:
Redemisti crucem passus:
Tantus labor non sit cassus... †
Ingemisco, tamquam reus:
Culpa rubet vultus meus:
Supplicanti parce Deus.
Qui Mariam absolvisti,
Et latronem exaudisti,
Mihi quoque spem dedisti,... †
Inter oves locum praesta,
Et ab haedis me sequestra,
Statuens in parte dextra.
Confutatis maledictis,
Flammis acribus addictis,
Voca me cum benedictis.
Oro supplex et acclinis,
Cor contritum quasi cinis:
Gere curam mei finis.

Think, kind Jesus – my salvation
caused Thy wondrous incarnation;
leave me not to reprobation.
Faint and weary Thou hast sought me;
on the cross of suffering bought me;
shall such grace be vainly brought me?...
Guilty, now I pour my moaning,
all my shame with anguish owning;
spare, O God, Thy suppliant groaning!
Through the sinful Mary shriven,
through the dying thief forgiven,
Thou to me a hope hast given...
With Thy sheep a place provide me,
from the goats afar divide me,
to Thy right hand do Thou guide me.
When the wicked are confounded,
doomed to flames of woe unbounded,
call me, with Thy saints surrounded.
Low I kneel with heart-submission;
see, like ashes, my contrition!
Help me in my last condition!

†Britten omitted 3 and 3 lines.

Sonnet On seeing a piece of our artillery brought into action

Be slowly lifted up, thou long black arm,
Great gun towering toward Heaven, about to curse;
[Sway steep against them, and for years rehearse
Huge imprecations like a blasting charm!]
Reach at that arrogance which needs thy harm,
And beat it down before its sins grow worse;
[Spend our resentment, cannon, yea, disburse
Our gold in shapes of flame, our breaths in storm.

Yet, for men's sakes whom thy vast malison
Must wither innocent of enmity,
Be not withdrawn, dark arm, thy spoilure done,
Safe to the bosom of our prosperity.]
But when thy spell be cast complete and whole,
May God curse thee, and cut thee from our soul!

Lacrimosa dies illa,
Qua resurget ex favilla
Judicandus homo reus:
Huic ergo parce Deus.

Ah! that day of tears and mourning!
From the dust of earth returning,
man for judgement must prepare him:
Spare, O God, in mercy spare him!

War Requiem, Op. 66 (1961)

Futility

Move him into the sun –
Gently its touch awoke him once,
At home, whispering of fields unsown.
Always it woke him, even in France,
Until this morning and this snow.
If anything might rouse him now
The kind old sun will know.

Think how it wakes the seeds, –
Woke, once, the clays of a cold star.
Are limbs, so dear-achieved, are sides,
Full-nerved – still warm – too hard to stir?
Was it for this the clay grew tall?
– O what made fatuous sunbeams toil
To break earth's sleep at all?

Pie Jesu Domine, dona eis requiem.	Lord, all-pitying, Jesu blest, grant them rest.
Amen.	Amen.

III. OFFERTORIUM

Domine Jesu Christe, Rex gloriae,	O Lord Jesus Christ, King of Glory,
libera animas omnium fidelium	deliver the souls of all the faithful
defunctorum de poenis inferni,	departed from the pains of hell
et de profundo lacu: libera eas	and from the depths of the pit: deliver
de ore leonis, ne absorbeat eas	them from the lion's mouth, that hell
tartarus, ne cadant in obscurum:	devour them not, that they fall not into darkness.
sed signifer sanctus Michael	But let the standard-bearer Saint Michael
repraesentet eas in lucem sanctam.	bring them into the holy light:
Quam olim Abrahae promisisti,	which, of old, Thou didst promise
et semini ejus.	unto Abraham and his seed.

The parable of the old men and the young

So Abram rose, and clave the wood, and went,
And took the fire with him, and a knife.
And as they sojourned both of them together,
Isaac the first-born spake and said, My Father,
Behold the preparations, fire and iron,
But where the lamb for this burnt-offering?
Then Abram bound the youth with belts and straps,

And builded parapets and trenches there,
And stretchèd forth the knife to slay his son.
When lo! an angel called him out of heaven,
Saying, Lay not thy hand upon the lad,
Neither do anything to him. Behold,
A ram, caught in a thicket by its horns;
Offer the Ram of Pride instead of him.
But the old man would not so, but slew his son, –
And half the seed of Europe, one by one.

Hostias et preces tibi Domine	We offer unto Thee, O Lord, sacrifices
laudis offerimus: tu suscipe pro	of prayer and praise: do Thou receive
animabus illis, quarum hodie	them for the souls of those whose memory
	we this day recall: make them, O Lord,
memoriam facimus: fac eas, Domine,	to pass from death unto life,
de morte transire ad vitam.	which of old Thou didst promise to
Quam olim Abrahae promisisti	Abraham and his seed.
et semini ejus.	

IV. SANCTUS

Sanctus, Sanctus Dominus Deus Sabaoth.	Holy, Holy, Holy, Lord God of Sabaoth.
Pleni sunt coeli et terra gloria tua.	Heaven and earth are full of Thy glory:
Hosanna in excelsis.	Glory be to Thee, O Lord most high.
	Blessed is he that cometh in the name of the
Benedictus qui venit in nomine Domini.	Lord.
Hosanna in excelsis.	Glory be to Thee, O Lord most high.

The end

After the blast of lightning from the East,
The flourish of loud clouds, the Chariot Throne;
After the drums of Time have rolled and ceased,
And by the bronze west long retreat is blown,

Shall life renew these bodies? Of a truth
All death will He annul, all tears assuage? –
Fill the void veins of Life again with youth,
And wash, with an immortal water, Age?

When I do ask white Age he saith not so:
'My head hangs weighed with snow.'
And when I hearken to the Earth, she saith:
'My fiery heart shrinks, aching. It is death.
Mine ancient scars shall not be glorified,
Nor my titanic tears, the sea, be dried.'

War Requiem, Op. 66 (1961)

Agnus Dei, qui tollis peccata mundi,   O Lamb of God, Who takest away the sins of the world,
dona eis requiem sempiternam.†   grant them eternal rest.

At a Calvary near the Ancre

One ever hangs where shelled roads part.
    In this war He too lost a limb,
But His disciples hide apart;
    And now the Soldiers bear with Him.

Near Golgotha strolls many a priest,
    And in their faces there is pride
That they were flesh-marked by the Beast
    By whom the gentle Christ's denied.

The scribes on all the people shove
    And bawl allegiance to the state,
But they who love the greater love
    Lay down their life; they do not hate.

†Britten interweaves the Latin text and Owen's poem.

VI. LIBERA ME

Libera me, Domine, de morte aeterna,   Deliver me, O Lord, from death eternal,
in die illa tremenda: in that fearful day:
                    When the heavens and the earth shall be shaken:
Quando coeli movendi sunt et terra: When Thou shalt come to judge the world by fire.
Dum veneris judicare saeculum per ignem. I am in fear and trembling
Tremens factus sum ego, et timeo   till the sifting be upon us, and the wrath to come.
dum discussio venerit, atque ventura ira.

Dies illa, dies irae, calamitatis   O that day, that day of wrath, of calamity
et miseriae, dies magna et amara valde.   and misery, a great day and exceeding bitter.

Strange meeting

It seemed that out of battle I escaped
Down some profound dull tunnel, long since scooped
Through granites which titanic wars had groined.
Yet also there encumbered sleepers groaned,
Too fast in thought or death to be bestirred.
Then, as I probed them, one sprang up, and stared
With piteous recognition in fixed eyes,
Lifting distressful hands as if to bless.
[And by his smile, I knew that sudden hall,
By his dead smile I knew we stood in Hell.
With a thousand pains that vision's face was grained;

            War Requiem, Op. 66 (1961)

Yet no blood reached there from the upper ground,]
And no guns thumped, or down the flues made moan.
'Strange friend,' I said, 'here is no cause to mourn.'
'None,' said the other, 'save the undone years,
The hopelessness. Whatever hope is yours,
Was my life also; I went hunting wild
After the wildest beauty in the world,
[Which lies not calm in eyes, or braided hair,
But mocks the steady running of the hour,
And if it grieves, grieves richlier than here.]
For by my glee might many men have laughed,
And of my weeping something had been left,
Which must die now. I mean the truth untold,
The pity of war, the pity war distilled.
Now men will go content with what we spoiled.
Or, discontent, boil bloody, and be spilled.
They will be swift with swiftness of the tigress,
None will break ranks, though nations trek from progress.
[Courage was mine, and I had mystery,
Wisdom was mine, and I had mastery;
To] miss the march of this retreating world
Into vain citadels that are not walled.
Then, when much blood had clogged their chariot-wheels
I would go up and wash them from sweet wells,
†[Even with truths that lie too deep for taint.
I would have poured my spirit without stint
But not through wounds; not on the cess of war.
Foreheads of men have bled where no wounds were.]
I am the enemy you killed, my friend.
I knew you in this dark; for so you frowned
Yesterday through me as you jabbed and killed.
I parried; but my hands were loath and cold.
Let us sleep now...'

In paradisum deductant te Angeli:	Into Paradise may the Angels lead thee:
in tuo adventu suscipiant te Martyres,	at thy coming may the Martyrs receive
et perducant te in civitatem sanctam	thee, and bring thee into the holy city
Jerusalem. Chorus Angelorum te suscipiat,	Jerusalem. May the Choir of Angels
et cum Lazaro quondam paupere aeternam	receive thee, and with Lazarus, once
habeas requiem.	poor, mayest thou have eternal rest.
	Rest eternal grant unto them, O Lord:
Requiem aeternam dona eis, Domine:	and let light eternal shine upon them.
et lux perpetua luceat eis.	May they rest in peace. Amen.
Requiescant in pace. Amen.	

†Britten replaces these lines with 'Even from wells we sunk too deep for war, / Even
the sweetest wells that ever were.'

War Requiem, Op. 66 (1961)   [223

Psalm 150, Op. 67 (1962)

This setting, for children's voices and instruments, was first performed on 24 June 1963 at the Aldeburgh Festival in the Jubilee Hall by the Northgate School Choir and Orchestra, conducted by Britten. It was written 'For the centenary celebrations of Old Buckenham Hall School – formerly South Lodge School, Lowestoft – July 1962'.

Psalm 150: O praise God

O praise God in his holiness: praise him in the firmament of his power.
Praise him in his noble acts: praise him according to his excellent greatness.
Praise him in the sound of the trumpet: praise him upon the lute and harp.
Praise him in the cymbals and dances: praise him upon the strings and pipe.
Praise him upon the well-tuned cymbals: praise him upon the loud cymbals.
Let everything that hath breath: praise the Lord.

The twelve apostles (1962)

This work was written for Pears and the London Boy Singers and was first performed by them and Britten on 16 June 1962 in Aldeburgh Parish Church at the Aldeburgh Festival. The solo lines exist in several versions; this one was collected in the Southern Appalachians by Cecil Sharp.

TRAD. *The ten commandments* 'The twelve apostles'

Solo I'll sing you one, oh.
Chorus Pray, what is your one, oh?
Solo One is one and all alone and ever more shall be so.
  I'll sing you two, oh.
Chorus What is your two, oh?
Solo Two, two the lily-white boys clothed all in green, oh.
  One is one and all all alone and ever more shall be so.
  I'll sing you three, oh.
Chorus What is your three, oh?
Solo Three, three the riders...
  Four the gospel preachers...
  Five the symbols at your door...
  Six the small belaters...
  Seven the seven stars in the sky...
  Eight the eight archangels...
  Nine the nine bright shiners...
  Ten the ten commandments...
  Eleven the eleven went up to heaven...
  Twelve the twelve apostles.

King Herod and the cock (1962)

Britten's arrangement of this folksong for unison voices and piano was dedicated 'For the London Boy Singers'. This setting was first performed at the Aldeburgh Parish Church on 16 June 1962 by the London Boy Singers with Britten at the piano.

ANON. *King Herod and the cock*

There was a star in David's land,
In David's land appeared,
And in King Herod's chamber
So bright it did shine there.

The wise men stood espièd it
And told the king on high
That a princely babe was born that night
No king shall e'er destroy.

'If this be truth,' King Herod said,
'That thou has said to me,
Then the roasted cock that stands in the dish
Shall crow full senses three.'

O the cock soon thrusten'd and feather'd well
By the work of God's own hand,
And he did crow full senses three
In the dish where he did stand.

Hymn to St Columba: Regis regum rectissimi (1962)

This hymn for chorus and organ was first performed on 2 June 1963 at Gartan, Co. Donegal, by The Ulster Singers, conducted by Havelock Nelson. It was dedicated 'For Derek Hill'.

Regis regum rectissimi   (tr. Ian Hamnett)   attributed to St Columba
'Hymn to St Columba'

Regis regum rectissimi
prope est dies domini,
dies irae et vindictae,
tenebrarum et nebulae,
Regis regum rectissimi,

Near is the Day of the Lord, the most righteous King of Kings, the Day of wrath and vengeance, of darkness and cloud, the Day of the most righteous King of Kings,

Diesque mirabilium
tonitruorum fortium,
dies quoque angustiae,
maeroris ac tristitiae.
Regis regum rectissimi,

The Day too of wonders, of strong thunderings, the Day also of distress, of woe and sadness, the Day of the most righteous King of Kings,

In quo cessabit mulierum
amor et desiderium,
nominumque contentio
mundi hujus et cupido,
Regis regum rectissimi.

In which love and desire for women will cease, and competition for fame, and longing for the things of this world, the Day of the most righteous King of Kings.

Cantata misericordium, Op. 69 (1963)

This cantata, for tenor and baritone solos, chorus, string quartet, orchestra and piano, was first performed on 1 September 1963 in Geneva, 'In honorem Societatis Crucis Rubrae'. Its first British performance was on 12 September, with Pears, Thomas Hemsley, BBC Chorus and the LSO, conducted by Britten. The work was dedicated to Fidelity Cranbrook.

PATRICK WILKINSON   *Cantata misericordium*

Chorus Beati misericordes.
Beati qui dolore corporis afflictis succurrunt.
Audite vocem Romani:

Tenor 'Deus est mortali iuvare mortalem.'

Chorus Audite vocem Iudaei:

Barytonus 'Proximum tuum, sicut te ipsum, ama.'

Tenor et barytonus At proximus meus quis est?

Chorus Iesu parabola iam nobis fiat fabula.

Chorus En viator qui descendit ab Ierusalem in Iericho.

Viator Ah quam longa est haec via, quam per deserta loca.
Terret me solitudo, terret omnis rupes, omne arbustum.
Insidias timeo. Heus, asine, propera, propera.

Chorus Blessed are the merciful.
Blessed are those who succour the afflicted in body.
Hear the voice of a Roman:
Tenor 'For man to love man is God.'
Chorus Hear the voice of a Jew:
Baritone 'Thou shalt love thy neighbour as thyself.'
Tenor and baritone But who is my neighbour?
Chorus Let us enact now a parable of Jesus.
Chorus Behold a traveller going down from Jerusalem to Jericho.
Traveller (Baritone) Ah how long this way is, how desolate the country!
I am afraid of the solitude, of every rock, of every shrub. I fear an ambush. Hey, donkey, hurry, hurry.

Chorus Cave, viator, cave! Latent istis in umbris latrones.
Iam prodeunt, iam circumstant. Cave, viator, cave!

Viator Qui estis homines? Cur me sic intuemini? Atat! Plaga!
Atatae! Pugnis, fustibus vapulo. Iam spolior, nudor.
Quo fugit asinus? Eheu relinquor humi prostratus, semivivus,
solus, inops.

Chorus Ubi nunc latrones isti? Quam cito ex oculis elapsi sunt.
Solitudo ubique, solitudo et silentium. Quis huic succurent in
tanta vasitate?

Chorus Beware, traveller, beware! Robbers are lurking in those shadows. Now they are
coming forward, now they are surrounding you. Beware, traveller, beware!
Traveller What men are you? Why do you look at me like that? Oh, a blow! Oh! Oh!
Fists and cudgels! Robbed and stripped! Where has my ass gone? Alas, I am left
prostrate on the ground, half dead, alone, helpless.
Chorus Where have those robbers gone? How quickly they have vanished. Solitude
everywhere, solitude and silence. Who will help this man in such a wilderness?

Chorus Bono nunc animo es, viator. Nam tibi appropinquat
iter faciens qui habitu est sacerdos. Is certe sublevabit.
Compella eum.

Viator Subveni, ah subveni: ne patere me mori.

Chorus Dure sacerdos, quid oculos avertis? Quid procul
praeteris? Ut praeterit, ut abit ex oculis homo sacerrimus.

Chorus Be of good cheer, traveller: there is someone approaching along the road who by
his dress is a priest. Surely he will rescue you. Hail him.
Traveller Help, oh help me: do not let me die.
Chorus Hard-hearted priest, why do you look away, why do you pass by on the other
side? See, he is passing by, he is vanishing from sight, the accursed holy man!

Chorus En alter in conspectum venit. Tolle rursus, abiecte,
animos.
Qui accedit est Levita. Is certe sublevabit.

Viator Fer opem, fer opem atrociter mihi vulnerato.

Chorus O ferrea hominum corda! Hic quoque conspexit
iacentem, praeteriit, acceleravit gradum. Timetne
cadaveris ne tactu polluatur? I nunc, sacrosancte
Levita, legis tuae praescriptiones inhumanas observa.

Chorus Look, another is coming in sight. Raise your spirits, outcast, again. The man
who is coming is a Levite. He surely will rescue you.
Traveller Give me aid, give me aid; I am terribly wounded.
Chorus Oh the hard hearts of men! This one too saw him lying there, passed by and
hastened his pace. Is he afraid of being polluted by touching a corpse? Go on, sacrosanct
Levite, observe the inhuman prescriptions of your law.

Cantata misericordium, Op. 69 (1963)   [229

Chorus Ecce, tertius apparet – sed languescit spes auxilii: nam propior
   videtur esse contemptus Samaritanus. Quid interest Samaritani Iudaei
   negotia suscipere molesta?

Viator Miserere mei, hospes, afflicti.

Samaritanus Ah, di bono! Quid audio? Quid ante pedes iam video? Iacet
   hic nescioquis immania passus. Age, primum haec vulnera adligem. Ubi
   mihi vinum? Ubi oleum? Sursum, iam sursum imponam te in tergum
   iumenti mei.

Chorus Vincit, ecce, vincit tandem misericordia. Hic pedes ipse comitatur
   eum in deversorium.

Chorus See now, a third is appearing – but hope of relief is fading: for from near he is
seen to be only a despised Samaritan. What interest has a Samaritan in taking up the
troublesome affairs of a Jew?
Traveller Pity me, stranger, pity me: I am suffering.
Samaritan (Tenor) Ah, good gods! What do I hear? What do I see before my feet? Here
lies someone who has been horribly treated. Come, first let me bind up these wounds.
Where is my wine, my oil? Up, now I will lift you up on to the back of my beast.
Chorus Triumph! Mercy is triumphing at last. This man is accompanying him to an inn
himself on foot.

Samaritanus Ohe, caupo, siquid audis: aperi portam. Viatorem
   adfero a latronibus spoliatum. Aperi, quaeso... Benigne.
   Para nobis cenam, caupo, para cubiculum, amabo.
   Mihi cras abeundum erit. Cura hunc dum convalescat.
   Dabo tibi duos denarios.

Viator Iam rursus revivesco. Iam spes in animum redit.
   Optime hospitum, quis es? Unde es gentium?
   Salvus quomodo tibi gratias referam dignas?

Samaritanus Quis sim, unde sim gentium, parce quarere.
   Dormi nunc, amice, dormi: iniuriarum obliviscere.

Samaritan Ho, innkeeper, do you hear? Open the door. I have with me a traveller who
has been stripped by robbers. Open, please... Thank you.
Prepare us supper, innkeeper, and a room, please. Tomorrow I shall have to go on. Look
after this man till he gets better. I will give you two denarii.
Traveller I am coming back to life again. Hope is reviving in me. Best of strangers, who
are you? From what people do you come? I am saved, and how can I thank you worthily?
Samaritan Who I am, and what my people, ask no more. Sleep now, my friend, sleep:
forget your injuries.

Chorus Mitis huius adiutoris qui servavit saucium
Proximumque sibi duxit hospitem incognitum,
O si similes existant ubicumque gentium!
Morbus gliscit, Mars incedit, fames late superat;
Sed mortales, alter quando alterum sic sublevat,
E dolore procreata caritas consociat.

Tenor et barytonus Quis sit proximus tuus iam scis.

Chorus Vade et tu fac similiter.

Chorus O that men like this gentle helper, who saved a wounded man and treated as his neighbour an unknown stranger, may be found all over the world. Disease is spreading, war is stalking, famine reigns far and wide.
But when one mortal relieves another like this, charity springing from pain unites them.
Tenor and baritone Who your neighbour is, now you know.
Chorus Go and do likewise.

Songs and Proverbs of William Blake, Op. 74 (1965)

The settings of these Songs and Proverbs, for baritone and piano, were first performed on 24 June 1965 at the Aldeburgh Festival by Dietrich Fischer-Dieskau and Britten. The texts were selected by Pears from Blake's *Songs of Experience, Auguries of Innocence* and *Proverbs of Hell*. Britten wrote to Peter du Sautoy: 'When I think of the wonderful words I feel rather inadequate.'

WILLIAM BLAKE   *Songs and Proverbs*

Proverbs 22–5

The pride of the peacock is the glory of God.
The lust of the goat is the bounty of God.
The wrath of the lion is the wisdom of God.
The nakedness of woman is the work of God.

London

I wander thro' each charter'd street,
Near where the charter'd Thames does flow
And mark in every face I meet
Marks of weakness, marks of woe.

In every cry of every Man,
In every Infant's cry of fear,
In every voice, in every ban,
The mind-forg'd manacles I hear.

How the Chimney-sweeper's cry
Every black'ning Church appalls,
And the hapless Soldier's sigh
Runs in blood down Palace walls.

But most thro' midnight streets I hear
How the youthful Harlot's curse
Blasts the new-born Infant's tear
And blights with plagues the Marriage hearse.

Proverb 21

Prisons are built with stones of Law, brothels
with bricks of Religion.

The Chimney-sweeper

A little black thing among the snow,
Crying 'weep 'weep in notes of woe!
'Where are thy father & mother? say?'
'They are both gone up to the church to pray.

'Because I was happy upon the heath,
'And smil'd among the winter's snow
'They clothed me in the clothes of death,
'And taught me to sing the notes of woe.

'And because I am happy & dance & sing
'They think they have done me no injury,
'And are gone to praise God & his Priest & King
'Who make up a heaven of our misery.'

Proverb 31

The bird a nest, the spider a web, man friendship.

A Poison Tree

I was angry with my friend:
I told my wrath, my wrath did end.
I was angry with my foe:
I told it not, my wrath did grow.

And I water'd it in fears,
Night & morning with my tears;
And I sunned it with smiles,
And with soft deceitful wiles.

And it grew both day and night,
Till it bore an apple bright.
And my foe beheld it shine,
And he knew that it was mine.

And into my garden stole
When the night had veil'd the pole:

In the morning glad I see
My foe outstretch'd beneath the tree.

Proverb 41

Think in the morning. Act in the noon.
Eat in the evening. Sleep in the night.

The Tyger

Tyger! Tyger! burning bright
In the forests of the night,
What immortal hand or eye
Could frame thy fearful symmetry?

In what distant deeps or skies
Burnt the fire of thine eyes?
On what wings dare he aspire?
What the hand dare seize the fire?

And what shoulder, & what art,
Could twist the sinews of thy heart?
And when thy heart began to beat,
What dread hand? & what dread feet?

What the hammer? what the chain?
In what furnace was thy brain?
What the anvil? What dread grasp
Dare its deadly terrors clasp?

When the stars threw down their spears,
And water'd heaven with their tears,
Did he smile his work to see?
Did he who made the Lamb make thee?

Tyger! Tyger! burning bright
In the forests of the night,
What immortal hand or eye
Dare frame thy fearful symmetry?

Proverbs 44, 18, 52

The tygers of wrath are wiser than the horses of instruction.
If the fool would persist in his folly he would become wise.
If others had not been foolish, we should be so.

Songs and Proverbs of William Blake, Op. 74 (1965)

The Fly

Little Fly,
Thy summer's play
My thoughtless hand
Has brush'd away.

Am not I
A fly like thee?
Or art not thou
A man like me?

For I dance,
And drink & sing,
Till some blind hand
Shall brush my wing.

If thought is life
And strength & breath
And the want
Of thought is death;

Then am I
A happy fly,
If I live,
Or if I die.

Proverbs 12, 11, 10

The hours of folly are measur'd by the clock;
  but of wisdom, no clock can measure.
The busy bee has no time for sorrow.
Eternity is in love with the productions of time.

Ah, Sun-flower

Ah, Sun-flower! weary of time,
Who countest the steps of the Sun,
Seeking after that sweet golden clime,
Where the traveller's journey is done:

Where the Youth pined away with desire,
And the pale Virgin shrouded in snow,
Arise from their graves, and aspire
Where my Sun-flower wishes to go.

Auguries of Innocence

To see a World in a Grain of Sand
And a Heaven in a Wild Flower,
Hold Infinity in the palm of your hand
And Eternity in an hour.
[A Robin Red breast in a Cage
Puts all Heaven in a Rage.
A dove house fill'd with doves & Pigeons
Shudders Hell thro' all its regions.
A dog starv'd at his Master's Gate
Predicts the ruin of the State.
A Horse misus'd upon the Road
Calls to Heaven for Human blood.
Each outcry of the hunted hare
A fibre from the Brain does tear.
A Skylark wounded in the wing,
A Cherubim does cease to sing.
The Game Cock clip'd & arm'd for fight
Does the Rising Sun affright.
Every Wolf's & Lion's howl
Raises from Hell a Human Soul... †
A truth that's told with bad intent
Beats all the Lies you can invent.
It is right it should be so;
Man was made for Joy & Woe;
And when this we rightly know
Thro' the World we safely go.
Joy & Woe are woven fine,
A Clothing for the Soul divine;
Under every grief & pine
Runs a joy with silken twine.
The Babe is more than swadling Bands;
Throughout all these Human Lands
Tools were made, & Born were hands,
Every Farmer Understands.
Every Tear from Every Eye
Becomes a Babe in Eternity;
This is caught by Females bright
And return'd to its own delight.
The Bleat, the Bark, Bellow & Roar
Are Waves that Beat on Heaven's Shore.
The Babe that weeps the Rod beneath
Writes Revenge in realms of death.

Songs and Proverbs of William Blake, Op. 74 (1965)

The Beggar's Rags, fluttering in Air,
Does to Rags the Heavens tear.
The Soldier, arm'd with Sword & Gun,
Palsied strikes the Summer's Sun.
The poor Man's Farthing is worth more
Than all the Gold on Afric's Shore.
One Mite wrung from the Labrer's hands
Shall buy & sell the Miser's Lands:
Or, if protected from on high,
Does that whole Nation sell & buy.
He who mocks the Infant's Faith
Shall be mock'd in Age & Death.
He who shall teach the Child to Doubt
The rotting Grave shall ne'er get out.
He who respects the Infant's faith
Triumphs over Hell & Death.
The Child's Toys & the Old Man's Reasons
Are the Fruits of the Two seasons.
The Questioner, who sits so sly,
Shall never know how to Reply.
He who replies to words of Doubt
Doth put the Light of Knowledge out.
The Strongest Poison ever known
Came from Caesar's Laurel Crown.
Nought can deform the Human Race
Like to the Armour's iron brace.
When Gold & Gems adorn the Plow
To peaceful Arts shall Envy Bow.
A Riddle or the Cricket's Cry
Is to Doubt a fit Reply.
The Emmet's Inch & Eagle's Mile
Make Lame Philosophy to smile.
He who Doubts from what he sees
Will ne'er Believe, do what you Please.
If the Sun & Moon should doubt,
They'd immediately Go out.
To be in a Passion you Good may do,
But no Good if a Passion is in you.
The Whore & Gambler, by the State
Licenc'd, build that Nation's Fate.
The Harlot's cry from Street to Street
Shall weave Old England's winding Sheet.

Songs and Proverbs of William Blake, Op. 74 (1965) [237

The Winner's Shout, the Loser's Curse,
Dance before dead England's Hearse.]
Every Night & every Morn
Some to Misery are Born.
Every Morn & every Night
Some are Born to sweet delight.
Some are Born to sweet delight,
Some are Born to Endless Night.
We are led to Believe a Lie
When we see not Thro' the Eye
Which was Born in a Night to perish in a Night
When the Soul Slept in Beams of Light.
God Appears & God is Light
To those poor Souls who dwell in Night;
But does a Human Form Display
To those who Dwell in Realms of day.

†32 lines omitted.

Songs and Proverbs of William Blake, Op. 74 (1965)

Voices for today, Op. 75 (1965)

This anthem, for chorus (men, women and children) and organ (ad lib.), was commissioned for the twentieth anniversary of the United Nations and was first performed on 24 October 1965 in London, by the LSO Chorus, choristers of Westminster Abbey, Ralph Downes, and conductors Istvan Kertesz and Douglas Guest; in Paris by the chorus and boys of the French Radio Choir, conductors Jacques Jauineau and Jean-Paul Kreder; and in New York by Schola Cantorum, Farmingdale Boys' Choir, Richard Foster, and conductors Hugh Ross and Arpad Darazs.

If you have ears to hear, then hear!
(JESUS CHRIST)

The Beloved of the Gods wishes that all people should be unharmed,
self-controlled, calm in mind, and gentle.
(ASOKA)

Love your enemies; do good to those that hate you.
(JESUS CHRIST)

Where is the equal of Love? Where is the battle he cannot win?
(SOPHOCLES)

The strong and mighty topple from their place,
The supple and weak rise above them all.
(LAO TZU)

Force is not a remedy.
(BRIGHT)

Justice is a better procurer of peace than war.
(PENN)

Dismantle the fort,
Cut down the fleet –
Battle no more shall be!
(MELVILLE)

The fruits of the spirit are slower to ripen than intercontinental missiles.
(CAMUS)

Burning stakes do not lighten the darkness.
(LEC)

Telling lies to the young is wrong.
Proving to them that lies are true is wrong.
The young know what you mean. The young are people.
(YEVTUSHENKO)

Everything that lives is holy.
(BLAKE)

Give us back a heart, a lasting hope in life. Innocent peace!
(HÖLDERLIN)

Ring out the thousand wars of old,
Ring in the thousand years of peace.
(TENNYSON)

How blessed are the peacemakers; God shall call them his sons.
(JESUS CHRIST)

Silence the raging battle with Heaven's melodies of peace.
(HÖLDERLIN)

We have nothing to lose, except everything. So let us go ahead.
This is the challenge of our generation.
(CAMUS)

The world's great age begins anew,
The golden years return.
(SHELLEY)

If you have ears to hear, then hear!

VIRGIL   (tr. John Connington)   *Eclogue IV*   'Ultima Cumaei'

[Sicelides Musae, paulo maiora canamus.
non omnis arbusta iuvant humilesque myricae;
si canimus silvas, silvae sint consule dignae.]
      Ultima Cumaei venit iam carminis aetas;
magnus ab integro saeclorum nascitur ordo.
iam redit et Virgo, redeunt Saturnia regna;
iam nova progenies caelo demittitur alto.
tu modo nascenti puero, quo ferrea primum
desinet ac toto surget gens aurea mundo,
casta fave Lucina: tuus iam regnat Apollo.
[teque adeo decus hoc aevi, te consule, inibit,
Pollio, et incipient magni procedere menses;
te duce, si qua manent sceleris vestigia nostri,
inrita perpetua solvent formidine terras.
ille deum vitam accipiet divisque videbit
permixtos heroas et ipse videbitur illis,
pacatumque reget patriis virtutibus orbem.]
      At tibi prima, puer, nullo munuscula cultu
errantes hederas passim cum baccare tellus
mixtaque ridenti colocasia fundet acantho.
ipsae lacte domum referent distente capellae
ubera, nec magnos metuent armenta leones;

If you have ears to hear, then hear!

[Muses of Sicily, let us strike a somewhat louder chord. It is not for all that plan-
tations have charms, or groundling tamarisks. If we are to sing of the woodland,
let the woodland rise to a consul's dignity.]
      The last era of the song of Cuma has come at length; the grand file of the ages
is being born anew; at length the virgin is returning, returning to the reign of
Saturn; at length a new generation is descending from heaven on high. Do but
thou smile thy pure smile on the birth of the boy who shall at last bring the race
of iron to an end, and bid the golden race spring up all the world over – thou,
Lucina – thine own Apollo is at length on his throne. [In thy consulship it is – in
thine, Pollio – that this glorious time shall come on, and the mighty months
begin their march. Under thy conduct, any remaining trace of our national guilt
shall become void, and release the world from the thraldom of perpetual fear. He
shall have the life of the gods conferred on him, and shall see gods and heroes
mixing together, and shall himself be seen of them, and with his father's virtues
shall govern a world at peace.]
      For thee, sweèt boy, the earth of her own unforced will shall pour forth a
child's first presents – gadding ivy and foxglove everywhere, and Egyptian bean
blending with the bright smiling acanthus. Of themselves, the goats shall carry
home udders distended with milk; nor shall the herds fear huge lions in the way.

ipsa tibi blandos fundent cunabula flores.
Occidet et serpens, et fallax herba veneni
occidet; Assyrium volgo nascetur amomum.
[At simul heroum laudes et facta parentis
iam legere et quae sit poteris cognoscere virtus.
molli paulatim flavescet campus arista,
incultisque rubens pendebit sentibus uva
et durae quercus sudabunt roscida mella.
pauca tamen suberunt priscae vestigia fraudis,
quae temptare Thetim ratibus, quae cingere muris
oppida, quae iubeant telluri infindere sulcos.
alter erit tum Tiphys, et altera quae vehat Argo
delectos heroas; erunt etiam altera bella
atque iterum ad Troiam magnus mittetur Achilles.]
    Hinc ubi iam firmata virum te fecerit aetas,
cedet et ipse mari vector, nec nautica pinus
mutabit merces; omnis feret omnia tellus.
non rastros patietur humus, non vinea falcem;
robustus quoque iam tauris iuga solvet arator;
nec varios discet mentiri lana colores,
ipse sed in pratis aries iam suave rubenti

Of itself, thy grassy cradle shall pour out flowers to caress thee. Death to the serpent, and to the treacherous plant of poisoned juice. Assyrian spices shall spring up by the wayside.

[But soon as thou shalt be of an age to read at length of the glories of heroes and thy father's deeds, and to acquaint thyself with the nature of manly work, the yellow of the waving corn shall steal gradually over the plain, and from briers, that know nought of culture, grapes shall hang in purple clusters, and the stubborn heart of oak shall exude dews of honey. Still, under all this show, some few traces shall remain of the sin and guile of old – such as may prompt men to defy the ocean goddess with their ships, to build towns with walls round them, to cleave furrows in the soil of earth. A second Tiphys shall there be in those days – a second Argo to convey the flower of chivalry; a second war of heroes, too, shall there be, and a second time shall Achilles be sent in his greatness to Troy.]

Afterwards, when ripe years have at length made thee man, even the peaceful sailor shall leave the sea, nor shall the good ship of pine exchange merchandise – all lands shall produce all things; the ground shall not feel the harrow, nor the vineyard the pruning-hook; the sturdy ploughman, too, shall at length set his bullocks free from the yoke; nor shall wool be taught to counterfeit varied hues, but of himself, as he feeds in the meadows, the ram shall transform his fleece, now into a lovely purple dye, now into saffron yellow – of its own will, scarlet shall clothe the lambs as they graze. [Ages like these, flow on! – so cried to their spindles the Fates, uttering in concert the fixed will of destiny.

murice, iam croceo mutabit vellera luto;
sponte sua sandyx pascentes vestiet agnos.
['Talia saecla' suis dixerunt 'currite' fusis
concordes stabili fatorum numine Parcae.
　　Adgredere o magnos (aderit iam tempus) honores,
cara deum suboles, magnum Iovis incrementum!]
aspice convexo nutantem pondere mundum
terrasque tractusque maris caelumque profundum;
aspice venturo laetentur ut omnia saeclo!
[o mihi tum longae maneat pars ultima vitae,
spiritus et, quantum sat erit tua dicere facta:
non me carbinimus vincet nec Thracius Orpheus,
nec Linus, huic mater quamvis atque huic pater adsit,
Orphei Calliopea, Lino formosus Apollo.
Pan etiam, Arcadia mecum si iudice certet,
Pan etiam Arcadia dicat se iudice victum.]
Incipe, parve puer, risu cognoscere matrem:
matri longa decem tulerunt fastidia menses.
incipe, parve puer: [cui non risere parentes,
nec deus hunc mensa, dea nec dignata cubili est.]

Assume thine august dignities – the time is at length at hand – thou best-loved offspring of the gods, august scion of Jove!] Look upon the world as it totters beneath the mass of its overhanging dome – earth and the expanse of sea and the deep of heaven – look how all are rejoicing in the age that is to be! [may my life's last days last long enough and breath be granted me enough to tell of thy deeds! I will be o'ermatched in song by none – not by Orpheus of Thrace, nor by Linus, though that were backed by his mother, and this by his father – Orpheus by Calliope, Linus by Apollo in his beauty. Were Pan himself, with Arcady looking on, to enter the lists with me, Pan himself, with Arcady looking on, should own himself vanquished.]

Begin, sweet child, with a smile, to take notice of thy mother – that mother has had ten months of tedious sickness and loathing. Begin, sweet child – [the babe on whom never parent smiled, never grew to serve the table of a god or the bed of a goddess!]

The Poet's Echo, Op. 76 (1965)

This group of poems by Alexandr Pushkin (set in Russian) was first performed on 2 December 1965 at the Conservatoire of Music, Moscow, by Galina Vishnevskaya and Mstislav Rostropovitch. It was dedicated 'For Galya and Slava'. Vishnevskaya said that Britten 'had succeeded in penetrating the very heart of the verse'. The subject of 'Epigram' was Count M.S. Vorontsov, Pushkin's chief in Odessa. He was brought up in England ('Half a milord') and had financial interests in Odessa ('half of a boss').

ALEXANDR SERGEEVICH PUSHKIN   (tr. Peter Pears)

ЭХО (*The poet's echo*)

Ревет ли зверь в лесу глухом,	From leafy woods the savage howl,
Трубит ли рог, гремит ли гром,	A distant horn, the thunder's roll,
Поет ли дева за холмом –	A maiden singing up the hill,
На всякий звук	To every sound
Свой отклик в воздухе пустом	Your answering cry the air doth fill
Родишъ ты вдруг.	In quick rebound.
Ты внемлешъ грохоту громов,	You listen for the thunder's voice,
И гласу бури и валов,	The ocean wave's wild stormy noise,
И крику сельских пастухов –	The distant mountain-shepherd's cries
И шлешъ ответ;	You answer free;
Тебе ж нет отзыва ... Таков	To you comes no reply. Likewise
И ты, поэт!	O poet, to thee!

Я ДУМАЛ, СЕРДЦЕ ПОЗАБЫЛО (*My heart*)

Я думал, сердце позабыло	My heart, I fancied it was over,
Слособность легкую страдать,	That road of suffering and pain,
Я говорил: тому, что было,	And I resolved: 'Tis gone for ever,
Уж не бывать! уж не бывать!	Never again! never again!
Прошли восторги, и печали,	That ancient rapture and its yearning,
И легковерные мечты ...	The dreams, the credulous desire ...
Но вот опять затрепетали	But now old wounds have started burning
Лред мощной властью красоты.	Inflamed by beauty and her fire.

АНГЕЛ (*Angel*)

В дверях здема ангел нежный	At Eden's gate a gentle angel
Главой поникшею сиял,	With lowered head stood shining bright,
А демон мрачный и мятежный	While Satan sullen and rebellious
Над адской бездною летал.	O'er Hell's abysses took his flight.

Дух отрицанъя, дух сомненъя
На духа чистого взирал
И жар невольный умиленья
Впервые смутно познавал.

« Прости, – он рек, – тебя я видел,
И ты недаром мне сиял:
Не всё я в небе ненавидел,
Не всё я в мире презирал».

Soul of negation, soul of envy,
He gazed at that angelic light,
And warm and tender glowed within him
A strange confusion at the sight.

'Forgive,' he said, 'now I have seen thee,
Not vainly didst thou shine so bright:
Not all in heaven have I hated,
Not all things human earn my spite.'

СОЛОВЕЙ И РОЗА (*The nightingale and the rose*)

В безмолвии садов, весной, во мгле ночей,
Поет над розою восточный соловей.
Но роза милая не чувствует, не внемлет,
И под влюбленный гимн колеблется и дремлет.
Не так ли ты поешь для хладной красоты?
Опомнись, о поэт, к чему стремишься ты?
Она не слушает, не чувствует поэта;
Глядишь – она цветет; взываешь – нет ответа.

The garden's dark and still; 'tis spring; no night wind blows.
He sings! the nightingale, his love song to the rose.
She does not hearken, his rose beloved, disdainful,
And to his amorous hymn, she dozes, nodding and swaying.
With such words would you melt cold beauty into fire?
O poet, be aware how far you would aspire!
She is not listening, no poems can entrance her;
You gaze; she only flowers; you call her; there's no answer.

ЭПИГРАММА (*Epigram*)

Полу-милорд, полу-купец,
Полу-мудрец, полу-невежда,
Полу-подлец, но есть надежда,
Что будет полным наконец.

Half a milord, half of a boss,
Half of a sage, half of a baby,
Half of a cheat; there's hope that maybe
He'll be a whole one by and by.

СТИХИ, СОЧИНЕННЫЕ НОЧЬЮ ВО ВРЕМЯ ВЕССОННИЦЫ
(*Lines written during a sleepless night*)

Мне не спится, нет огня;
Всюду мрак и сон докучный.
Ход часов лишь однозвучный
Раздается близ меня,
Парки бабье лепетанье,
Спящей ночи трепетанье,
Жизни мышья беготня ...
Что тревожишь ты меня?
Что ты значишь, скучный шопот?
Укоризна, или ропот
Мной утраченного дня?
От меня чего ты хочешь?
Ты зовешь или пророчишь?
Я понять тебя хочу,
Смысла я в тебе ищу ...

Sleep forsakes me with the light;
Shadowy gloom and haunting darkness;
Time ticks on its way relentless
And its sound invades the night.
Fateful crones are at their mumbling,
Set the sleepy night atrembling,
Scurrying mouse-like, life slips by ...
Why do you disturb me, say?
What's your purpose, tedious whispers?
Do you breathe reproachful murmurs
At my lost and wasted day?
What is this you want to tell me?
Do you prophesy or call me?
Answer me, I long to hear!
Voices, make your meaning clear ...

The 'Golden Vanity', Op. 78 (1966)

This 'vaudeville for boys and pianos after the old English ballad' was written at the request of the Vienna Boys' Choir, who particularly asked that they should not play girls parts. It was first performed by them, conducted by Anton Neyder, at The Maltings, Snape, during the Aldeburgh Festival on 3 June 1967. It was dedicated 'Für die Wiener Sängerknaben'.

COLIN GRAHAM *The 'Golden Vanity'*

A ship I have got in the North Country
And she goes by the name of the *Golden Vanity*,
O I fear she'll be taken by a Spanish Ga-la-lee,
    As she sails by the Low-lands low.

To the Captain then upspake the little Cabin-boy,
He said, 'What is my fee, if the galley I destroy?
The Spanish Ga-la-lee, if no more it shall annoy,
    As you sail by the Low-lands low.'

'Of silver and gold I will give to you a store;
And my pretty little daughter that dwelleth on the shore,
Of treasure and of fee as well, I'll give to thee galore,
    As we sail by the Low-lands low.'

Then they row'd him up tight in a black bull's skin,
And he held all in his hand an augur sharp and thin,
And he swam until he came to the Spanish Gal-a-lin,
    As she lay by the Low-lands low.

He bored with his augur, he bored once and twice,
And some were playing cards, and some were playing dice,
When the water flowèd in it dazzled their eyes,
    And she sank by the Low-lands low.

So the Cabin-boy did swim all to the larboard side,
Saying 'Captain! take me in, I am drifting with the tide!'
'I will shoot you! I will kill you!' the cruel Captain cried,
    'You may sink by the Low-lands low.'

Then the Cabin-boy did swim all to the starboard side,
Saying, 'Messmates, take me in, I am drifting with the tide!'
Then they laid him on the deck, and he closed his eyes
and died,
    As they sailed by the Low-lands low.

They sew'd his body tight in an old cow's hide,
And they cast the gallant cabin-boy out over the ship side,
And left him without more ado to drift with the tide,
    And to sink by the Low-lands low.

The building of the house, Op. 79 (1967)

This setting of Psalm 127 was written for the Inaugural Concert of the new Maltings Concert Hall, Snape, and was performed by the English Chamber Orchestra and a chorus of East Anglian choirs, conducted by Britten, on 2 June 1967.

PSALM 127   *Except the Lord the house doth make*
'The building of the house'
(adapted by Imogen Holst from the *Whole Book of Psalms*, 1613)

Except the Lord the house doth make,
And thereunto doth set his hand,
What men do build it cannot stand:
Likewise in vain men undertake
Cities and holds to watch and ward,
Except the Lord to be their safeguard.

Though ye rise early in the morn
And so at night go late to bed,
Feeding full hardly with brown bread,
Yet were your labour lost and worn:
But they shall thrive whom God doth bless,
Their house shall stand through storm and stress,
                                        Amen

THE BIBLE, PSALM 127   *Except the Lord build the house*

Except the Lord build the house: their labour is but lost that build it.
Except the Lord keep the city: the watchman waketh but in vain.
It is but lost labour that ye haste to rise up early, and so late take rest, and
    eat the bread of carefulness: for so he giveth his beloved sleep.
Lo, children and the fruit of the womb: are an heritage and gift that cometh
    of the Lord.
Like the arrows in the hand of the giant: even so are the young children.
Happy is the man that hath his quiver full of them: they shall not be
    ashamed when they speak with their enemies in the gate.

The oxen (1967)

This carol for women's voices and piano was dedicated 'For Cecily Smithwick [Peter Pears's sister] and the East Coker W.I.'

THOMAS HARDY   *The oxen*

Christmas eve and twelve of the clock.
   'Now they are all on their knees,'
An elder said as we sat in a flock
   By the embers in hearthside ease.

We pictured the meek mild creatures where
   They dwelt in their strawy pen,
Nor did it occur to one of us there
   To doubt they were kneeling then.

So fair a fancy few would weave
   In these years! Yet, I feel,
If someone said on Christmas Eve,
   'Come; see the oxen kneel

'In the lonely barton by yonder coomb
   Our childhood used to know,'
I should go with him in the gloom,
   Hoping it might be so.

Children's crusade, Op. 82 (1968)
(Kinderkreuzzug)

This ballad for children's voices, percussion, two pianos and chamber/ electronic organ was 'Written for the members of Wandsworth School Choir and Orchestra (director Russell Burgess) to perform on the 50th Anniversary of The Save The Children Fund at St Paul's Cathedral, 19th May 1969'. It was conducted by Burgess. It was dedicated 'To Hans Werner Henze'.

BERTOLT BRECHT   (tr. Hans Keller, with Britten & Pears)

Children's crusade

In Poland, in nineteen thirty-nine,
There was the bloodiest fight:
Turning every town and village
Into a wilderness of night.

Young sisters had lost their brothers,
Young wives their men at war;
In the blaze and the heaps of rubble
Children found their parents no more.

Nothing has come out of Poland,
Letter or printed report;
But in the East runs a story
Of the most curious sort.

Snow fell as they told one another
There in an Eastern town,
About a children's crusade:
Deep in Poland, wandering round.

Lost children were scuttling, hungry;
In little formations were seen.
There they gathered with others
Standing where villages once had been.

They wanted to fly from the fighting,
Let the nightmare cease;
And one fine day they'd come
Upon a land, where there was peace.

They had their little leader,
Keeping them on the go,
But he'd a terrible worry:
The way he just did not know.

A little Jew was found marching in step:
He had a velvety collar,
He was used to the whitest bread,
And yet he showed much valour.

Once two brothers joined the pack,
Tried strategic campaigning
When they stormed a peasant's empty shack,
They left it because it was raining.

A thin, grey boy kept himself apart,
He avoided provocation.
He was marked by a fearful guilt:
He came from the Nazi legation.

And there was among them a drummer boy,
He found drum and drumsticks in a village shop
        that had been raided,
The troop allowed no drumming:
Noise would have betrayed it.

And there was a dog,
They'd caught him to eat him;
Kept him on as an eater:
That was the only way to treat him.

They had their symphony
By a waterfall in the snow:
Our drummer boy could use his drumsticks,
Since nobody could hear him, no!

And then there was some loving.
She was twelve, he was fifteen; there,
In a ruined cottage,
She sat and combed his hair.

But love, it is not for ever –
Not in the biting cold,
For how can the saplings blossom
With so much snow to hold?

Then there was a war,
War against some other children on the run;
And the war just simply ended:
Sense it had none.

And then there was a trial,
On either side burned a candle.
What an embarrassing affair!
The judge condemned! – What a scandal!

Then there was a funeral,
Velvet Collar it was whom they buried,
The body by Polish and German bearers
To burial was carried.

Protestants and Catholics, and Nazis were there,
To consign him to his mother earth.
At the end they heard a little socialist
Talk with confidence of mankind's rebirth.

So there was faith, there was hope too,
But no meat or bread.
Had people who cuffed them for stealing
Offered them shelter instead!

But none should rebuke the needy man
Who would not part with a slice:
For fifty-odd children you need flour,
Flour, not sacrifice.

They wandered steadily southward.
South is there, where the sun
Stands high at midday
For everyone.

Once, to be sure, they found a soldier
Wounded, in pinewoods he lay.
They tended him seven days,
So that he could tell them the way.

He spoke up clearly, 'To Bilgoray!'
His fever made him rave.
An eighth day he did not live to see:
For him too they dug a grave.

Children's crusade, Op.82 (1968)

True, there was a signpost also:
Deep in the snow they found.
In fact it had ceased to show the way:
Someone had turned it round.

And when they hunted for Bilgoray
Nowhere could they find it.

They stood there, around their leader.
He looked at the snow-laden air,
And made a sign with his little hand,
And told them: it must be there.

Where once the south-east of Poland was
In raging blizzard keen.
There were our five-and-fifty
Last to be seen.

Whenever I close my eyes
I see them wander
There from this old farmhouse destroyed by the war
To another ruined house yonder.

High above them, in the clouded sky
I see others swarming, surging, many!
There they wander, braving icy blizzards,
(Homes and aims they haven't any)

Searching for a land where peace reigns,
No more fire, no more thunder,
Nothing like the world they're leaving,
Mighty crowds too great to number.

In Poland, in that same January,
They caught a dog, half strangled:
A cord was hung from his scraggy neck,
And from it a notice dangled.

Saying this: PLEASE COME AND HELP US!
WHERE WE ARE, WE CANNOT SAY.
WE ARE THE FIVE-AND-FIFTY.
THE DOG KNOWS THE WAY.

The writing was in a childish hand.
Peasants had read it over.
Since then more than a year has gone by.
The dog starved: he didn't recover.

Children's crusade, Op.82 (1968)   [253

Who Are these Children?, Op. 84 (1969)

This work for tenor and piano was first performed on 4 May 1971 at the National Gallery of Scotland, Edinburgh, by Pears and Britten. It was dedicated 'To Tertia Liebenthal'.

WILLIAM SOUTAR *Lyrics, rhymes and riddles*

A riddle

There's pairt o' it young
And pairt o' it auld:
There's pairt o' it het
And pairt o' it cauld:

There's pairt o' it bare
And pairt o' it claid:
There's pairt o' it quick
And pairt o' it dead.

(Answer: *the earth*)

A laddie's sang

hillsides above	O! it's owre the braes abüne our toun
	Whan the simmer days come in;
streams roll down	Whaur the blue-bells grow, and the burnies row,
golden, gorse	And gowdan is the whin.
cuckoo, birch copse	The gowk sings frae the birken–schaw,
lark, above	And the laverock far aboon:
hum, plovers	The bees bummer by, the peesies cry,
sparkling waterfall leaps	And the lauchin linn lowps doun.

Nightmare

The tree stood flowering in a dream:
Beside the tree a dark shape bowed:
As lightning glittered the axe-gleam
Across the wound in the broken wood.

The tree cried out with human cries:
From its deepening hurt the blood ran:

The branches flowered with children's eyes
And the dark murderer was a man.

There came a fear which sighed aloud;
And with its fear the dream-world woke:
Yet in the day the tree still stood
Bleeding beneath the axe-man's stroke.

Black day

beating

A skelp frae his teacher
For a' he cudna spell:
A skelp frae his mither

upsetting, broth

For cowpin owre the kail.

A skelp frae his brither

bashing, fine

For clourin his braw bat:
And a skelp frae his faither

knows

For the Lord kens what.

Bed-time

Cuddle-doun, my bairnie;

doleful

The dargie day is düne:

silver star

Yon's a siller sternie

below

Ablow the siller müne:

spider

Like a wabster body
Hingin on a threed,
Far abüne my laddie

truckle

And his wee creepie-bed.

Slaughter

Within the violence of the storm
The wise men are made dumb:
Young bones are hollowed by the worm:
The babe dies in the womb.

Above the lover's mouth is pressed
The silence of a stone:
Death rides upon an iron beast†
And tramples cities down.

And shall the multitudinous grave
Our enmity inter;

These dungeons of misrule enslave
Our bitterness and fear?

All are the conquered; and in vain
The laurel binds the brow:
The phantoms of the dead remain
And from our faces show.

†Soutar later changed 'Death' to 'Fate'.

A riddle

It was your faither and mither,
Yet it wasna weddit:
It was your sister or brither
Though nane were beside it.

Wit and wisdom it lent ye,
learned   Yet it wasna lairéd:
died, knew   And though it dee'd or it kent ye
It was never buried.

(Answer: *the child you were*)

The larky lad

The larky lad frae the pantry
great hall   Skipp't through the muckle ha';
He had sma' fear o' the gentry,
And his respec' was sma'.

He cockit his face richt merry;
And as he jiggit on
His mou' was round as a cherry
Like he whistled a braw tune.

And monie a noble body
Glower'd doun frae his frame o' gowd
mischievous   On the plisky pantry-laddie
rude   Wha was sae merry and royd.

Who are these children?

With easy hands upon the rein,
And hounds at their horses' feet,
The ladies and the gentlemen
Ride through the village street.

Brightness of blood upon the coats
And on the women's lips:
Brightness of silver at the throats
And on the hunting whips.

Is there a dale more calm, more green
Under this morning hour;
A scene more alien than this scene
Within a world at war?

Who are these children gathered here
Out of the fire and smoke
That with remembering faces stare
Upon the foxing folk?

Supper

bread sops   Steepies for the bairnie
soft   Sae moolie in the mou':
Parritch for a strappan lad
To mak his beard grow.

potatoes   Stovies for a muckle man
To keep him stout and hale:
fellow   A noggin for the auld carl
make   To gar him sleep weel.

Bless the meat, and bless the drink,
And the hand that steers the pat:
And be guid to beggar-bodies
gate   Whan they come to your yett.

The children

Upon the street they lie
Beside the broken stone:
The blood of children stares from the broken stone.

Death came out of the sky
In the bright afternoon:
Darkness slanted over the bright afternoon.

Again the sky is clear
But upon earth a stain:
The earth is darkened with a darkening stain:

A wound which everywhere
Corrupts the hearts of men:
The blood of children corrupts the hearts of men.

Silence is in the air:
The stars move to their places:
Silent and serene the stars move to their places:

But from earth the children stare
With blind and fearful faces:
And our charity is in the children's faces.

The auld aik

oak

The auld aik's doun:
The auld aik's doun:
Twa hunner year it stüde, or mair,
But noo it's doun, doun.

The auld aik's doun:
The auld aik's doun:
We were sae shair it wud aye be there,
But noo it's doun, doun.

Who Are these Children?, Op. 84 (1969)

Canticle IV: Journey of the Magi, Op. 86 (1971)

This Canticle for counter-tenor, tenor, baritone and piano, was first performed, on 26 June 1971, at the Aldeburgh Festival by James Bowman, Pears, John Shirley-Quirk and Britten. It was dedicated 'To James, Peter and John'.

T.S. ELIOT *Journey of the Magi*

'A cold coming we had of it,
Just the worst time of the year
For a journey, and such a long journey:
The ways deep and the weather sharp,
The very dead of winter.'
And the camels galled, sore-footed, refractory,
Lying down in the melting snow.
There were times we regretted
The summer palaces on slopes, the terraces,
And the silken girls bringing sherbet.
Then the camel men cursing and grumbling
And running away, and wanting their liquor and women,
And the night-fires going out, and the lack of shelters,
And the cities hostile and the towns unfriendly
And the villages dirty and charging high prices:
A hard time we had of it.
At the end we preferred to travel all night,
Sleeping in snatches,
With the voices singing in our ears, saying
That this was all folly.

Then at dawn we came down to a temperate valley,
Wet, below the snow line, smelling of vegetation;
With a running stream and a water-mill beating the darkness,
And three trees on the low sky,
And an old white horse galloped away in the meadow.
Then we came to a tavern with vine-leaves over the lintel,
Six hands at an open door dicing for pieces of silver,
And feet kicking the empty wine-skins.
But there was no information, and so we continued

And arrived at evening, not a moment too soon
Finding the place; it was (you may say) satisfactory.

All this was a long time ago, I remember,
And I would do it again, but set down
This set down
This: were we led all that way for
Birth or Death? There was a Birth, certainly,
We had evidence and no doubt. I had seen birth and death,
But had thought they were different; this Birth was
Hard and bitter agony for us, like Death, our death.
We returned to our places, these Kingdoms,
But no longer at ease here, in the old dispensation,
With an alien people clutching their gods.
I should be glad of another death.

Canticle IV: Journey of the Magi, Op. 86 (1971)

Canticle V: The death of St Narcissus, Op. 89 (1974)

This Canticle was composed for tenor and harp, one reason being that Britten could no longer play the piano. It was first performed on 15 January 1975 at Schloss Elmau, Upper Bavaria, by Pears and Osian Ellis. It was dedicated 'In loving memory of William Plomer'.

T.S. ELIOT *The death of Saint Narcissus*

Come under the shadow of this gray rock –
Come in under the shadow of this gray rock,
And I will show you something different from either
Your shadow sprawling over the sand at daybreak, or
Your shadow leaping behind the fire against the red rock:
I will show you his bloody cloth and limbs
And the gray shadow on his lips.

He walked once between the sea and the high cliffs
When the wind made him aware of his limbs smoothly
    passing each other
And of his arms crossed over his breast.
When he walked over the meadows
He was stifled and soothed by his own rhythm.
By the river
His eyes were aware of the pointed corners of his eyes
And his hands aware of the pointed tips of his fingers.

Struck down by such knowledge
He could not live men's ways, but became a dancer before God
If he walked in city streets
He seemed to tread on faces, convulsive thighs and knees.
So he came out under the rock.

First he was sure that he had been a tree,
Twisting its branches among each other
And tangling its roots among each other.

Then he knew that he had been a fish
With slippery white belly held tight in his own fingers,
Writhing in his own clutch, his ancient beauty
Caught fast in the pink tips of his new beauty.

Then he had been a young girl
Caught in the woods by a drunken old man
Knowing at the end the taste of his own whiteness
The horror of his own smoothness,
And he felt drunken and old.

So he became a dancer to God.
Because his flesh was in love with the burning arrows
He danced on the hot sand
Until the arrows came.
As he embraced them his white skin surrendered itself to
    the redness of blood, and satisfied him.
Now he is green, dry and stained
With the shadow in his mouth.

Sacred and Profane, Op. 91 (1974–5)

This setting of eight medieval lyrics for unaccompanied voices was first performed on 14 September 1975 at The Maltings, Snape, by the Wilbye Consort directed by Pears. Dedicated 'For P.P. and the Wilbye Consort'.

ST GODRIC (12th century) *St Godric's hymn*

Sainte Marye Virgine,

Moder Jesu Christes Nazarene,

receive   Onfo, schild, help thin Godric,

having received, on high,   Onfang, bring heyilich with thee in Godes

kingdom   Riche.

bower   Sainte Marye, Christes bur,

virgin among maidens,   Maidenes clenhad, moderes flur,

flower among mothers

blot out, reign, heart,   Dilie min sinne, rix in min mod,

Bliss   Bring me to winne with the self God.

ANON. (13th century) *I mon waxe wod*

wood   Foweles in the frith,

The fisses in the flod,

I must go mad   And I mon waxe wod:

Mulch sorw I walke with

For beste of bon and blod.

ANON. (13–14th centuries) *Lenten is come*

spring   Lenten is come with love to toune,

song   With blosmen and with briddes roune,

happiness   That all this bisse bringeth.

Dayeseyes in this dales,

Notes swete of nightegales,

each   Uch fowl song singeth.

thrush wrangles   The threstelcock him threteth oo.

their   Away is huere winter wo

woodruff   When woderofe springeth.

wonderfully well   This fowles singeth ferly fele,

warble, abundant, joy   And wliteth on huere wynne wele,

That all the wode ringeth.

puts on, complexion	The rose raileth hire rode,
bright	The leves on the lighte wode
	Waxen all with wille.
sends forth, radiance	The mone mandeth hire ble,
lovely	The lilye is lossom to se,
thyme	The fennel and the fille,
woo	Wowes this wilde drakes,
animals cheer, mates	Miles murgeth huere makes,
flows	Ase strem that striketh stille.
passionate man moans	Mody meneth; so doth mo;
I know	Ichot ich am on of tho
becomes	For love that likes ille.

	The mone mandeth hire light,
	So doth the semly sonne bright,
gloriously	When briddes singeth breme.
wet	Deawes donketh the dounes,
animals, secret cries	Deores with huere derne rounes
for telling their tales	Domes for to deme.
ground	Wormes woweth under cloude,
wonderfully	Wimmen waxeth wounder proude,
suit	So well it wol hem seme.
be without what I will	Yef me shall wonte wille of on,
happiness	This wunne wele I wole forgon,
banished	And wiht in wode be fleme.

ANON. (13th century)   *The long night*

pleasant	Mirie it is, while sumer ilast,
birds	With fugheles song.
but now draws nigh	Oc nu necheth windes blast,
	And weder strong.
	Ey! ey! what this night is long!
very great	And ich, with well michel wrong,
sorrow	Soregh and murne and fast.

ANON. (14th century)   *Yif ic of luve can*

cross	Whanne ic se on Rode
lover	Jesu, my lemman,
	And besiden him stonden
	Marye and Johan,
back is scourged	And his rig iswongen

Sacred and Profane, Op. 91 (1974–5)

pierced	And his side istungen,
	For the luve of man;
ought	Well ou ic to wepen,
abandon	And sinnes for to leten,
know	Yif ic of luve can,
	Yif ic of luve can,
	Yif ic of luve can.

ANON. (14th century)   *A maiden in the mor lay*   'Carol'

Maiden in the mor lay,
In the mor lay;
Sevenight fulle,
Sevenight fulle,
Maiden in the mor lay;
In the mor lay,
Sevenightes fulle and a day.

Welle was hire mete.
What was hire mete?

primrose	The primerole and the –
	The primerole and the –

Welle was hire mete.
What was hire mete?
The primerole and the violet.

Welle was hire dring.
What was hire dring?

cold	The childe water of the –
	The chelde water of the –

Welle was hire dring.
What was hire dring?
The chelde water of the welle-spring.

Welle was hire bowr.
What was hire bowr?
The rede rose and the –
The rede rose and the –
Welle was hire bowr.
What was hire bowr?
The rede rose and the lilye flour.

ANON. (14th century)   *Ye that pasen by*

                Ye that pasen by the weiye,
while   Abidet a little stounde.
                Beholdet, all my felawes,
like me   Yef any me lik is founde.
                To the Tre with nailes thre
                Wol fast I hange bounde;
                With a spere all thoru my side
                To mine herte is mad a wounde.

ANON. (13th century)   *A death*

                Wanne mine eyhnen misten,
ears hiss   And mine heren sissen,
                And my nose coldet,
                And my tunge foldet,
face   And my rude slaket,
                And mine lippes blaken,
grins   And my muth grennet,
spittle runs And my spotel rennet,
                And mine her riset,
trembles   And mine herte griset,
shake   And mine honden bivien,
stiffen   And mine fet stivien –
                Al to late! al to late!
bier   Wanne the bere is ate gate.

pass   Thanne I schel flutte
shroud   From bedde to flore,
                From flore to here,
                From here to bere,
grave   From bere to putte,
closed up   And te putt fordut.
rests, upon Thanne lyd mine hus uppe mine nose.
jot   Of al this world ne give I it a pese!

Sacred and Profane, Op. 91 (1974–5)

A Birthday Hansel, Op. 92 (1975)

Set for voice and harp, 'These songs were written at the special wish of H.M. The Queen for her mother's seventy-fifth birthday, 4th August 1975'. They were first performed privately at Sandringham by Pears and Osian Ellis and then on 19 March 1976 at the Cardiff Festival. Britten slightly altered the titles of some of these songs.

ROBERT BURNS To John Maxwell, Esq, of Terraughty, on his birthday

'Birthday song'

Health to the Maxwells' vet'ran Chief!
Health, ay unsour'd by care or grief:
Inspir'd, I turn'd Fate's sibyl leaf,
    This natal morn,
proof   I see thy life is stuff o' prief,
    Scarce quite half-worn:

[This day thou metes threescore eleven,
And I can tell that bounteous Heaven
know   (The second sight, ye ken, is given
every   To ilka Poet)
term, lease On thee a tack o' seven times seven
    Will yet bestow it.

gallants   If envious buckies view wi' sorrow
Thy lengthen'd days on this blest morrow,
May Desolation's lang-teeth'd harrow,
    Nine miles an hour,
Rake them, like Sodom and Gomorrah,
brimstone dust   In brunstane stoure.

But for thy friends, and they are mony,
Baith honest men and lasses bonie,
comfortable, frugal May couthie Fortune, kind and cannie,
    In social glee,
Wi' mornings blythe and e'enings funny
    Bless them and thee!]

good fellow Fareweel, auld birkie! Lord be near ye,

dare not touch And then the Deil, he daurna steer ye:

Your friends ay love, your faes ay fear ye,
                For me, shame fa' me,
If neist my heart I dinna wear ye
                While Burns; they ca' me.

befall
next

A rose bud 'My early walk'

A rose bud by my early walk
Adown a corn-inclosèd bawk,
Sae gently bent its thorny stalk,
            All on a dewy morning.
Ere twice the shades o' dawn are fled,
In a' its crimson glory spread,
And drooping rich the dewy head,
            It scents the early morning.

open space

Within the bush her covert nest
A little linnet fondly prest,
The dew sat chilly on her breast
            Sae early in the morning.
[She soon shall see her tender brood,
The pride, the pleasure o' the wood,
Amang the fresh green leaves bedew'd,
            Awauk the early morning.]

awake

So thou, dear bird, young Jeany fair,
On trembling string or vocal air
Shall sweetly pay the tender care
            That tents thy early morning.
So thou, sweet Rose bud, young and gay,
Shalt beauteous blaze upon the day,
And bless the Parent's evening ray
            That watch'd thy early morning.

guards

Wee Willie Gray

Wee Willie Gray, and his leather wallet,
Peel a willow-wand, to be him boots and jacket;
The rose upon the breer will be him trews and doublet,
The rose upon the breer will be him trews and doublet.

Wee Willie Gray, and his leather wallet,
Twice a lily-flower will be him sark and cravat;
Feathers of a flee wad feather up his bonnet,
Feathers of a flee wad feather up his bonnet.

shirt

A Birthday Hansel, Op. 92 (1975)

My Hoggie

A young sheep before it
is first shorn.

What will I do gin my Hoggie die,
    My joy, my pride, my Hoggie?

if

My only beast, I had nae mae,

vain
    And vow but I was vogie.

live-long
The lee-lang night we watch'd the fauld,
    Me and my faithfu' doggie;

water-fall
We heard nocht but the roaring linn,

scrub-covered hillsides
    Among the braes sae scroggie.

owl
But the houlet cry'd frae the castle wa',

snipe
    The blitter frae the boggie;

fox
The tod reply'd upon the hill –
    I trembled for my Hoggie.

When day did daw, and cocks did craw,
    The morning it was foggie;

strange dog
An unco tyke lap o'er the dyke,

almost
    And maist has killed my Hoggie.

Afton Water

I charge you, O ye daughters of Jerusalem, that ye stir
not, nor awake my love – my dove; my undefiled! The
flowers appear on the earth, the time of the singing of
the birds is come, and the voice of the turtle is heard in
our land.

hillsides
Flow gently, sweet Afton, among thy green braes,
Flow gently, I'll sing thee a song in thy praise;
My Mary's asleep by thy murmuring stream,
Flow gently, sweet Afton, disturb not her dream.

Thou stock dove whose echo resounds thro' the glen,
Ye wild whistling blackbirds in yon thorny den,
Thou green crested lapwing thy screaming forbear,
I charge you disturb not my slumbering Fair.

[How lofty, sweet Afton, thy neighbouring hills,
Far mark'd with the courses of clear, winding rills;
There daily I wander as noon rises high,

cottage
My flocks and my Mary's sweet Cot in my eye.

How pleasant thy banks and green vallies below,
Where, wild in the woodlands, the primroses blow;
There oft as mild ev'ning weeps over the lea,

birch   The sweet-scented birk shades my Mary and me.]

Thy crystal stream, Afton, how lovely it glides,
And winds by thy cot where my Mary resides;
How wanton thy waters her snowy feet lave,
As gathering sweet flowerets, she stems thy clear wave.

Flow gently, sweet Afton...

The winter it is past 'The winter'

The winter it is past, and the summer comes at last,
    And the small birds, they sing on ev'ry tree;
Now ev'ry thing is glad, while I am very sad,
    Since my true love is parted from me.

The rose upon the brier, by the waters running clear,
    May have charms for the linnet or the bee;
Their little loves are blest, and their little hearts at rest,
    But my true love is parted from me.

Leezie Lindsay

Will ye go to the Hielands, Leezie Lindsay?
    Will ye go to the Hielands wi' me?
Will ye go to the Hielands, Leezie Lindsay,
    My pride and my darling to be?

Phaedra, Op. 93 (1975)

The dramatic cantata for mezzo soprano and small orchestra was first performed on 16 June 1976 in The Maltings, Snape, at the Aldeburgh Festival, by Dame Janet Baker and the English Chamber Orchestra, conducted by Steuart Bedford. It was dedicated 'For Janet Baker'.

Lowell described this as a 'free' translation of Racine's *Phèdre*, since, in his view, 'Racine's plays are generally and rightly thought to be untranslatable'. Britten's much abbreviated version is a monologue.

Phaedra, the wife of Theseus, falls desperately in love with her stepson, Hippolytus. When he rejects her, she falsely accuses him of trying to assault her. Theseus prays to Poseidon, the sea-god, to destroy Hippolytus. Phaedra confesses and kills herself.

ROBERT LOWELL after RACINE *Phaedra*
(Act I)

l.120 [*Phaedra* Nurse, I am in love. The shame
kills me. I love the... Do not ask his name.

Oenone Who?

Phaedra Nurse, you know my old loathing for the son
of Theseus and the barbarous amazon?

Oenone Hippolytus! My God, oh my God!

Phaedra You, not I, have named him.

Oenone What can you do, but die?
Your words have turned my blood to ice.
Oh righteous heavens, must the blasphemies
of Pasiphaë fall upon her daughter?
Her Furies strike us down across the water.
Why did we come here?

Phaedra My evil comes from farther off.] In May,
in brilliant Athens, on my marriage day,
I turned aside for shelter from the smile
of Theseus. Death was frowning in an aisle –
Hippolytus! I saw his face, turned white!

My lost and dazzled eyes saw only night,
capricious burnings flickered through my bleak
abandoned flesh. I could not breathe or speak.
I faced my flaming executioner,
Aphrodite, my mother's murderer!
I tried to calm her wrath by flowers and praise,
I built her a temple, fretted months and days
on decoration. [I even hoped to find
symbols and stays for my distracted mind,
searching the guts of sacrificial steers.
Yet when my erring passions, mutineers
to virtue, offered incense at the shrine
of love, I failed to silence the malign
Goddess.] Alas, my hungry open mouth,
thirsting with adoration, tasted drouth –
Venus resigned her altar to my new lord –
[and even while I was praying, I adored
Hippolytus above the sacred flame,
now offered to his name I could not name.
I fled him, yet he stormed me in disguise,
and seemed to watch me from his father's eyes.
I even turned against myself, screwed up
my slack courage to fury, and would not stop
shrieking and raging, till half-dead with love
and the hatred of a stepmother, I drove
Hippolytus in exile from the rest
and strenuous wardship of his father's breast...]

(Act II)

l.96   [*Hippolytus* ... What are you saying, Madam?
         You forget my father is your husband!

         Phaedra I have let
            you see my grief for Theseus! How could I
            forget my honor and my majesty,
            Prince?

         Hippolytus Madam, forgive me! My foolish youth
            conjectured hideous untruths from your truth.
            I cannot face my insolence. Farewell... (Exit)]

         Phaedra You monster! You understood me too well!
            Why do you hang there, speechless, petrified,

polite! My mind whirls. What have I to hide?
Phaedra in all her madness stands before you.
I love you! Fool, I love you, I adore you!
Do not imagine that my mind approved
my first defection, Prince, or that I loved
your youth light-heartedly, and fed my treason
with cowardly compliance, till I lost my reason.
[I wished to hate you, but the gods corrupt
us; though I never suffered their abrupt
seductions, shattering advances, I
too bear their sensual lightnings in my thigh...
At first I fled you, and when this fell short
of safety, Prince, I exiled you from court.]
Alas, my violence to resist you made
my face inhuman, hateful. I was afraid
to kiss my husband lest I love his son.
I made you fear me (this was easily done);
you loathed me more, I ached for you no less.
Misfortune magnified your loveliness.
[I grew so wrung and wasted, men mistook
me for the Sibyl. If you could bear to look
your eyes would tell you. Do you believe my passion   .
is voluntary? That my obscene confession
is some dark trick, some oily artifice?...]
The wife of Theseus loves Hippolytus!
See, Prince! Look, this monster, ravenous
for her execution, will not flinch.
I want your sword's spasmodic final inch.

(Act III)

l.18   *Phaedra* Oh Gods of wrath,
            how far I've travelled on my dangerous path!
            I go to meet my husband; at his side
            will stand Hippolytus. How shall I hide
            my thick adulterous passion for this youth,
            who has rejected me, and knows the truth?
            [Will the stern Prince stand smiling and approve
            the labored histrionics of my love
            for Theseus, see my lips, still languishing
            for his, betray his father and his King?]
            Will he not draw his sword and strike me dead?

Suppose he spares me? What if nothing's said?...
Can I kiss Theseus with dissembled poise?
[I think each stone and pillar has a voice.]
The very dust rises to disabuse
my husband – to defame me and accuse!
Oenone, I want to die. Death will give
me freedom; oh it's nothing not to live;
death to the unhappy's no catastrophe!
[I fear the name that must live after me,
and crush my son until the end of time.
Is his inheritance his mother's crime,
his right to curse me, when my pollution stains
the blood of heaven bubbling in his veins?
The day will come, alas, the day will come,
when nothing will be left to save him from
the voices of despair. If he should live
he'll flee his subjects like a fugitive...

(Act V)

[*Theseus* Ah Phaedra, you have won. He's dead. A man
was killed. Were you watching? His horses ran
him down and tore his body limb from limb.
Poseidon struck him, Theseus murdered him.
I served you! Tell me why Oenone died?
Was it to save you? Is her suicide
A proof of your truth? No, since he'd dead, I must
accept your evidence, just or unjust.
I must believe my faith has been abused;
you have accused him; he shall stand accused.
He's friendless even in the world below.
There the shades fear him! Am I forced to know
the truth? Truth cannot bring my son to life.
If fathers murder, shall I kill my wife
too? Leave me, Phaedra. Far from you, exiled
from Greece, I will lament my murdered child...
                                I know the gods are hard
to please. I pleased you. This is my reward:
I killed my son. I killed him! Only a god
spares enemies, and wants his servants' blood!

Phaedra, Op. 93 (1975)

Phaedra No, Theseus, I must disobey your prayer.
Listen to me. I'm dying. I declare
Hippolytus was innocent.

Theseus Ah Phaedra, on your evidence, I sent
him to his death. Do you ask me to forgive
my son's assassin? Can I let you live?]

Phaedra My time's too short, your highness. It was I,
who lusted for your son with my hot eye.
The flames of Aphrodite maddened me;
[I loathed myself, and yearned outrageously
like a starved wolf to fall upon the sheep.
I wished to hold him to me in my sleep
and dreamt I had him.] Then Oenone's tears,
troubled my mind; she played upon my fears,
until her pleading forced me to declare
I loved your son. [He scorned me. In despair,
I plotted with my nurse, and our conspiracy
made you believe your son assaulted me.
Oenone's punished; fleeing from my wrath,
she drowned herself, and found a too easy path
to death and hell. Perhaps you wonder why
I still survive her, and refuse to die?]
Theseus, I stand before you to absolve
your noble son. Sire, only this resolve
upheld me, and made me thrown down my knife.
I've chosen a slower way to end my life –
Medea's poison; chills already dart
along my boiling veins and squeeze my heart.
A cold composure I have never known
gives me a moment's poise. I stand alone
and seem to see my outraged husband fade
and waver into death's dissolving shade.
My eyes at last give up their light, and see
the day they've soiled resume its purity.

[*Panope* She's dead, my lord.

Theseus   Would God, all memory
of her and me had died with her! Now I
must live. This knowledge that has come too late
must give me strength and help me expiate
my sacrilegious vows. Let's go, I'll pay

my son the honors he has earned today.
His father's tears shall mingle with his blood.
My love that did my son so little good
asks mercy from his spirit. I declare
Aricia is my daughter and my heir.]

Welcome Ode, Op. 95 (1976)

This ode, for young people's chorus and orchestra, was first performed on 11 July 1977 at The Corn Exchange, Ipswich, in the presence of Her Majesty The Queen, on the occasion of her Silver Jubilee visit to Suffolk. It was performed by the Suffolk Schools' Choir and Orchestra conducted by Keith Shaw.

THOMAS DEKKER AND JOHN FORD *Summer pastimes*
(from *The Sun's Darling*)

'March'

Haymakers, rakers, reapers and mowers,
   Wait on your summer-queen,
Dress up with musk-rose her eglantine bowers,
   Daffodils strew the green.
      Sing, dance and play,
      'Tis holiday;
The sun does bravely shine
      On our ears of corn.
      Rich as a pearl
      Comes every girl:
This is mine, this is mine, this is mine,
Let us die ere away they be borne.

Bow to the sun, to our queen, and that fair one
   Come to behold our sports.
[Each bonny lass here is counted a rare one
   As those in princes' courts.
      These and we
      With country glee
Will teach the woods to resound,
And the hills with echoes hollow.]
      Skipping lambs
      Their bleating dams
'Mongst kids shall trip it round,
For joy thus our wenches we follow.

[Wind, jolly huntsmen, your neat bugles shrilly,
   Hounds make a lusty cry:

Spring up, you falconers, the partridges freely,
Then let your brave hawks fly.
Horses amain
Over ridge, over plain,
The dogs have the stag in chase.
'Tis a sport to content a king.
So hot ho! through the skies
How the proud bird flies
swooping   And sousing kills with a grace.
Now the deer falls, hark how they ring!]

ANON. *The fairies' roundel*
(from *The Maid's Metamorphosis* 1600)

'Roundel'

Round about, round about, in a fine ring a:
Thus we dance, thus we dance, and thus we sing a.
Trip and go, to and fro, over this green a:
All about, in and out, for our brave queen a.

Round about, round about, in a fine ring a:
Thus we dance, thus we dance, and thus we sing a.
Trip and go, to and fro, over this green a:
All about, in and out, for our brave queen a.
We have danc'd round about, in a fine ring a:
We have danc'd lustily and thus we sing a.
All about, in and out, over this green a:
To and fro, trip and go, to our brave queen a.

HENRY FIELDING   *Ode to the New Year*

'Canon'

This is a day, in days of yore
Our fathers never saw before;
This is a day; 'tis one to ten
Our sons will never see again.
Then sing the day,
And sing the song,
And thus be merry
All day long.

     Welcome Ode, Op. 95 (1976)

This is the day,
And that's the night,
When the sun shall be gay,
And the moon shall be bright.
The sun shall rise
All in the skies:
The moon shall go
All down below.
Then sing the day,
And sing the song,
And thus be merry
All day long.

Eight Folk Song Arrangements (1976)

TRAD. *Lord! I married me a wife*

Lord, Lord, Lord. I married me a wife,
She gave me trouble all her life;
Made me work in the cold rain and snow,
Rain and snow, rain and snow,
Made me work in the cold rain and snow.

TRAD. *She's like the swallow*

She's like the swallow that flies so high,
She's like the river that never runs dry,
She's like the sunshine on the lee shore,
I love my love and love is no more.

'Twas out in the garden this fair maid did go,
Apicking the beautiful primrose;
The more she plucked the more she pulled
Until she got her apron full.

It's out of those roses she made a bed,
A stony pillow for her head.
She laid her down, no word did say,
Until this fair maid's heart did break.

She's like the swallow...

TRAD. *Lemady*

One midsummer's morn as I were awalking
The fields and the meadows were covered with green,
The birds asweetly singing so pleasant and so charming,
So early in the morning by the break of the day.

Arise, arise, go pluck your love a posy
Of the prettiest flowers that grows in yonder green.
O yes I'll arise and pluck lillies, pinks and roses
All for my dearest Lemady, the girl I adore.

O Lemady, Lemady, what a lovely lass thou art,
Thou art the fairest creature that ever my eye did see.
I'll play you a tune all on the pipes of ivory
So early in the morning by the break of the day.

TRAD. *Bonny at morn*

The sheep's in the meadows,
The kye's in the corn,
Thou's ower lang in thy bed,
Bonny at morn.
> *Canny at night, bonny at morn,*
> *Thou's ower lang in thy bed, Bonny at morn.*

The bird's in the nest,
The trout's in the burn,
Thou hinders thy mother
In many a turn.

We're all laid idle
Wi' keeping the bairn,
The lad winnot work
And the lass winnot lairn.

I was lonely and forlorn Bugeilio'r Gwenith Gwyn
(tr. from Welsh by Osian Ellis)

I was lonely and forlorn
Among the meadows mourning;
For I had wooed her oft and long,
Yet others reaped her loving.

Not to me this maid did come
To cure my painful yearning.
Yet I had watched, the fields among,
Her beauty and her blooming.

While the seas do ebb and flow
And minutes do not falter;
And while my heart beats in my breast,
My 'fliction ne'er will alter.

Ne'er shall I kiss her cheeks so fair,
Nor feel her arms embracing;
For I had watched the ripening wheat,
Yet others reaped her loving.

David of the white rock   Cariog
(tr. from Welsh by Thomas Oliphant and Osian Ellis)†

Life and its follies are fading away,
Love has departed, why then should I stay?
Cold is my pale cheek, and furrowed with care,
Dim is my eye-sight, and snow white my hair.

Near me, in silence, my harp lies unstrung,
Weak are my fingers and falt'ring my tongue.
Tuneful companion we parted must be;
Thou canst no longer bring comfort to me.

Yet ere we sever, thy master would fain
Swan-like expire in a last dying strain;
And where above him the cypress boughs wave,
Spirits shall murmur it over his grave.

†This is not a folk song but a melody by David Owen

The false knight upon the road

The knight met a child on the road.
'O where are you going to?' said the knight in the road.
'I'm a-going to my school,' said the child as he stood.
He stood and he stood and it's well because he stood.
'I'm a-going to my school,' said the child as he stood.

'O what are you going there for?'
'For to learn the Word of God.'

'O what have you got there?'
'I have got my bread and cheese.'

'O won't you give me some?'
'No, ne'er a bite nor a crumb.'

'I wish you was on the sands.'
'Yes, and a good staff in my hands.'

'I wish you was in the sea.'
'Yes, and a good boat under me.'

'I think I hear a bell.'
'Yes, and it's ringing you to hell.'

Eight Folk Song Arrangements (1976)

Bird scarer's song

Shoo all 'er birds you be so black,
When I lay down to have a nap.
  Shoo arlo arlo arlo birds.

Out of master's ground into Tom Tucker's ground.

Out of Tom Tucker's ground into Luke Coles's ground,

Out of Luke Coles's ground into Bill Veator's ground.

Ha! Ha!

Bibliography & Indices

Britten's Library

This bibliography lists all the books in Britten's and Pears's large library from which Britten took the texts he set to music.

ANTHOLOGIES

Auden, W.H. (ed.) *The Oxford Book of Light Verse*, 1939
Auden, W.H. and Garrett, J. (eds.) *The Poet's Tongue*, 1935
Ault, N. (ed.) *Elizabethan Lyrics*
The Benedictines of Solesmes, Tournai, *The Liber Ususalis*, 1956
Boas, F.S. (ed.) *Songs and Lyrics from the English Playbooks*, 1945
The Book of Common Prayer
Braithwaite, W.S. (ed.) *The Book of Elizabethan Verse*, 1908
Budd, F.E. (ed.) *A Book of Lullabies*, 1300–1900, 1930
Bullett, G. (ed.) *English Galaxy of Shorter Poems*, 1939
Davies, R.T. (ed.) *Medieval English Lyrics*, 1963
Dearmer, P., Vaughan Wiliams, R., and Shaw, M. (eds.) *The Oxford Book of Carols*, 1928
de la Mare, W. (ed.) *The Augustan Books of Modern Poetry*
  Behold this Dreamer, 1945
  Come Hither, 1928
  Songs of Childhood, 1926
  Tom Tiddler's Ground, 1931
Drinkwater, J. (ed.) *The Way of Poetry*
Fellowes, E.H. (ed.) *English Madrigal Verse*, 2nd ed. 1939
Gregory, H. (ed.) *The Triumph of Life, Poems of Consolation*, 1943
M.M. & J.M.D. (eds.) A Book of Lighter Verse
  English Lyrical Verse, 1936
Methuen, A. (ed.) *An Anthology of Modern Verse*, 1927
Pollard, A.W. (ed.) *English Miracle Plays Moralities and Interludes*, 1927
Rickert, E. (ed.) *Ancient English Christmas Carols*, 1928
Rutter, J. (ed.) *An Anthology of Flower Poems*, 1937
Quiller-Couch, A. (ed.) *The Oxford Book of Ballads*, 1910
  The Oxford Book of English Verse, 1927
Sisam, K. (ed.) *Fourteenth Century Verse and Prose*, 1921
Squire, J.C. (ed.) *Songs from the Elizabethans*, 1924
Stainer, J. & Martin, G.C. (eds.) *The Versicles and Responses as used in St Paul's Cathedral*

Sternhold, T., Hopkins, J. *et al* (eds.) *The Whole Book of Psalms*, 1613
Stewart, C. (ed.) *Poems of Sleep and Dream*, 1947
Waley, A. (transl.) *Chinese Poems*, 1946

INDIVIDUAL POETS

Auden, W.H. *Another Time*, 1940
  Collected Shorter Poems 1925–1957
  For the Time Being, 1945
  Look Stranger, 1936
Auden, W.H. & Isherwood, C. *On the Frontier*, 1938
Barnfield, R. *The Poems of*, 1936
Beaumont, F. & Fletcher J. *The Works of*, 1872
Blake, W. *The Poetical Works of*, 1960
Brecht, B. *Gedichte und Lieder*, 1962
Buonarroti, M.A. *The Sonnets of Michael Angelo*, transl. Symonds, J.A.
Burns, R. *Poetical Works of*, 1958
Crabbe, G. *Poetical Works of*, 1851
Cotton, C. *Poems from the Works of*, 1922
Crozier, E. *Saint Nicholas, Patron Saint of Children*, 1949
de la Mare, W. *Complete Poems*
Donne, J. *Complete Poetry and Selected Prose*, 1941
Duncan, R. The Solitudes, 1960
Eliot, T.S. *Collected Poems* 1909–1962, 1963
  Poems Written in Early Youth, 1967
Graves, R. *Poems* 1926–30
Hardy, T. *Collected Poems of*, 1923
Herbert, G. *The Works*, 1941
Hölderlin, F. *Gedichte*, 1955
  Samliche Werke, 1961
  Poems and Fragments, transl. Hamburger, M. 1966
Lowell R. *Phaedra*, 1963
Owen, W. *The Poems of*, 1955
Pushkin, A. *Selected Verse*, 1964
Rimbaud, A. *Les Illuminations*, 1936
Sitwell, E. *The Canticle of the Rose*, 1950
Smart, C. *Poems*
Soutar, W. *But the Earth Abideth*, 1943
  Collected Poems, 1948
Walton, I. *Songs from 'The Compleat Angler'*, 1929

Index of Authors

Anonymous 11, 14, 20–22, 25–26, 33, 34, 35, 37, 39, 40, 41, 43, 91–3, 95, 104, 107, 129, 143, 154, 161, 162, 226, 263–6, 278
Asquith, Herbert (1881–1947) 3
Auden, Wystan Hugh (1907–73) 42, 43, 45, 47, 49–55, 60, 63–9, 85, 88, 111, 145

Barnfield, Richard (1574–1627) 148
Beaumont, Francis (c.1584–1616) 153
Beddoes, Thomas Lovell (1803–49) 86
Belloc, Hilaire (1870–1953) 10
Blake, William (1757–1827) 104, 126, 152, 232–6
The Bible 248
The Book of Common Prayer (1559) 32, 207, 224
Brecht, Bertolt (1898–1956) 250
Brontë, Emily (1818–48) 57
Burns, Robert (1759–96) 1, 126, 211, 267–70
Burra, Peter (1909–37) 56

Carey, Henry (c.1690–1743) 209
Cariog (John Ceiriog Hughes 1832–87) 282
Clare, John (1793–1864) 144, 160
Coleridge, Samuel Taylor (1772–1834) 185
Columba, St (521–97) 227
Cornyshe, William (c.1465–c.1523) 95
Cotton, Charles (1630–87) 102
Crabbe, George (1754–1832) 158
Crozier, Eric (1914–) 133–42

Dekker, Thomas (c.1572–c.1632) 277
De la Mare, Walter (1873–1956) 6–8, 18–19
Donne, John (1572–1631) 114–17
Duncan, Ronald (1914–82) 46, 112–13, 118, 155

Eliot, Thomas Stearns (1888–1965) 259, 261

English Missal 216–23

Farjeon, Eleanor (1881–1965) 40
Fielding, Henry (1707–54) 278
Fletcher, John (1579–1625) 153
Ford, Ford Madox (1873–1939) 9
Ford, John (1586–c.1639) 277

Godric, St (c.1065–1170) 263
Goethe, Johann Wolfgang von (1749–1832) 195
Graham, Colin (1931–) 246
Graves, Robert (1895–1985) 31
Greene, Robert (1558–92) 127

Hardy, Thomas (1840–1928) 171–6, 249
Herbert, George (1593–1633) 179
Herrick, Robert (1591–1674) 145, 157
Hölderlin, Friedrich (1770–1843) 192–4
Hopkins, Gerard Manley (1844–89) 71–5
Hugo, Victor (1802–85) 4–5

Jonson, Ben (1572–1637) 105

Keats, John (1795–1821) 106, 188

Longfellow, Henry Wadsworth (1807–82) 2
Lowell, Robert (1917–77) 271–6
Lu Yu (1125–1210) 182

MacNeice, Louis (1907–63) 90
Michelangelo (1475–1564) 81–4
Middleton, Thomas (1580–1627) 185
Milton, John, (1608–74) 144
Moore, Thomas (1779–1852) 202–6

Nashe, Thomas (1567–1601) 144

Owen, Wilfred (1893–1918) 188, 216–22

Peele, George (c.1558–98) 144, 151
Phillips, John (1631–1706) 128
Po Chü-i (772–846) 62, 181–2

Pushkin, Alexandr Sergeevich (1779–1837) 244–5

Quarles, Francis (1592–1644) 27, 124

Racine, Jean (1639–99) 271–6
Randolph, Thomas (1605–35) 128
Ravenscroft, Thomas (1592–1640) 44
Rimbaud, Arthur (1854–91) 76–80
Rossetti, Christina (1830–94) 24

Shakespeare, William (1564–1616) 190, 196–201, 212
Shelley, Percy Bysshe (1792–1822) 184
Sitwell, Edith (1887–1964) 176–8
Slater, Montagu (1902–56) 47
Smart, Christopher (1722–71) 100
Soutar, William (1898–1943) 254–8
Southwell, Robert (1561?–95) 15, 93–4
Spenser, Edmund (1552–99) 143
Stubbs, C.W. (1845–1912) 16
Swingler, Randall (1909–1967) 61, 67, 69

Taylor, Jane (1783–1824) 35
Tennyson, Alfred, Lord (1809–92) 103, 184

Thackeray, William Makepeace (1811–63) 34
Traditional 12, 36, 91, 96–9, 119–23, 129–32, 180, 208, 210, 213–15, 225, 280, 281
Tusser, Thomas (c.1520–c.1580) 26

Udall, Nicholas (1504–56) 37

Vaughan, Henry (1622–95) 13, 145
Verlaine, Paul (1844–96) 4–5
Virgil, Publius (70–19 BC) 241

Waley, Arthur (1889–1966) 62, 181–3
Walton, Izaak (1593–1683) 38
Wedderburn, James, John, & Robert (c. 1548) 92
Weelkes, Thomas (c. 1575–1623) 44
Wilkinson, Patrick (1907–85) 228
Wither, George (1588–1667) 28
Wordsworth, William (1770–1850) 186
Wu-ti (157–87 BC) 182

Yeats, William Butler (1865–1939) 96

Index of Titles

This index gives the authors' own or the commonly accepted titles of the poems (some shortened); and also Britten's titles, where these differ. The titles of his works which include a number of poems are given in capitals. 'The' and 'A' are not listed alphabetically.

A che più debb'i omai 82
Across the darkened sky 61
Advance democracy 61
Afton Water 269
Ah, Sun-flower 235
A.M.D.G. 71
Angel 244
Anthem for doomed youth 217
Antiphon 179
Antique 78
As dew in Aprille 93
The ash grove 99
As it is, plenty 51
At a Calvary near the Ancre 222
At day-close in November 171
At the mid hour of night 204
At the railway station 174
At the round earth's imagin'd corners 116
Auguries of innocence 236
The auld aik 258
Autumn 6
The autumn wind 182
Avenging and bright 202

The ballad of green broom 161
BALLAD OF HEROES 67
The ballad of little Musgrave and Lady Barnard 107
Balulalow 92
Batter my heart 114
Be kind and courteous 199
Bed-time 255
Before life and after 175
Begone, dull care 34
Being beauteous 79
La belle 121
Beware 2

The big chariot 181
The birds 10
Bird scarer's song 283
A BIRTHDAY HANSEL 267
Birthday song 267
Birthday song for Erwin 118
Black day 255
Blow, bugle, blow 103
Bonny at morn 281
The bonny Earl o' Moray 97
A BOY WAS BORN 20
A boy was born: Puer natus 20
The brisk young widow 208
The building of the house 248
But that night, when on my bed 186

Ca' the yowes 211
Calypso 66
Canon 278
Cantata misericordium 228
Canticles
    I My beloved is mine 124
    II Abraham and Isaac 162
    III Still falls the rain 176
    IV Journey of the Magi 259
    V The death of St Narcissus 261
Carol 265
The carol of King Cnut 16
A CEREMONY OF CAROLS 91
Chanson d' Automne 5
A charm 128
A CHARM OF LULLABIES 126
The children 257
Children's crusade 250
The chimney-sweeper 233
The choirmaster's burial 173
Christ's nativity 13

Christmas 26
A Christmas carol 27
Come you not from Newcastle? 132
The company of heaven 57
A cradle song 126
Cradle song for Eleanor 90
Cuck-oo 35

Dance song 183
Danse macabre 67
David of the White Rock 282
A day dream 57
Dear harp of my country 204
A death 266
Death be not proud 117
The death of Saint Narcissus 226
Deo gracias 95
Départ 80
Depression 182
Die Heimat 192
Die Jugend 193
Die Linien des Lebens 194
Dirge for Wolfram 86
The driving boy 144

Early one morning 210
Eclogue IV 241
Ee-oh! 35
Eho! Eho! 122
EIGHT FOLK SONG ARRANGEMENTS 280
Either I mistake your shape 196
Elegy 104
The end 221
Epigram 245
Epilogue 45
Epitaph 3
Evening 112
The evening primrose 160
Evening quatrains 102
Ev'n like two little bank-dividing brooks
    124
Except the Lord 248

Fair and fair 151
The fairies' roundel 278
The false knight 282
Fancie 212
Fanfare 76
Festival Te Deum 32
Fileuse 120

First, April, she with mellow flowers 157
Fish in the unruffled lakes 53
Fishing song 38
FIVE FLOWER SONGS 157
The fly 235
The foggy, foggy dew 131
FOLK SONG ARRANGEMENTS:
    VOL.1 BRITISH ISLES 96
    VOL.2 FRANCE 119
    VOL.3 BRITISH ISLES 129
    VOL.4 IRELAND 202
    VOL.5 BRITISH ISLES 208
    VOL.6 ENGLAND 213
FOUR CABARET SONGS 63
FRIDAY AFTERNOONS 34
Funeral blues 65
Futility 220

God's grandeur 73
The 'Golden Vanity' 246
Groves of Blarney 205

Hälfte des Lebens 194
Hawking for the partridge 44
Heaven-haven 75
The herd-boy 182
The Highland balou 126
Hodie Christus natus est 91
The holly and the ivy 180
THE HOLY SONNETS OF JOHN DONNE 114
How sweet the answer 203
The humming of the ban 202
Hymn to Diana 105
Hymn to St Cecilia 88
Hymn to St Columba 227
Hymn to St Peter 178
A hymn to the Virgin 11

I know a bank 198
I lov'd a lass 28
I mon waxe wod 263
I mun be married a Sunday 37
I was lonely and forlorn 281
I will give my love an apple 213
If it's ever spring again 176
If thou wilt ease 86
If we shadows have offended 200
Il est quelqu'un sur terre 121
The impatient maid 144
In freezing winter night 94

In the bleak mid-winter 24
Jazz-man 40
Jesu, as Thou art our Saviour 22
Johnny 65
Journey of the Magi 259
Jubilate Deo: Psalm 100 207

Kate Tyrrel 204
The kind ghosts 188
King Herod and the cock 226
The Kraken 184

La belle est au jardin 121
A laddie's song 254
La Noël passée 119
The larky lad 256
The last rose of summer 205
L'enfance 5
Le roi s'en va-t-en chasse 121
LES ILLUMINATIONS 76
Leezie Lindsay 270
Lemady 280
Lenten is come 263
Lift-boy 31
The Lincolnshire poacher 210
Lines written during a sleepless night 245
The little Musgrave and Lady Barnard
   107
The little old table 172
Little Sir William 96
London 232
London, to thee I do present 153
The long night 264
Lord! I married me a wife 280
The lover's journey 159
A love sonnet 28
Lullay, Jesu 20
Lully, lulley 25
A lyke-wake dirge 104
Lyrics, rhymes and riddles 254

A maiden in the mor lay 265
March 277
Marine 78
Marsh flowers 158
Master Kilby 214
May 33
Menschenbeifall 192
The merry cuckoo 143
Messalina 44

Midnight on the Great Western 171
Midnight's bell goes ting 185
A MIDSUMMER NIGHT'S DREAM 196
Mid-winter 24
The miller of Dee 130
The minstrel boy 203
Missa pro defunctis 216
Molly, my dear 204
Morning 112
The morning star 144
Mother comfort 47
My early walk 268
My heart 244
My Hoggie 269

New Prince, new pompe 15
A New Year carol 36
The next war 218
Night 113
Night covers up 60
The nightingale and the rose 245
Nightmare 254
Nocturne 51, 103
NOCTURNE 184
Noel 25
Not even summer yet 56
Now is Christmas ycome 22
Now is the month of maying 33
Now the hungry lion roars 199
Now the leaves are falling 49
Now, until the break of day 200
Nuits de Juin 4
The nurse's song 128

O can ye sew cushions? 97
O Deus, ego amo te 74
O tell me the truth 63
O that I had ne'er been married 1
O Waly, Waly 131
Ode to the New Year 278
Oft in the stilly night 205
Oh my blacke soule 114
Oh might those sighes 115
Oh, to vex me 115
Old Abram Brown 41
The old lute 181
Oliver Cromwell 99
On a poet's lips I slept 184
ON THIS ISLAND 49
Oratio Patris Condren 71

Index of Titles

O the sight entrancing 206
OUR HUNTING FATHERS 43
Out on the lawn 145
Over hill, over dale 196
The oxen 249

Pacifist march 46
The parable of the old men 220
Parade 79
Pastoral 102
Phaedra 271
Phrase 77
Planxty Sudley 206
The plough boy 129
Poems 216
Poems in depression 182
THE POET'S ECHO 244
A poison tree 233
The poor and their dwellings 158
Preparation 14
Prologue 43
Proud songsters 174
Proverbs 232–5
Psalm 127: Except the Lord 248
Psalm 150: O praise God 224

Quand j'étais chez mon père 123
QUATRE CHANSONS FRANÇAISES 4

The rainbow 18
Rats away 43
The red cockatoo 62
Regis regum rectissimi 227
Rejoice in the Lamb 100
Rendete agli occhi mei 83
Residence in France 186
Rich and rare 204
A riddle 254, 256
The ride-by-nights 18
Rosa mystica 71
A rose bud 268
Roundel 278
Royauté 78

SACRED AND PROFANE 263
The sacrifice of Isaac 162
Sagesse 4
The sailor and the soldier 216
Sail on, sail on 202
Sailor-boy 213

SAINT NICOLAS 133
The salley gardens 96
Sally in our alley 209
Seascape 50
SECHS HÖLDERLIN-FRAGMENTE 192
Sephestia's lullaby 127
SERENADE 102
SEVEN SONNETS OF MICHELANGELO 81
A shepherd's carol 111
She's like the swallow 280
Shine out, fair Sun 143
The ship of Rio 19
The shooting of his dear 215
The shower (II) 145
The sick rose 104
Si come nella penna 81
Silver 7
Since she whom I lov'd 116
Sith sickles 44
SIX HÖLDERLIN FRAGMENTS 192
Slaughter 255
Sleep and poetry 188
Sokrates und Alcibiades 193
The soldier 74
The soldier and the sailor 215
Song 49, 56, 178
Song: Lift-boy 31
Song – Night covers up 60
A song of enchantment 6
The song of the women 9
Song – On May morning 144
Song on the water 86
Song – Underneath the abject willow 47
SONGS AND PROVERBS OF WILLIAM BLAKE 232
SONGS FROM THE CHINESE 181
Sonnet 106
Sonnet: On seeing a piece of our artillery 219
Sonnet 43: When most I wink 190
Sound the flute 152
Spirto ben nato 84
Spring 152
Spring carol 95
SPRING SYMPHONY 143
Spring, the sweet Spring 144
St Godric's hymn 263
Still falls the rain 176
Still though the scene 69

Index of Titles

Strange meeting 222
The succession of the four sweet months
    157
Sumer is icumen in 154
The summer is coming 204
Summer pastimes 277
S'un casto amor 84
The sun shines down 55
Supper 257
Sweet Polly Oliver 129
Sweet was the song 14
The sycamore tree 12

The teares of an affectionate shepheard
    148
Te Deum in C 32
Tell me where is Fancie bred 212
The ten commandments 225
That yonge child 92
Thee, God, I come from 73
There is no rose 92
There's none to soothe 129
There was a man of Newington 37
There was a monkey 40
These are the forgeries 197
This little Babe 93
THIS WAY TO THE TOMB 112
Thou hast made me 117
The three kings 22
THREE TWO-PART SONGS 18
THY KING'S BIRTHDAY 13
TIT FOR TAT 6
Tit for tat 8
To daffodils 157
To John Maxwell, Esq. 267
To lie flat on the back 54
To sleep 106
To violets 145
A tragic story 34
The trees they grow so high 98
Tu sa' ch'i' so, signor mie 83
The twelve apostles 225
TWO BALLADS 47
TWO PART-SONGS 28

TWO SONGS 86
The tyger 234

Ultima Cumaei venit 241
Um Mitternacht 195
Underneath the abject willow 47
The useful plough 39

Veggio co' be' vostr'occhi 82
Vigil 7
Villes I 76
Voices 217
VOICES FOR TODAY 239
Voici le printemps 120
The volunteer 3

Wagtail and the baby 172
The wanderings of Cain 185
WAR REQUIEM 216
Waters above 145
A Wealden trio 9
A wedding anthem 155
Wee Willie Gray 268
Welcome, maids of honour 145
WELCOME ODE 277
Welcome Yule 26
What if this present 116
What is more gentle 188
What's in your mind? 85
When will my May come 148
When you're feeling... 42
WHO ARE THESE CHILDREN? 254
Who are these children? 256
The winter 270
The winter it is past 270
WINTER WORDS 171
Wolcum Yule 91
Worship we this holy day 21
The wren 203

Ye that pasen by 266
Yif ic of love can 264
You spotted snakes 198
You who stand at your doors 67

Index of First Lines

This index lists the first line (mostly shortened) of each poem as set by Britten and, where they differ, the first line of the longer poem from which Britten took his text. 'The' and 'A' are not listed alphabetically.

Abraham, my servante, Abraham 162
A che più debb'i' omai 82
Across the darkened sky 61
Adam lay ibounden 95
After the blast of lightning 221
Ah, Sun-flower 235
And when it pleaseth thee 149
As I sat under a sycamore tree 12
As it fell on one holy-day 107
As it is, plenty 51
As sweet Polly Oliver 129
As the soldier and the sailor 215
Assez vu. La vision... 80
At Eden's gate 244
At the mid hour of night 204
At the round earths imagin'd corners 116
The auld aik's doun 258
Autumn wind rises 182
Avenging and bright 202
Awake, glad heart! get up and sing! 13
Ay me, alas, heigh ho 44

A baby watched a ford 172
Batter my heart 114
Be kind and courteous 199
Be slowly lifted up 219
Beati misericordes 228
Begone dull care 34
Behold a silly tender babe 15, 94
Below the thunders 184
The bird a nest 233
Blood, mud and bitterness 46
A boy was born in Bethlehem 20
Bugles sang 217
But that night, when on my bed 187

Ca' the yowes to the knowes 211
Ce sont des villes 76

Christmas eve and twelve of the clock 249
A cold coming we had of it 259
Come under the shadow 261
Come you not from Newcastle 132
A country life is sweet 39
Crash and Clang 40
Creak, little wood thing 172
Cuck-òo, Cuck-òo 35
Cuddle-doun, my bairnie 255

Da ich ein Knabe war 193
Dark is the night 7
The day's grown old 102
Dear harp of my country 204
Dear, shall we talk 47
Death be not proud 117
Des drôles très solides 79
Devant une neige 79
Die Linien des Lebens sind verschieden 194
Don't help-on the big chariot 181
Down by the salley gardens 96
Down yonder green valley 99
Driver, drive faster 66

Early one morning 210
Easter day was a holiday 96
Eho! Eho! Eho! 122
Either I mistake your shape 196
Encinctured with a twine 185
Ev'n like two little bank-dividing brooks 124
Except the Lord 248

Fair and fair 151
Fair daffodils, we weep 157
Fair was the morning 159
First, April 157

Fish in the unruffled lakes 53
A flaxen-headed cowboy 129
Flow gently, sweet Afton 269
Foweles in the frith 263
The fox and his wife 35
Froh kehrt der Schiffer heim 192
From leafy woods 244

The garden's dark 245
Get ivy and hull, woman 26
Glory to God on high 27
Good day, good day 25
Gracieux fils de Pan 78

Half a milord 245
Have you been catching 8
Haymakers, rakers, reapers 277
Health to the Maxwells' 267
Hee-balou, my sweet 126
He often would ask us 173
Here lies the clerk 3
Here the strong mallow strikes 158
Here we bring new water 36
Herod that was both wild 21
Hodie Christus natus est 91
The holly and the ivy 180
The hours of folly 235
How now, spirit 196
How sweet the answer 203

I command all the rats 43
I have desired to go 75
I hug my pillow 182
I know a bank 198
I know a maiden fair to see 2
I'll sing you one, oh 225
I loved a lass, a fair one 28
I mun be maried a Sunday 37
I saw the lovely arch 18
I sing of a maiden 93
I wander 232
I was angry with my friend 233
I was lonely and forlorn 281
I will give my love an apple 213
If it's ever spring again 176
If thou wilt ease thine heart 86
If we shadows have offended 200
If you have ears to hear 239
Il est quelqu'un sur terre 121
In a garden shady 88

In Chester town 208
In May, in brilliant Athens 271
In Poland, in nineteen thirty-nine 250
In the bleak mid-winter 24
In the heat of the day 214
In the southern village 182
In the third-class seat 171
Ist nicht heilig mein Herz 192
It seemed that out of battle 222
It's farewell to the drawing-room 67
It was a beautiful and silent day 186
It was your faither and mither 256

J'ai seul la clef 76
J'ai tendu des cordes 77
Jesu that dost in Mary dwell 71
Jesu, Jesu, Jesu, Jesu 22

The knight met a child 282

La belle est au jardin 121
La Nöel passée 119
The larky lad 256
Le ciel est, par-dessus le toit 4
L'enfant chantait 5
Lenten is come with love 263
L'Été, lorsque le jour a fui 4
Le roi s'en va 121
Les chars d'argent 78
Les sanglots longs 5
Let me tell you the story 31
Let the florid music praise 49
Life and its follies 282
A little black thing 233
Little Fly 235
Lo! yonder shed 158
London, to thee I do present 153
Look, stranger 50
Lord, Lord, Lord 280
Lorsque j'étais jeunette 120
Lullaby baby 128
Lully, lulley 25

Maiden in the mor lay 265
The merry Cuckoo 143
Midnight's bell goes ting 185
The minstrel boy 203
Mirie it is 264
Mit gelben Birnen hänget 194
Morning is only 112

Index of First Lines

[297

Move him into the sun 220
My heart, I fancied 244
My subject is war 216

Night covers up the rigid land 59
Night is no more 113
Not even summer yet 56
Now is Christmas ycome 22
Now is the month of maying 33
Now let us sing gaily 155
Now the bright morning star 144
Now the hungry lion roars 199
Now the leaves are falling 49
Now through night's caressing grip 51
Now, until the break of day 200
Nurse, I am in love 271

O be joyful in the Lord 207
O can ye sew cushions 97
O God, I love thee 74
O come all you young fellows 215
O! it's owre the braes 254
O lift your little pinkie 111
O my deare Hert 92
O, merry rang the hymn 16
O might those sighes 115
O praise God 224
O Rose, thou art sick 104
O soft embalmer 106
O that I had ne'er been married 1
O the gallant fisher's life 38
O the sight entrancing 206
O the valley in the summer 65
O wow for day 107
Of all the girls 209
Of cord and cassia-wood 181
Of on that is so fayr 11
Oft in the stilly night 205
Oh my blacke Soule 114
Oh, to vex me 115
Oh would to God 148
Old Abram Brown is dead 41
Oliver Cromwell 99
On a poet's lips I slept 184
On a sunny brae alone I lay 57
One ever hangs 222
One midsummer's morn 280
Our eyes are blinded 133
Our hunting fathers 45
Out on the lawn I lie 145

Out there, we've walked 218

Pleasure it is 95
Praised be the God of Love 179
The pride of the peacock 232
Prisons are built 233

Quand j'étais chez mon père 123
Queen and huntress 105
Quiet, sleep! 128

The red fox 112
Regis regum rectissimi 227
Rejoice in God 160
Rendete agli occhi miei 83
Requiem aeternam dona eis 216
Rich and rare were the gems 204
A rose bud by my early walk 268
'The Rose in a mystery' 71
Round about, round about 278

Sail on, sail on 202
Sainte Marye Virgine 263
See how the sun 118
Sent as a present 62
The sheep's in the meadows 281
She sleeps on soft 188
She's like the swallow 280
Shine out, fair Sun 143
A ship I have got 246
Shoo all 'er birds 283
Sicelides Musae 241
Si come nella penna 81
Since she whom I lov'd 116
Sith sickles and the shearing 44
A skelp frae his teacher 255
Sleep forsakes me 245
Sleep, my darling, sleep 90
Sleep! sleep! beauty bright 126
Slowly, silently 7
So Abram rose 220
So blessed a sight it was 20
Some say that Love's a little boy 63
A song of enchantment I sang 6
Sound the Flute 152
Spirto ben nato 84
The splendour falls 103
Spring, the sweet Spring 144
Steepies for the bairnie 257
Still falls the Rain 176

Still though the scene 69
Stop all the clocks 64
Sumer is icumen in 154
S'un casto amor 83
The sun shines down 55
Sweet was the song 14

Tell me where is Fancie 212
The ten hours' light 171
That yonge child 92
Thee, God, I come from 73
There came three kings 22
There is a wind 6
There is no rose 92
There is not much 174
There lived a sage 34
There's none to soothe 129
There's pairt o' it young 254
There was a jolly miller 130
There was a man 37
There was an old man 161
There was a monkey 40
There was a ship of Rio 19
There was a star 226
These are the forgeries 197
They are our past 43
Think in the morning 234
This ae nighte 104
This is a day 278
This little Babe 93
Thou hast made me 117
Thou shalt make them 178
A thousand thousand 58
The thrushes sing 174
A time there was 175
Tis the last rose 205
To lie flat on the back 54
To see a World in a Grain 236
The tree stood flowering 254
The trees they grow so high 98
Tu sa' ch'i' so 83
The tygers of wrath 234
Tyger! Tyger! 234

Ultima Cumaei venit 241
Um Mitternacht ging ich 195
Un beau matin 78

Underneath the abject willow 47
The unicorn's hoofs 183
Up on their brooms 18
Upon the street they lie 257

Veggio co' be' vostr'occhi 82
Voici le printemps 120

Wanne mine eyhnen misten 266
Warum huldigest du 193
The water is wide 131
Waters above! 145
We are the darkness 178
We go walking 213
We praise thee, O God 32
Wee Willie Gray 268
Weep not, my wanton 127
Welcome be thou 26
Welcome, maids of honour 145
Whanne ic se on Rode 264
What if this present 116
What is more gentle 188
What passing bells 217
What's in your mind 85
What will I do 269
When as the rye reach'd 144
When I was a bachelor 131
When I was bound apprentice 210
When Jesus Christ 10
When most I wink 190
When once the sun sinks 160
When ye've got a child 9
When you're feeling 42
Wild with passion 86
Will ye go to the Hielands 270
The winter it is past 270
With easy hands 256
Within the violence of the storm 255
Wolcum be thou hevene king 91
The world is charged 73

Ye Hielands and ye Lowlands 97
Ye that pasen by the weiye 266
Yes. Why do we all 74
Yet if His Majesty, our sovran lord 14
You spotted snakes 198
You who stand at your doors 67